Stephen Haseler is Emeritus Professor of Government and Director of the Global Policy Institute at London Metropolitan University. He holds a PhD from the London School of Economics and has held Visiting Professorships at Georgetown University and Johns Hopkins University. He has been active in public life in Britain (Labour candidate, GLC Committee Chair and founder member of the SDP) and has appeared regularly on TV (including BBC *Newsnight*) and radio (*Today*). He lives in West London.

He is the author of 15 books on British and European politics, including *The Battle for Britain: Thatcher and the New Liberals* (I.B.Tauris), *The End of the House of Windsor* (I.B.Tauris); *Super-State: The New Europe and the Challenge to America* (I.B.Tauris); *The Super-Rich: The Unjust World of Global Capital; Sidekick: British Global Strategy from Churchill to Blair; The Death of British Democracy and Meltdown: How the Masters of the Universe Destroyed the West's Power and Prosperity.*

BOOKS BY STEPHEN HASELER

The Gaitskellites
The Death of British Democracy
Euro-Communism
The Tragedy of Labour
Anti-Americanism
The Politics of Giving
The Battle For Britain: Thatcher and the New Liberals
The End of the House of Windsor
The English Tribe
The Super-Rich: The Unjust World of Global Capitalism
Super-State: The New Europe and its Challenge to America
Sidekick: British Global Strategy from Churchill to Blair
*Meltdown: How the Masters of the Universe Destroyed the West's
    Power and Prosperity*
Meltdown UK: There Is Another Way

The
Grand
Delusion

Britain After Sixty
Years of Elizabeth II

Stephen Haseler

I.B. TAURIS

LONDON · NEW YORK

Published in 2012 by I.B.Tauris & Co. Ltd
6 Salem Road, London W2 4BU
175 Fifth Avenue, New York NY 10010
www.ibtauris.com

Distributed in the United States and Canada Exclusively by Palgrave
Macmillan, 175 Fifth Avenue, New York NY 10010

ISBN 978 1 78076 073 5

A full CIP record for this book is available from the British Library
A full CIP record for this book is available from the Library of Congress
Library of Congress catalog card: available

Typeset in Sabon by Dexter Haven Associates Ltd, London
Printed and bound in Sweden by ScadBook AB

CONTENTS

ACKNOWLEDGEMENTS

I wish to thank Andrew Blick and Jon Temple for their invaluable research help, Jo Godfrey, my patient editor at I.B.Tauris, Robert Hastings and Gretchen Ladish for their excellent editorial work. And, of course, I owe a debt of gratitude too to all those in the university and think-tank world, in politics and in journalism, who, over the years, have shared and added to my interest and understanding of the compelling, if sometimes dispiriting, story of post-war British politics and our ruling establishment. In view of my no-doubt somewhat 'unorthodox' views on the sensitive issue of the Queen's role in this story, I had better emphasise that the views expressed here are mine and mine alone.

PREFACE

This book, written to coincide with the diamond jubilee, is a political history of Britain in the 'reign' of Elizabeth II. It is not a history of the Queen, but in any story of post-war Britain 'Queen and country' are inseparable. To write about post-war British politics and its leaders without writing about the Queen, her values and her influence, is to look at British history through a half-shut eye.

The story of the Queen is essentially a story of survival – and survival against the odds. Monarchy, particularly the kind of imperial and celebrity monarchy of Britain, is a very odd institution for an advanced industrial and commercial democracy to tolerate, let alone celebrate. Yet the British monarchy has indeed survived. And in jubilee year, looking back over her time in office, Queen Elizabeth, from her own and her family's vantage-point, can count her reign a real success. In a sense she was lucky to come to the throne at all. The house of Windsor survived both the abdication of Edward VIII and the war. And it also survived, intact and without even a hint of attempted reform, the post-war 'socialist' Attlee government.

The Queen and monarchy also survived both the period of 'modernisation', with its 'anti-establishment' rhetoric, of the mid-1960s, led by the modernising governments of Harold Wilson. And then, more impressively still, Britain's monarchy was to survive the era of 1970s extremism, with its strikes and 'states of emergency', when the insurgent left in the trade unions and in the Labour Party were seeking an 'irreversible shift of wealth and power to working people and their families'. Evidently, and revealingly, the Windsors were not even a target for the radicals and reformers, let alone the left-wing militants, of those years. The old establishment sailed on, as did its 'grand delusion'.

It was Margaret Thatcher and her 1980s 'revolution' that posed the first real problem for the Queen and the royal family. Thatcher's era saw the erosion of deference in Britain, and her 'free market', middle-class 'revolution' had little time for traditional England, particularly its rural attachments. Thatcherism, certainly when it met resistance to change, developed a decidedly 'anti-aristocratic' and 'anti-establishment' impulse. Thatcher clashed with the Anglican establishment over her economic policies and with the Queen over her disdain for the Commonwealth. The perceptive Irish commentator Conor Cruise O'Brien went as far as to describe Thatcher as resembling 'Old Ironsides', Oliver Cromwell.

But, most impressively of all, the Queen and the monarchy survived the era of Diana Spencer. This 'people's princess' – as she was dubbed by prime minister Tony Blair – captured the imagination of a large section of British public opinion, and by establishing what amounted to an alternative royalty – one much more human, modern and accessible than the up-tight Windsors – she held a dagger to the heart of the Queen herself. And it was during the aftermath of Diana's sudden death in the autumn of 1997 that this threat to the monarchy burst into the open. The behaviour of the Queen ahead of Diana's funeral – remaining in Scotland, seemingly formal, cold and unmoved – led to an estrangement from the more emotional public. This was the lowest point of her reign, so low in fact that a credible case can be made that the new prime minister, by studiously avoiding opening a debate on the issue of monarchy itself, saved both the Queen and the traditional monarchy for which she stood.

So the legacy of Elizabeth II, the great survivor, is already becoming clear. When she dies or abdicates she will hand over a monarchy and an unwritten constitution that has hardly changed since she 'ascended' the throne in 1952. Britain's monarchy – which still plays such an important part in the life of Britain and still sets the tone of the country and of its view of itself – has exactly the same powers as it had when she took over, and probably more influence. Even such independent, charismatic and powerful prime ministers as Margaret Thatcher and Tony Blair needed to take care not to fall foul of her. As Blair himself remarked in a revealing aside, reported in Alistair Campbell's memoirs, she still has 'the power to put us in our place'.

THE 'GRAND DELUSION'

However, the Queen, and the values and culture she represents, has done more than just survive. She, and the monarchy, continue to define us as a country and a people. They define our past, and they project an image to the world of our present. And, crucially, she has increasingly set the tone and limits for our ruling groups.

And from the coronation onwards, it has been a grand and imperial tone. As I argue in Chapter 1, this coronation in 1953, the first TV spectacular, presented post-war Britain to the world, and there was little in it that was modest or realistic. The ceremony was an extraordinary affair – a combination of medieval divine kingship and nineteenth-century imperial pomp. Its extravagance and grandeur was fit for an imperial queen/empress rather than the head of state of a modern European country; and its Ruritanian rituals, to the modern eye at least, border on the absurd. And it served to reveal a sad truth: that in post-war, post-colonial Britain the new head of state, and the English establishment behind her, could simply not recognise that the country's far-flung empire was indeed lost. For on that June day in 1953 it was on full display – as was the country's certainty of its exceptional place in the world. The authorities had had one whole year, since the Queen's 'accession' to the throne, to plan for the coronation. And they decided to celebrate the past rather than signal a future role for the country.

This coronation was a perfect representation of the 'grand delusion': for the reality of Britain was very, very different from the image this spectacular portrayed. Two world wars had left the country in a seriously reduced state; Britain had lost an empire, and had become, in effect, an economic, and thus political, dependency of the USA. By 1953, following the US loan, the Marshall aid programme and the formation of NATO, the country was, in truth, part of the American empire not the centre of its own. And its society was nothing like the picture-postcard portrayal inherent in the 'grand delusion' – a world of lords and ladies, palaces and thatched cottages; rather it was a highly urbanised and industrialised working-class country. Yet the Queen and her coronation were reflecting a completely different image – a wrong image, a 'grand delusion'.

The central theme of this book is the proposition that this 'grand delusion' has, remarkably, continued to hold sway long after coronation year was over – and that its grip on the minds of our elites has remained unloosened right through the reign and up until today. *The Grand*

Delusion attempts to show how prime minister after prime minister and their governments, with some very few exceptions, have seen themselves as leaders of a world power; and that when confronted with reality have then adopted the conceit of aiming to 'punch above our weight' rather than attempting to adjust to our new position and status.

Rather than properly adjust, Britain's post-war political class has created substitutes, or surrogates, for empire. One such is the Commonwealth of Nations. This Commonwealth became a useful mechanism for continuing the 'world role', and was a theme that ran through the coronation events of 1953 (it was then called 'the British Commonwealth'). Both the new Queen and successive Archbishops of Canterbury have been strongly attached to the Commonwealth, and over the years have formed a strong bias at the heart of the English establishment in its favour. And this is not surprising, seeing as the Queen is its head and the Archbishop is the leader of the worldwide Anglican communion, which has more supporters in Africa than in Britain.

The Commonwealth allows not just the Queen and Archbishop, but our political leaders too, to play a role on the world stage. It is perhaps a testimony to the continuing power of the old establishment, particularly the Queen herself, that this delusion of self-importance has been cross-party. It was, after all, a Labour prime minister, Harold Wilson, who famously said as late as the mid-1960s, when Labour was debating whether to withdraw from 'east of Suez', that 'our frontiers are on the Himalayas'. This was an axiom of British foreign and imperial policy operating at the height of Victorian colonial times when British troops were fighting and dying on the North-West frontier with Afghanistan. That, over a hundred years later, it could still be so is testimony to the persistence of this 'world role' ideology.

As with the role played by the Commonwealth, the other surrogate for empire has been the 'special relationship' with the USA. Very soon after the war Britain's foreign-policy establishment came to the view that only through hitching our star to the USA could the 'world role' fixation be realised. Yet the power relationship in this 'alliance' was, though, so one-sided that Britain effectively ceased to be an independent country – and became more like a pole of influence within the American empire. Later both Margaret Thatcher and Tony Blair took this relationship with the USA to new heights. Under Thatcher in the 1980s Britain started down a road of deregulating the City of London which would ultimately lead to the country entering what amounted to the Wall Street-led global financial empire. And Blair deepened this relationship – and added a political/military dimension to it – when, under the influence of Washington, he ordered British troops to fight alongside Americans in the invasion of Iraq.

FROM EMPIRE TO EMPIRE IN SIXTY YEARS

In Part 1 I try to show how this obsession with a 'world role' ran through the thinking of Britain's leading post-war strategic decision-makers – Ernest Bevin, Winston Churchill and Anthony Eden. And, only three years after the coronation, how their vastly overblown idea of the country's power led, when it collided with cold reality, to the defeat and humiliation at Suez in 1956. I then show how this 1956 national defeat was, in Anthony Nutting's cute double entendre, 'no end of a lesson'.

In Parts 2 and 3 I attempt to chronicle the era of 'modernisation' – the tumultuous time of social and intellectual change and ferment, starting in the mid-1960s, which saw the rise of the meritocrats, the erosion of deference and the growth of trade-union militancy. This was also an era of steep economic decline which saw a polarisation in the 1970s and 1980s between an extremist left and fundamentalist Thatcherism – and the rise of a new 'Thatcherite' middle class with few attachments to the old hierarchies. Such a process of social change and modernisation in which the old imperial classes both died out and were replaced could have reasonably been expected seriously to erode the post-imperial 'grand delusion' which was, after all, largely the product of these classes. New classes with new values – say the meritocracy represented by Harold Wilson and Edward Heath, or the new entrepreneurial business class favoured by Thatcher – would surely discard the pretence and pomp of British power and find it much easier to adjust to the reality of Britain as a medium-sized European country.

But it was not to be. As I attempt to show in Part 4, in Elizabeth's late-twentieth-century Britain – and partly because of her influence on top elites – old habits died hard. The new groups and classes that emerged in the 1970s and 1980s, instead of forging a cultural revolution, simply took on many of the values of the people they were replacing. Thatcher's revolution may indeed have both represented and induced a hard-headed new business class contemptuous of older traditionalist values, but it was always less radical than met the eye. Her middle-class 'revolution' did not spread the wealth nearly as much as it originally promised; her governments, no matter their anti-aristocratic rhetoric, did not erode the power and fortunes of the British super-rich, including the landowners; and, no matter the tensions, Margaret Thatcher avoided a serious financial row with the Queen.

What her Janus-faced 'revolution' did do, however, was to reinforce old prejudices and myths – especially the 'grand delusion'. For the continuing stubborn hold of this myth on the national imagination was to be helped by the notion, popular in the 1990s, that 'Britain was back' – that Thatcher had 'turned round' the economy and that, compared to France and Germany, whose economies were regularly traduced as sclerotic, Britain was a success story. And during the administration of her annointed successor, John Major, the 'grand delusion' of British importance and exceptionalism not only endured but was taken to new heights – as Rupert Murdoch's press unleashed a visceral form of 'Euroscepticism' and tabloid xenophobia into the country's political discourse.

A NEW EMPIRE OF FINANCE AND CREDIT

But Britain's story since the 1980s, after it emerged from the traumas and extremism of the 1970s, is, in essence, the story of the financialisation of both the economy and society – a deadly process that came to a head in the crash of 2008. This financialisation of Britain, based upon an over-extended City of London, is so central to the latter part of the history of the reign of Elizabeth II that I have devoted Part 5 to it – and called it 'An empire of finance'.

During the last two decades – either side of the turn of the millennium – Britain's political elites, now joined by the just as powerful financial elites, have remained largely mentally unreconstructed. Still gripped by the 'grand delusion' – indeed a myth reinforced by the Euroscepticism and xenophobia unleashed during the early 1990s – British longing for empire was whetted by new imperial vistas opening up – this time in the form of global and globalised finance. From the 1980s onwards a new generation of privately educated Britons (many from the same public schools as serviced the old elite), never keen on industry and manufacturing, and much preferring 'a career in the City', flocked to this new frontier of finance. It all lead to another imperial over-reach: to the huge and unsustainable over-extension of British banks and the financial industry.

This new dash for a global role through a financial empire reached its zenith during the premiership of Tony Blair. During the mid-1990s a central objective of Blair's project of New Labour was to secure a deal, a

Faustian pact, with the City of London – which would later lead to Blair as prime minister becoming the City's champion, and the leading supporter of 'light-touch' financial regulation and reckless over-extension.

Blair was one of nature's 'grand delusionists'. He warmed to a world role for Britain as a way of securing a world role for himself, and indeed he succeeded in becoming a global celebrity. In Chapter 14 I outline his problems with the Queen and the royals; but it is easy to understand how, after he had in effect saved the Windsors following the death of Diana, he sought to enlist the Queen, and her world role, in his own project. But, as I argue in Chapter 16, the New Labour prime minister's 'fatal attraction' to power – to global power (and with it global celebrity) led him into his second Faustian pact, this time with American global military power – so much so that he led his country, and incredibly his own Labour Party, to support the 2003 invasion of Iraq, a country that did not threaten the West. Britain's role in this invasion remains an extraordinary episode in the post-war history of Britain. And it stands testimony to the continuing hold of the 'grand delusion' on Britain's elites of this type.

THE DIAMOND JUBILEE: GLORIOUS, AND ISOLATED

The final two parts of the book (6 and 7) look at the dire consequences of our inability to shake free from the 'grand delusion' over the length of the reign. As I argue that the consequences are primarily economic and social, these chapters are necessarily mainly about the economy and society, about how our reckless financial and credit over-extension has hollowed out our economy and ruined family budgets. Under the influence of global finance Britain became the most globalised major economy in Europe. And the imperatives of globalisation – the search for arbitrage and lower and lower costs – has 'hollowed out' the real economy, eroded its manufacturing base, lost jobs and placed downward pressure on wages and therefore demand. And the only way that successive governments could keep demand up, and therefore growth up, was by a credit boom. This credit mountain has now collapsed, and has brought us low – in a deep and enduring recession or depression. It has created a perfect storm that is now crashing around us – in, of all years, diamond jubilee year.

But this perfect economic storm is coinciding with another feature of the the country's overly financialised economy – that is the rapid growth in inequality. For, as the 'hollowing out' has squeezed, and disintegrated, the middle class, inordinate concentrations of wealth have appeared at the top of British society. A new super-rich and mega-rich class – comprising both the 'new money' of City-based finance and the enhanced money of traditional English inherited fortunes – has formed what amounts to a new plutocracy. These dramatic social changes are a recipe for social instability, and are a clue that the British, as they face the recession/depression, may not be 'all in this together'.

Traditionalists, of course, argue that binding the nation together, making us feel 'all in this together', is a role for monarchy. And, perhaps fortuitously, the British in 2012 are being asked to celebrate a royal diamond jubilee with an extra day of bank holiday. The problem is that the house of Windsor's particular style of monarchy – grand and global, with a super-rich celebrity lifestyle – may not really be right for the times. Nor might great displays of national importance.

Another problem with the jubilee is the role of the Queen herself. It is now generally agreed that the Queen has played an important role in the country's public life. As head of state she has set the tone for the nation, and on policy issues she has used her real influence behind the scenes. So, as she has taken this lead – now for over half a century – it is only reasonable that she needs to take some of the responsibility for the state of the nation. And it is also only reasonable that commentators and analysts should feel able to hold her to account.

For this writer, an insistent question remains: can Britain ever properly adjust to the modern age while this grandiose 'imperial' monarchy still sets the tone? And can Britain ever puncture the 'grand delusion' while the house of Windsor still stands as a powerful rebuke to the modesty and realism needed to see the country through the crisis. More importantly still, in the coming era of inequality, with huge gaps of wealth and income growing in Britain, can our 'rich and famous' celebrity monarchy any longer be a rallying point for national unity? Can we ever genuinely 'all be in this together?'

By her account, Elizabeth Windsor stands for continuity, tradition, service and national unity. But she also stands for national grandeur, social hierarchy and super-rich inherited wealth. Yet, the country – certainly since the loss of empire and now since the global financial crash – needs as a matter of urgency to adjust to a new age: one involving a more limited role abroad and a more equal society at home. But can it so adjust while the grand, lavish and pervasive monarchy she represents still represents our face to the world. In this sense, rather than help us forward, she represents a problem, not a solution – and is a real obstacle to change.

PART 1
Pride and empire

1 CORONATION: PRETENCE AND POMP

There is no source from which we can raise sufficient funds to enable us
to live and spend on the scale we contemplate except the United States.

John Maynard Keynes, August 1945

Queen Elizabeth II was crowned on 2 June 1953, having 'ascended'
to the throne to become monarch over a year earlier on 6 February
1952. The coronation ceremony, held in Westminster Abbey, anointed
and crowned the British head of state. But Elizabeth Windsor was at the
same time crowned Queen of Canada, Australia, New Zealand, South
Africa, Ceylon and Pakistan, and also became Head of what was then
called the British Commonwealth of Nations and 'Supreme Governor'
of the Church of England. This ceremony was a truly important event
– certainly for the post-war British.

The ceremonial opened as Elizabeth took her seat on the Chair of
Estate, and then she stood along with the Garter Principal King of Arms,
the Archbishop of Canterbury, the Lord Chancellor, the Lord Great
Chamberlain, the Lord High Constable and the Earl Marshall, and then
the Garter Principal King of Arms 'presented' the Queen to the audience
to the east, south, west and north of the Abbey. He intoned, 'Sirs, I here
present unto you Queen Elizabeth, your undoubted Queen.' And those
present then 'acclaimed' their 'sovereign'. Then the Archbishop asked of
Elizabeth, 'Will you solemnly promise and swear to govern the Peoples
of the United Kingdom of Great Britain and Northern Ireland, Canada,
Australia, New Zealand, the Union of South Africa, Pakistan and Ceylon,
and of your Possessions and other Territories to any of them belonging

3

or pertaining, according to their respective laws and customs?' She then pledged to 'maintain the laws of God and the true profession of the gospel' and the 'inviolable settlement of the Church of England'.

And then the coronation ceremony moved on to the mysterious 'anointing' and 'crowning'. The 'anointing' was particularly mystical. Elizabeth's crimson robe was removed and she proceeded to King Edward's Chair wearing the anointing gown. This part of the ceremony was not televised (and in 1937 at the preceding coronation was not even photographed). The official explanation was that this element of the coronation service is considered sacred, and so concealed from public gaze. The Dean of Westminster had the task of pouring consecrated oil – described as 'holy oil' – from an eagle-shaped ampulla into a spoon – the filigreed spoon, the only component of the medieval crown jewels that survived Cromwell's revolution – and the Archbishop of Canterbury anointed 'the sovereign' on the hands, breast and head. This anointing was completed while the assembled sang 'Zadok the Priest'. The Queen was then invested with the royal bracelets and the royal robe, the sovereign's orb, the queen's ring, the sceptre with the cross and the sceptre with the dove. She was 'crowned' by the Archbishop of Canterbury as the assembled sang 'God Save the Queen'. Thus was made legitimate – through this ancient ceremony – the new British head of state, Elizabeth II. Both the new Queen herself and the British political class took all of this extremely seriously. It was the foundation stone upon which Elizabeth II was to 'reign', and to represent the country as its head of state for the rest of the century and well beyond.

Almost as central to this ceremony as the new Queen herself was the role played by the Archbishop of Canterbury. For it was on his authority – acting, that is, on behalf of the national church and the divine power – that the British head of state was, so to speak, sworn in. At no point in the ceremony was the new head of state's authority, even symbolically, deemed to rest upon the assent of 'the people' or institutions representative of 'the people'. Intriguingly, reference to parliament was completely absent from the ceremonial. There was a point in the coronation called 'the Recognition' at which the assembled dignitaries on the four sides of 'the Theatre' (as the raised coronation platform was appropriately named) were actually asked to recognise 'your undoubted Queen' – but they were then instructed by the ceremony rules to shout, 'God save Queen Elizabeth.' As Randolph Churchill wrote in his book *The Story of the Coronation*, published to coincide with the great event, the coronation proves that 'the dynastic principle has triumphed and is enshrined in the very heart of the theory of a modern constitutional monarchy, as it is, if we search our hearts, in ourselves.'[1]

The whole procedure was, in fact, 'sanctified by the church' – a kind of solemn contract between the Archbishop, representing both the established church and the divine, and the new Queen. Although the powers of royal 'divine right' to rule were long gone from Britain's constitution, the office of monarch or 'sovereign' itself was still as late as 1953 legitimated by God. Elizabeth's oath was to the Almighty and her office and authority was derived from Him.

THE ILLUSION OF GREATNESS

This ceremony possessed far more significance than simply establishing a new monarch. It was the first great public event of the mass television era, broadcast through the country, and watched later by film throughout the world (the Canadians saw it later that night) and celebrated from New York (where the Duke and Duchess of Windsor attended a coronation party) to Korea (where it was reported from the Korean War front that Commonwealth soldiers fired red, white and blue smoke shells at the enemy). It was showing Britain's face to the world.

With this lavish, part-medieval, part-imperial, ceremony, offering few symbolic concessions to either the democratic age or post-war Britain, the message from the British establishment to the world was clear and unmistakable: Britain, which had been the greatest power in the world from the Napoleonic wars until the rise of American and German power, had survived the war, and the post-war austerity, and was back. The country, represented by her Queen, was still not just a great country, but a great power, indeed a world power. And on the eve of the coronation, at 11.30 on the morning of 29 May 1953, the imperial 'world leadership' role was nicely reinforced by the news that Edmund Hillary (with loyal Sherpa Tenzing at his side) had reached the top of Mount Everest. The newspapers talked of a 'new Elizabethan age' and it was obvious, as Harold Wilson was to argue over a decade later, that 'Britain's frontiers still 'lay on the Himalayas'.

And Britain's establishment was also affirming through this resplendent ceremony that the country's old-fashioned class system was still in order, that there was indeed a continuing upper class with a firm view about its role both in post-war Britain, and indeed in the world which it used to rule.

This bombastic coronation-cum-theatre was not just a Conservative government extravaganza, or piece of Churchillian theatre (although Churchill had a hand in constructing this royal show); rather it was a genuine expression of an all-party consensus. The Labour government's Defence White Paper of 1948 described Britain as remaining a 'great power', and in 1949 the Labour Minister of Defence described the country as 'a centre of world influence and power'. In March 1946 the Chiefs of Staff (Cunningham, Alanbrook and Tedder) had outlined a breathtaking and grandiose vision of a global Commonwealth defence system that would consist of four 'world zones', each with its own command structure (rather in the manner of the US Department of Defense during the Cold War and after): Mediterranean and Middle East; India; South East Asia; Australia and New Zealand. These unreconstructed 'Masters of the Universe' in the Foreign Office and the service ministries continued during 1947 to 'pipe the imperial march and beat the world-power drum'.[2]

And the Labour government supported them. Just after becoming prime minister in 1945 Clement Attlee shocked his colleagues by arguing in a cabinet paper that Britain's reduced strength as a country meant that its commitments should also be reduced. 'The British Commonwealth and Empire is not a unit that can be defended by itself. It was the creation of sea power,' he argued.[3] But he was to be overruled in cabinet, not least by the new Foreign Secretary Ernest Bevin. And by September 1947 the Labour Ministry of Defence was proposing, for 1949, to have a strength of 339,000 troops, with as many as 80,000 stationed outside Europe for the 'world role', and only 70,000 in Germany facing the increasingly menacing Soviet Union. And under Labour the defence build-up in 1951 for the Korean War had been so extravagant that even Churchill demurred at the cost.

THE REALITY: A BANKRUPT AMERICAN DEPENDENCY

What these cross-party fantasists could not bring themselves to understand was that, for Britain, the war had been an unmitigated catastrophe. It saw Britain's economy devastated and its power in the world seriously diminished. Britain's war leader Winston Churchill, in some moods, at least recognised the magnitude of the country's changed circumstances – in a poignant commentary at the very end of the war he ruefully suggested that his life's work of defending the empire might all have been for naught. He also worried that his victory over Nazi Germany might have been bought at the price of allowing a new tyranny, the Soviet Union, to dominate Europe.[4] Soviet Russia did indeed become the pre-eminent European power in the early months of post-war Europe – a stark fact that led most Western European governments to welcome the other new superpower as a balancing force. And as a result Britain's real post-war strategic position – as opposed to its fantasy role – was, in Attlee's words, as 'an easterly extension of a strategic area the centre of which is the American continent'.[5]

In fact, Britain's entry into an American-dominated sphere had been going on for some time. Britain's decline and the USA's rise had been almost a century-long story. In 1870, at the height of Victorian power and prosperity, Britain's share of world manufacturing exports was 45 per cent; by 1950 it had fallen to 26 per cent; by 1989 to only 9 per cent. Britain's share of manufacturing output reached 22.9 per cent of the world level in 1880; by 1913, on the eve of the Great War, it was 13.6 per cent; by 1938, on the eve of World War II, it was 10.7 per cent. In 1890 Britain was second only to the USA in iron and steel production (producing eight million tons of pig iron) but by 1913 the country was ranked third (producing only 7.7 million tons of steel, compared with Germany's 17.6 million and the USA's 31.8 million.

By the end of the nineteenth century, Britain still possessed something akin to a worldwide empire, but it was becoming a strung-out and somewhat ungainly, rickety affair. As early as 1884 the writer J.R. Seeley saw a future in which 'they [Russia and America] will surpass in power the states now called great as much as the great country-states of the sixteenth-century surpassed Florence.'[6] Some of Britain's more acute political leaders, like Tory prime minister Lord Salisbury, sensed this growing weakness, and could see the writing on the wall well before the First World War. Joseph Chamberlain also saw the fragility of the empire and believed Britain's imperial decline to be unavoidable unless the empire could be transformed into an imperial preference system – a trade bloc – that would compete with growing American economic power. And his son Neville, prime minister between 1937 and 1940, constructed a whole foreign policy based upon an assumption of British imperial weakness; his strategy of appeasement was a forlorn attempt to save what he could of the resources of the empire.[7]

For most of the first half of the twentieth century, though, British imperial propaganda was pumping out a different message – particularly to the young in the elite education system. In 1921 the South African

General Smuts told the British that they had emerged from the Great War 'quite the greatest power in the world'. As one young public schoolboy, educated to run the empire, later recalled, 'Naturally we believed in the greatness of Britain and the permanence of the Empire. I think we believed in our hearts...that the creation of the British empire was the best thing that ever happened to mankind.'[8] Greatness; and goodness too. In the 1930s schoolchildren were being informed that 'We're all subjects and partakers in the great design, the British empire...The British empire has always worked for the peace of the world. This was the job assigned to it by God.'[9] In other words, the empire was 'all that was noble and good' – naturally so, as it was run by the successors of those Victorian colonial Englishmen who were, according to the historian R.C.K. Ensor, among 'the most religious the world has ever known'.[10] And it is more than likely that the future Queen, the young Elizabeth, would have had this kind of thinking, even its extreme form, imbued in her by her nannies and parents.

Yet by the early 1940s, co-existing with this message of imperial power – and goodness – was a new and stark reality: for Britain – 'quite the greatest power in the world' – was becoming increasingly dependent upon an outside power. There were two phases in this unfolding dependence. The first began when the country's wartime rearmament programme became reliant upon American industry and technology. American machinery was needed to equip British industry for the production of tanks, aero engines and weapons. Britain also needed American steel, the essential ingredient for war-making. By 1940 Britain was effectively bankrupt. As the chancellor of the exchequer reported in February 1940, 'we are in great danger of our gold reserves being exhausted.'[11] By the end of 1940, with the Luftwaffe over the skies of England, the reserves had almost gone, and Britain started its slide into debt – with the USA as creditor. The British cabinet had a 'confident expectation of abundant American help'.[12] It was already clear what the war had wrought. The relationship between Britain and the USA had changed forever. As Correlli Barnett put it, 'in that summer of heroic attitudes...when the English scanned the skies for the Luftwaffe and the sea for the German army...England's existence as an independent, self-sustaining power was reckoned by the government to have just four months to run.'[13] Britain went bankrupt in December 1940 when the gold and dollar reserves ran out.

And after 1940 Britain's war effort – particularly the output of guns and aircraft – would become dependent on the American machine-tool industry: the country's domestic machine-tool industry was simply too inefficient and unskilled to produce the quality and output of guns and aircraft needed. The design and manufacture of British tanks (particularly the Covenanter) remained a problem, and by the summer of 1942 the famous British 8th Army was equipped with almost twice as many American (Grants and Stuarts) as British (Crusader) tanks. Even in the sensitive and crucial radar industry Britain became reliant upon North America for sophisticated parts – such as magnetrons for the airborne interception radar for night fighters. It was estimated in 1943 that annual imports of radio components and equipment from the USA equalled four-fifths of British production. As with other war technologies, British inventive and theoretical science was first rate, but production and design were often below the standards of allies and potential competitors.

Britain also became reliant upon American financial goodwill. British reserves had run out by the early spring of 1941 and the country was in no position to repay America for war supplies. However, the Defense of the United States Act – otherwise known as 'lend-lease' – was passed by congress in March 1941, and thenceforth, for the rest of the war, Britain no longer needed to wage war within her own means. She became as dependent upon American strength as a patient on a life-support machine. Barnett described the dependence as being on a 'heart-lung machine'.[14]

By 1944 the USA had hundreds of thousands of American troops in Britain, and had become the only sizeable foreign army to be stationed on British soil since the Norman invasion. It was soon clear that Britain would be unable to prosecute a second front without the USA, and this new subordinate position was soon confirmed when an American, General Eisenhower, became the supreme allied commander. In such circumstances the idea – central to the ideology of the English ruling classes – of Britain as an independent, 'sovereign' nation was extremely difficult to sustain. At the height of war Winston Churchill boldly stated that 'I have not become the King's first minister in order to preside over the liquidation of the British empire.'[15] And at the end of the war he proclaimed that the empire had emerged 'safe, undiminished and united from a mortal struggle'.[16] The truth was that the empire was over. And with it went British independence. The historian, John Charmley summed up Britain's situation in 1945, 'Churchill stood for the British empire, for British independence and for an "anti-Socialist" vision of Britain' (and he could have added a fourth point, that Churchill also stood for eliminating or weakening the Soviet Union). He then suggests that 'by July 1945 the first of these was on the skids, the second was dependent solely on America and the third had just vanished in a Labour election victory' (and he could have added that Churchill's anti-Soviet vision had also just vanished, for the result of the war meant that the Soviet Red Army was now right at the heart of Europe).[17]

CHURCHILL, BEVIN AND 'GREATNESS': SUBSERVIENT BULLDOGS (1942–51)

Winston Churchill was marginalised by the Americans virtually from the first day that US troops arrived in Britain. He was a minor player at the wartime conferences of the 'big three' at both Tehran and Yalta; his idea for invading Germany through the 'soft under-belly' of Yugoslavia was vetoed, as was his vision of a bold forward thrust following D-Day; and his attempt to secure an agreement with the Soviet Union on Poland before the Red Army arrived there was ignored. The Americans, under both Roosevelt and Truman, saw Churchill's various manoeuvres during the war as trying to secure a British sphere in the post-war settlement. The Americans, quite naturally, were keen to secure their own interests, which they saw as best pursued in Europe through a American–Russian condominium.

Churchill saw all this. He was no innocent. And out of dire necessity he accepted this new reality – and became the architect of Britain's 'junior partnership' with the USA. For Britain as well as Churchill the war may well have been 'our finest hour'. But it also saw the end of Britain's independent sovereign ability to defend itself – for the country had been saved by forces and resources outside its control. It had, in effect, become a dependent of the new superpower in the West. For Churchill, and for most of the British, such dependency was a price well worth paying. But it was a price nonetheless. And as the war dragged on, in decision after decision Churchill was overruled by his American allies. He was called 'the Last Lion' by Churchill's American biographer William Manchester, and his reputation in the USA was unsurpassed (and has remained so). Yet this great lion of a man was, on policy matters and geostrategy, effectively tamed. As power passed to the Americans during the war, Churchill's wartime foreign secretary, Anthony Eden, once plaintively asked, 'Can we not have our own foreign policy?' And he further believed that 'the common language should not delude the British into believing that the Americans also had common interests.'[18]

After 1945 Churchill continued to represent an image of British power and greatness when, in fact, he had presided over Britain's 'defeat' – if 'defeat' is to be defined in the way Churchill and Britain's imperialists defined it: losing the independent ability to defend the empire and oneself and conduct an independent foreign policy. For Churchill it was, as Charmley argues, truly the 'end of glory'; and Churchill knew it – and said so in his own words in the very title of his war history: 'triumph and tragedy.'

Yet, long after the war, establishment British historians were continuing with the story not just of British resolve and heroism but also of the myth of Churchill and the British as being 'victorious'. The approved narrative was that Churchill, not the Americans or Russians, 'saved' the country. It was an image that was to become a great source of post-war pride, but also a great source too of illusions about the country's true place in the world.

American troops left the whole of Europe – including Britain – very shortly after the German surrender, and commentators could be forgiven for thinking that, maybe, with America gone, Britain could regain her independence and reclaim her 'sovereignty'.

It was not to be. In the first few weeks of peace, post-war Britain was to be reminded of her new, reduced, status. On 21 August 1945 Washington announced a surprise decision to bring Britain's credit facilities in the lend-lease deal to an abrupt end, and to do so without even consulting the British government. According to historian John Dickie the US action amounted to a 'diktat', which caused even in the timid-looking Clement Attlee an unlikely outburst of public rage. In London, Washington's post-war treatment of her great ally was seen as hugely unfair. After all, during the war Britain had borne a far greater burden than had its US ally in the common cause of defeating Hitler. British casualties were over twice the American figure, and those killed and missing were three times higher; Britain's losses in external investment were a huge 35 times greater than those of America; and Britain's total expenditure on the war was 50 per cent greater than that of the USA. The British felt that such abrupt treatment was shabby, and even Churchill made a complaint about American high-handedness. In a rather forlorn and unusually critical statement the great man summed up Britain's new position: he found it difficult to believe that 'so great a nation...would proceed in such a rough and harsh manner as to hamper a faithful ally'.[19]

Britain needed a new loan to survive, and John Maynard Keynes summed up the country's humiliation – and dependence on the USA – when, as chief UK negotiator in the loan negotiations with the USA, he argued that 'the conclusion is inescapable that there is no source from which we can raise sufficient funds to enable us to live and spend on the scale we contemplate except the United States.'[20] Britain secured the loan, but at a huge price. The terms set by Washington as it flexed its new geopolitical muscles were stiff – and they required of their wartime ally the full implementation of the long-held American strategic goal of ending Britain's imperial-preference trading system.[21]

Ernest Bevin told the cabinet that he was 'reluctant to agree to any settlement that would leave us subject to economic direction from the US'. But he did agree – using the argument that 'were we to reject these terms' it would mean 'further sacrifices from the British people'.[22] Again, as with Churchill before him, Bevin reckoned he had 'no alternative' but to accept the terms of American leadership.

Bevin, though, had one great advantage over Churchill in his dealings with the Americans. He had fewer sentimental ties, and fewer illusions. During his time as a trade-union leader Bevin had travelled in the USA meeting fellow unionists – the working men and women who mostly hailed from non-Anglo background: Irish-Americans, Italian-Americans and the like. He quickly came to understand that America was not England – certainly not the England of the great houses and country lawns of the American Anglos whom Churchill would have known. Bevin came to understand during his early time as foreign secretary that the new superpower pursued her own interests, not Britain's – and that in Washington's approach to Britain sentiment played a very small role indeed. And, in return, calculation, not sentiment, governed his attitude towards America.

While foreign secretary Bevin had some tough fights with the US administration – particularly over his opposition to the establishment of the state of Israel (Britain abstained in the UN vote setting up the Zionist state). But his overriding preoccupation in the early post-war years was to oppose Soviet power in Europe, and he did so by taking the lead after 1947 in creating NATO and bringing the power of America back into the European continent. He was Britain's top cold-warrior, and as such he could be little other than a supporter of American power in the world.

Ernest Bevin was also a patriot. A 'Great Brit' nationalist who, with Attlee, took the decision to build the British nuclear bomb, he was, as Hugo Young put it, 'the only man in the Attlee cabinet who faintly resembled Winston Churchill'.[23] He was, in all senses, a big man – at ease with himself, confident, steadfast, direct. But in his relations with the Americans he was – for understandable reasons – another subservient bulldog. He knew that in the Cold War Britain survived and prospered only by courtesy of American power.

2 THE QUEEN, THE COMMONWEALTH AND THE BOMB

Only the English-speaking peoples count: that together they can rule the world.

Winston Churchill, State Department dinner, April 1954

When Winston Churchill returned to power in 1951 the very first decision he took was to abort the decolonisation process set in train by Labour. Under Churchill's influence the Conservatives in opposition had voted against the independence of India and Burma, and now, back in power, were not about to see any more imperial losses. As we have seen, Churchill had stated bluntly during the war that he did not plan 'to preside over the liquidation of the British empire' – and he stuck to this position right up till leaving office in 1955.[1] Although there were rumblings among the progressives in the Tory Party (from the youngish Rab Butler in particular), Churchill remained an imperialist to the end.

This decision was eloquent. For it perfectly represented the inability of the post-war British governing classes to adjust to their diminished world role. Edmund Wilson, the perceptive American man of letters who visited Britain soon after the end of the war, noticed this unreconstructed mood. His encounters with the top people of the period surprised him, as they were, in his view, completely 'unreconciled to the post-war diminishment of Britain'.[2] In 1947 it certainly seemed for a while as though the British Labour government was withdrawing from its world role. In February Bevin gave notice that Britain would be handing the Palestine issue over to the UN; shortly following this the government decided that British aid to Greece and Turkey was not to be renewed;

and in the same year it was announced that Britain would be ending the imperial control of India and Burma by June 1948. Yet, as it turned out, this, for the moment, was to be the extent of withdrawal. And it was a withdrawal that was forced on Labour by the exigencies of its economic and political position rather than by a real change of heart. Bevin's biographer, Alan Bullock, set out what was later to become a central charge against the post-war politicians.

> Instead of straining to keep up the part she had played as a leading power since the 18th century, so the argument runs, Labour should have taken the opportunity to withdraw from all overseas commitments in the shortest possible time and concentrate the country's energies on rebuilding her economy and foreign trade.[3]

It was not to be. And, with Churchill's Conservatives back in office there emerged for a time a cross-party consensus about the need to keep some kind of truncated world role. As the British elite looked at their position in the very early 1950s it saw a Britain that may well have been diminished, but also one that could preserve something of its former greatness. The country was a permanent member of the Security Council of the UN, still had an empire in Africa and a powerful presence, with bases, east of Suez. The trick was to accept the 'junior partner' position to the USA that was on offer, but use it to bolster this retrenched imperial role. Britain would piggyback on the USA.

And following the foundation of NATO, with the American connection now firmly established, Britain's leadership could set about constructing its new, updated, and virtual, world role. By the mid-1950s the three key institutions which would both embody and sustain this great pretence of a 'world role' and 'world leadership' were in place, and, intriguingly, are still there today: the Queen, the Commonwealth and the bomb.

QUEEN AND COMMONWEALTH

Britain's new Queen was more than willing to play the role of symbolic leader of a great world power. She had solemnly promised in the coronation oath to 'govern' the peoples of far-flung states from the United Kingdom to Canada, Australia, New Zealand, South Africa, Pakistan, and Ceylon and her 'Possessions and other Territories according to their respective laws and customs'. She had proclaimed herself 'Queen and Head of the Commonwealth' and would later show a continuing personal resolve to stress the importance of the newly created 'British Commonwealth of Nations' and to place her headship of the organisation at the centre of her view of her constitutional role. And from early in her reign she took her duty to visit this far-flung Commonwealth extremely seriously.

The coronation introduced to a wider public this new concept of a 'British Commonwealth' as a successor to, and subtle continuation of, the empire. The idea of some sort of 'Commonwealth' had been around well before the Second World War. It had first been mooted by Lord Rosebery in 1884 when he introduced the idea as a means of prolonging the empire by binding in the white dominions, which, upon independence, might well have considered totally breaking with Britain. 'There is no need for any nation, however great, leaving the empire,' he stated, 'because the empire is a commonwealth of nations.'[4]

Later, Lord Milner's so-called 'kindergarten' of bright young imperial thinkers from Oxbridge, brought together to reconstruct South Africa after the Boer War, had also re-thought the contours of empire with a view to prolonging it (including toying with outlandish ideas like an 'Anglo-Saxon world state' which would encompass the white dominions and North America). Lionel Curtis's *Project of a Commonwealth* was published in 1915, and an odd grouping known as the Round Table, which included such notables as Lord Lothian and Geoffrey Dawson, took up the idea. At the Imperial War Conference of 1917 the notion of the dominions as autonomous nations within something called an 'Imperial Commonwealth' was formally floated. In 1921 the prime minister of South Africa, Jan Smuts, echoed the views of other white dominions that the empire's days were numbered and that 'it will no longer be an empire but a society of free and equal sister states.'[5]

The idea that a white 'Commonwealth of Nations' could be adapted to include non-whites was floated during the inter-war years. That quintessential British imperial figure T.E. Lawrence (of Arabia) put forward the idea of creating 'brown dominions' and, under Curtis's influence, the concept of a 'multiracial Commonwealth' began to be propagated. And the present multiracial 'Commonwealth of Nations' was indeed born when India, Pakistan and Ceylon joined in (Burma refused). As Kathryn Tidrick, in a most perceptive analysis of the British and empire, put it, the Commonwealth 'gracefully combined the idea of imperial unity with that of national autonomy'.[6]

Yet there was a big story behind all this: for these British pioneers of the idea of a 'Commonwealth' (white or multiracial) sought not to end or even reduce, but to continue, Britain's global role, but with much looser, more indirect, relationships. In official Britain there was not even any suggestion that Britain should bring to an end its global reach and become instead a continental power.

For Attlee's post-war Labour government the idea of a new multi-racial 'British Commonwealth' was a godsend: for it could serve to square the growing moral opposition to colonialism within the British left with the continuing desire for British global grandeur (seemingly contradictory instincts often carried within the same British breast). British post-war left-wing internationalism always had a large tinge of moralising globalism about it. Labour left-wingers Fenner Brockway and Michael Foot were serious exponents of decolonisation – but they also genuinely believed in British global leadership by moral example (for instance by adopting unilateral nuclear disarmament).

THE BOMB

With this imperial mentality still dominant, it was not surprising that Britain's post-war establishment should also unite behind the need for Britain to possess 'the bomb'. The decision that Britain should become a nuclear power was taken in January 1947 by Attlee together with Bevin and only four other ministers (and without even reference to the cabinet). The British bomb was announced to the world by Churchill in February 1952, with the first successful test taking place in October of the same year.

The British felt that as British science had played a leading role in the creation, through the Manhattan Project, of the American atomic programme that led to the bombs unleashed on Japan in 1945, they had every right to belong to the nuclear club. But, more importantly, they were convinced that possessing a nuclear weapon was the key to the country remaining at the 'top table' and continuing with an independent global role, no matter how minimal. There was, intriguingly, much talk at the time, in late 1946, of the need for the bomb as a symbol of British independence *from the USA*. Lord Portal, the wartime Chief of the Air Staff, had declared that 'We could not afford to acquiesce in an American monopoly of this new development.'[7]

At one of the preliminary meetings which approved the bomb Bevin declared that it was necessary so that future British foreign secretaries could retain their dignity in relations with their US counterparts. Hugh Dalton and Stafford Cripps were opposed to building the bomb on grounds of cost, but Bevin won round his colleagues by reportedly declaring, 'I don't mind for myself, but I don't want any foreign secretary of this country to be talked at or by a secretary of state in the United States as I have just had [sic] in my discussions with Mr Byrnes.' Bevin insisted that the bomb be built and that 'we've got to have the bloody Union Jack flying on top of it.'[8]

Yet these concerns for independence from the USA did not last. Bevin's outburst against Byrnes was to amount to little more than a spasm, a blowing off of steam. And Attlee himself later argued that when the decision for the bomb had been taken he had not been worried so much about Britain controlling its own bomb but rather about America reverting to isolationism and leaving Britain high and dry. 'There was no NATO then,' he declared to interviewer Kenneth Harris.[9]

Any idea of Britain developing a truly independent nuclear system was soon to be stopped in its tracks. During the 1950s Britain's delivery systems became a major problem. The original 'V-bombers', and the missiles (Blue Steel, Blue Streak) became progressively redundant, and the delivery problems were only solved by the country's 'independent deterrent' becoming utterly dependent on American technology. It was during Harold Macmillan's premiership that Britain ceded effective control over its nuclear weapons to the USA when the prime minister arranged a deal with President John Kennedy for Britain to use the US Polaris system. Ever since then the country has been dependent upon a US guidance system for its targeting. But this key deal was fine for a British political class only interested in the appearance, and not the reality, of global power. By comparison French nuclear weapons systems have remained genuinely independent.

By the mid-1950s, as Churchill handed over to Anthony Eden, the word from the heart of the post-war British establishment – from the Queen, her court, from war leader Churchill and the opposition Labour party – was clear: there was to be no radical readjustment to a new role in the world, or a new view of ourselves, our standing or our power. The myth of British global power was to continue its fateful grip. And, on the face of it, for a broader public looking at life through newspaper headlines, post-war movies and the new medium of television, Britain was indeed still a great world power. The Churchill era may well have ended with the great war victor leaving Downing Street, but his successor, Anthony Eden – the wartime foreign secretary and a man totally associated in the public mind with Churchill and great-power politics – still looked the imperial part. And was soon to act upon it.

THE IMPERIAL MIND AT MID-CENTURY

This lingering sense of empire was – as we shall see – widely shared throughout British post-war society, but it was most keenly felt within the country's political and ruling classes. Most countries' foreign policies are still dictated by relatively small groups, and Britain's foreign policy at mid-century was no exception. What was remarkable, though, was the tightly knit social background, and the consequent uniform ideology, of this elite. The country's Foreign Office, its intelligence services and its governing political class were all drawn from an exceedingly narrow social background – overwhelmingly peopled by ex-public schoolboys educated at a very small number of elite schools. And so tightly drawn was this class that over the period 1918–50 over 80 per cent of all Tory cabinets were populated from public schools, and almost 50 per cent from two – two! such schools: Eton and Harrow. By 1960, 15 years into the post-war peace, an incredible 83.2 per cent of top army positions, 65 per cent of top civil servants and 82.6 per cent of ambassadors came from public schools.[10]

This small dominant class which governed the country in the 1950s was an imperial class. Many of their number had direct experience of empire, for they had, after all, been young men in the early part of the century, some before the First World War. Others were imbued with the imperial mentality in the 1920s and 1930s when the empire was still a going concern. Indeed, almost all of them had had an education specifically designed for an imperial ruling class – a training that it was considered would equip them to deal with the exigencies of ruling and administering a far-flung empire.

This 'education for empire' had been designed in the late-nineteenth-century English public schools, and carried over into the public schools in the new century. That its influence lasted well into the late twentieth century may well be due in part to the sheer rigour of its earlier application. Correlli Barnett went so far as to argue that 'except for young Nazis or Communists no class of leaders in modern times has been so subjected to prolonged moulding of character, personality and outlook as British public school boys in this era.'[11] Kathryn Tidrick echoes essentially the same sharp point. She argues that 'the public school system worked to produce Führers on the wholesale principle' and that these schools developed so that 'the imperial demand for leadership met with an unfailing supply' and also 'operated to rivet upon the British political system a governing class through which the leadership ethos was thoroughly diffused'.[12]

Of course these young men, as they came to power in mid or late life in mid-century Britain, had lived through some shattering events – particularly the Second World War – which had sapped Britain's power and wealth. And they had also seen this power pass to other countries, like Russia and the USA, whose support for Britain during the war had ensured that she did not go under. Yet, even so, this generation never truly experienced overt, unadorned defeat, the sharp, total experience of loss and impotence felt by the people on the continent. And even the obvious emergence of the USA as a world power, and its growing supplanting of the British empire, did not undermine the confidence of the class. Indeed, it had a rub-off effect. The English elite could – and did – claim pride of authorship of this newly powerful nation on the other side of the Atlantic. In the immediate post-war period, during American world supremacy, the levers of power and culture in the USA were still largely controlled by anglophile white Anglo-Saxon Protestants – in the hands, that is, of the 'cousins'. And, by the late 1960s these 'cousins', although themselves still very anti-colonialist, were beginning to see the value to themselves of the remnants of Britain's empire east of Suez, and, ever so subtly, encouraging the British to stay.

AN IMPERIAL PEOPLE

The wider public were also still smitten by empire. Although, as H.G. Wells could assert in *Mr Britling Sees It Through*, 'the middle class and most of the lower class knew no more of the empire than they did of the Argentine republic or the Italian Renaissance', this would also have been true of their knowledge of much of their own government.[13] A direct experience of ruling an empire was not necessary in order to feel part of a great nation which had conquered a third of the globe, and to feel, no matter how inchoately, superior culturally and racially to lesser breeds, and to believe that England and Britain were the centre of the world.

The depth of popular support for the empire can be gauged by the interesting fact that before World War II no section of British life ever turned decisively against the empire – not the Scots, the Welsh, the English, the industrial proletariat, the middle class, the nineteenth-century Conservatives or Liberals, and, incredibly, not even the radicals. There were votes in social-unity imperialism and in imperial preference. And there was no serious anti-colonial protest movement in the country until well into the second half of the twentieth century, not until after the

Second World War made the empire economically impossible. Indeed, the empire possessed a popular constituency right up to and beyond the Second World War. The Conservatives remained the party of empire right up until Winston Churchill died, and neither the Liberals nor Labour (nor even the socialist intellectuals before the Second World War) attempted any systematic rejection of the principle of empire.

And after 1945 the empire remained a constant source of images and tales in the mass popular media. Messages about the innate superiority of white Englishmen were produced and recycled in educational texts and popular newspapers right up into the 1960s. And in the working-class areas of the cities – after the large council-house-building programmes of the 1930s – the Pretoria Avenues, Khyber Crescents and Mafeking Roads acted as a constant reminder of British imperial superiority. Through association with empire the working classes could feel superior to others – the black and brown races.

These mid-century British lived in a world in which the map was still painted red, in which Africa, Asia, the Middle East and even parts of Latin America, were still run from London. They also inhabited a national culture which was still pumping out its imperial messages – particularly to the young. And even in the mid-1950s and 1960s it was impossible to think of Britain without thinking of the empire – secondary schoolchildren throughout the country were still assembling for 'Empire Day' to be told that they were the inheritors of a world power. It was a point massively reinforced by the imperial culture and trappings of the British monarchy, and the new Queen, in the new mass television age.

TWO WARS

It was also underpinned by the story the British began telling themselves about their role during the Second World War. Although the world wars had drastically reduced Britain's geostrategic position, for many people these great conflicts simply served to renew the country's greatness. The fires of patriotism, and nationalism, were restoked as war reinforced the sensibility of not only a separate but also a special virtuous English and British identity.

The sheer nationalistic fervour of 1914–18, when millions volunteered to fight (and die), is, to much contemporary thinking, still inexplicable. Yet it was very real. And so too was the full engagement in the war effort of the country's ruling-class youth. Quite simply the 'Great War' against

Germany saw the English 'public-school gentlemen' go to war en masse – thus precluding a re-run of the eighteenth-century radical taunt that the upper classes were unpatriotic. And the 'classlessness' of this sacrifice may help explain why the ineptness and bungling of many within the senior officer corps during the carnage of the trenches provoked very little anger once the war was over.

World War II also served to revive national, and nationalist, sentiment – particularly from its low point when pacifism and internationalism suffused the culture during the inter-war years. The 'British' brand came out of Hitler's war very well. The country faced, alone for some time, a clear, unambiguously evil, enemy. And 'unlike France' it successfully repelled an invasion. Also, 'it won the war', thus providing the country and, through the glamorous lens of the burgeoning film media, the wider world with British heroes. The Churchill 'bulldog' and the handlebar-moustached RAF fighter pilot-type became world famous as 'victors' and 'winners' – hardly the stuff of a declining empire.

The month of May 1945, with the economy in ruins and its world role draining away, nonetheless provided an image of a country of power and greatness. Field Marshall Bernard Montgomery was an Ulsterman, but could easily pass – by accent and bearing – as an archetypical public-school Englishman. And on 5 May, commanding the 21st Army Group, he presided over the surrender of all German forces in North-West Germany, Holland and Denmark. Three days later, Winston Churchill – the ultimate symbol of warrior Englishness – appeared alongside the royal family on the balcony of Buckingham Palace to salute 'Victory in Europe'. The British people could be forgiven for believing that the country had not just survived but prevailed – that it had pulled it off yet again; that it was still the most powerful nation under the sun; and that the culture of Englishness, personified in the 'English bulldog' personality of Winston Churchill and the decent 'English reticence' of King George VI, would resonate around the globe as emblems of a democracy to be copied.

Indeed following the war a major myth-making industry did emerge to feed the illusion of British centrality in the defeat of the Germans. To some extent national myths can serve the function of hiding bitter and awkward truths. Britain played an important though subsidiary part in the Battle of Normandy in 1944; and Normandy itself was a secondary front. The 'turning point of the war' was more likely located in the 1942 Battle of Stalingrad. Yet the post-war British media vastly exaggerated the British contribution, as they did the role of Winston

Churchill – who, as his own records more than abundantly testify, was very much the junior partner to Roosevelt and Truman throughout the last three-and-a-half years of the war. Churchill's post-war standing, particularly in America, where he became a statesman-hero (and rivalled the posthumous popularity of Roosevelt), did wonders for the country's reputation as a 'winner' and as a great power. The American media was still referring to the 'British empire' as a world player as late as the 1960s.

SUPERIORITY AND RACE

Yet the 'victory' in two wars only confirmed, and continued, the unbroken culture of imperialism. Had the country been defeated and occupied it might have been a different story, as the British might well have been able to put the imperial past fully and finally behind them. As it was they were not able to do so. And the values and prejudices of empire marched on well into the late part of the twentieth century.

Two prejudices of empire stand out and can help explain why, by comparative standards, a particularly exceptional type of nationalism endured in Britain. The first is a superiority complex different in kind from that of most other peoples in developed countries. The British, like the Americans, have a narrative of exceptionalism. But an empire controlling a third of the world on which the sun never sets is heady stuff. And the British came to believe they were not just exceptional, but superior too. Americans tend to believe their ideas particularly 'democracy', are superior; the British, of this type, vest superiority in the people themselves. In the imperial experience British and English contact with 'foreigners' was always minimal. The English did not mix, they conquered, and then they ruled. So the colonial experience – though technically an internationalising phenomenon – hardly encouraged cosmopolitan instincts among the rulers.

Lord Hugh Cecil, English landowner, imperialist and high Tory, is a perfect representative of this English sense of superiority – class, national and racial. In 1912 he proffered a view of the English mission which nicely represented the sentiment of his fellow rulers during the height of empire. In what was the very stuff of the ideology of Englishness he argued that 'our vocation in the world...[is] to undertake the government of vast, uncivilised populations and to raise them gradually to a higher level of life.'[14]

And another imperialist, Rudyard Kipling, revealed a similar mental framework in his famous poem 'The White Man's Burden':

Take up the White Man's burden –
Send forth the best ye breed –
Go bind your sons to exile
To serve your captives' need;
To wait in heavy harness
On fluttered folk and wild –
Your new-court sullen peoples,
Half-devil and half-child.

Thus English superiority was not simply cultural; it was racial as well. And the era of empire saw the emergence in England not only of a general prejudice in favour of English and white racial superiority (Lord Hugh Cecil's views would have received near-universal support) but also of strains of literary racism (in, among others, the works of H.G. Wells) philosophic racism (exemplified by the works of G.K. Chesterton), even systematic, scientific racism (of which Houston Stewart Chamberlain was a leading exponent).

General theories of race – like general theories of politics – did not catch on among the English, and scientific racism became unacceptable to the political class following the experience of the 1939–45 war and Nazism. However, a profound basic racial prejudice remained. As one contemporary theorist has put it,

with or without a theory of biological racism, whether derived from the work of Count Gobineau (1915) or some other source, a deep-seated unrefined belief in racial difference in performance, and in standards, probably owes its origin to the colonial relationship between white master and black subordinate ... The white man's civilising presence, the need to develop backward nations, the missionaries' vocation to convert the heathen acted as powerful justification for continued imperial domination. Such ideas deeply penetrated the culture of the British population and survive to the present day.[15]

Winston Churchill, the country's last unashamedly imperial leader, possessed a decidedly racist side – one shared at mid-century by many of his contemporaries in the higher reaches of English public life. The historian Andrew Roberts writes of Churchill, in a passage worthy of quoting at length, that his views on race did not spring up fully formed when he regained office in 1951, but were held consistently during his long political career. By the standards of today – and possibly even of his own time – Winston Churchill was a convinced racist... For Churchill Negroes were 'niggers' or 'blackamoors', Arabs were 'worthless', Chinese were 'chinks' or 'pigtails', and other black races were 'baboons' or 'Hottentots', Italians were 'mere organ-grinders'... As the great tribal leader of 1940 his [Churchill's] speeches were peppered with references to the British race... Sir David Hunt, one of his Private Secretaries during his 1951–55 period of office, recalls 'Churchill was on the whole rather anti-black. I remember him sending a telegram to [South African president] Dr Malan and asking me whether he should say 'My dear Mr President, Alles sal rect hom ["All is well"]. Keep on skelping the kaffirs!'

'Blackamoor' was also a term in normal upper class usage – indeed was used by another prominent figure of the fag end of empire, Elizabeth Bowes-Lyon (later 'the Queen Mother').[16]

This kind of 'unrefined' racial superiority existed in Britain well into the late twentieth century, and was revived by the arrival of mass third-world immigration into the country, a process begun in the late 1950s. And notions of racial and national superiority at the heart of imperial Englishness were complemented by a mild and understated antisemitism. Victorian English society developed a certain tolerance for very rich Jews like the Sassoons, the Rothchilds and the Oppenheimers (as its 'practical-man' persona tolerated big money from any quarter). Yet a disdain for Jewish people still surfaced regularly among English leadership groups. Even as late as 1959 the then prime minister, Harold Macmillan, could claim that 'the Jews, the planners and the old cosmopolitan element' were playing 'no small part in the [European] Commission.'[17] A standard view, even as late as the 1970s would be that 'everyone knew very well that there was a gaping chasm between them and us', and that although Jewish people are 'not really Jewish here in England... of course they're not really English either'.[18]

Yet superiority had its obligations. The imperial version of Englishness, conscious that it was the English role to administer large tracts of the globe and 'the vast uncivilised populations', developed a cult of rulership. Englishmen would be trained in the arts of leadership. They would be trusted. And, like the feudal nobility, in return for the loyalty of their subjects, they would rule paternalistically – over both the brown and black races and the domestic whites. They would be 'firm but fair' – incredibly, as late as 1974 a paternalistic election slogan of the Conservative Party in the February 1974 general election. This idea of rulership, of *noblesse oblige* leadership, still produces faint echoes in the political language of the country well into the twenty-first century: as in 'leading in Europe' and 'giving a lead to the world'.

And this notion of rulership would often involve leading by example, and the setting of standards of behaviour for lower ranks and lesser orders to follow. This idea that rulers needed to lead by personal example had been present earlier in English history, but came into its own during imperial rule in India – when the needs of administration coincided with the rapid growth, at home, of evangelical religion. And the British governing class of India 'owed much of its character to evangelical religion', particularly its concept of authority, which 'was rooted in the evangelical cult of personal example'.[19] Some aspects of this imperial culture of rulership can be seen in contemporary thinking about 'humanitarian' or 'liberal interventionism' – the idea that Britain has a moral 'duty' to intervene militarily in less developed parts of the world – which surfaced in sharp form many decades later under the premiership of Tony Blair.

3 EDEN: NO END OF A LESSON

I think Suez, more than anything, punctured the Great Power illusion once and for all.

> Joe Garner, permanent under-secretary,
> Commonwealth Office, 1981

I want to tell you that in the Middle East our great enemies are the Americans.

> Enoch Powell to Anthony Eden, some time in the 1940s

ANTHONY EDEN: AN ENGLISH GENTLEMAN'S WORLD ROLE

In April 1955, Anthony Eden became prime minister of Britain. Churchill, the unapologetic aristocratic imperialist was succeeded by no less a child of empire and aristocracy – though from a somewhat lower rank than his illustrious predecessor. Born into minor aristocracy in 1897, the family home, Windlestone near Durham, was surrounded by only 8000 acres, a smallish holding by the standards of the time. Eden had the full establishment education. He went to preparatory school in Surrey, thence to Eton, then saw service in the Great War (described by a biographer as 'selfless, courageous and modest'), and then went up to Oxford University, to Christchurch College (then often dubbed 'Eton by the Cherwell').[1]

Not surprisingly the young Anthony Eden had all the orthodox attributes of English superiority, separateness and standoffishness. There was some slight radical dissidence in him – qualities of sensitivity, asceticism and intellectuality that led him to think beyond the narrow confines of his upbringing – but, at root, like all those destined to secure political influence in the Conservative party in mid-century Britain, he was thoroughly imperial in mindset, brought up and immersed in the power and superiority of his class and country.[2]

Eden had become Churchill's foreign secretary – and heir apparent – when the Conservatives returned to office in 1951. The Conservatives, Churchill aside, had difficulties in settling into the new junior-partner relationship. The British, and particularly Eden, still saw something of an independent role for themselves – based upon Churchill's formulation of the country being at the centre of 'three intersecting circles': the Commonwealth, America and Europe. From the American point of view the Cold War was now the overriding issue, the 'Western world' through NATO was in a struggle that demanded unity, and the USA was the only country that could give leadership to the West. Britain's role was to be supportive in the struggle.

Washington believed it would be helpful to have Britain as a European sidekick willing to advance its interests both in Europe and through its residual imperial position east of Suez. And in the early 1950s Washington was also warming to the idea of a united Europe as a potential strategic ally. The US administration was constantly urging Britain to join in early moves towards European unity. After 1952, the new American administration's secretary of state John Foster Dulles was so keen on European defence integration that he threatened to change US policy if unity in Europe should lose momentum. 'If the European Defence Community should not become effective; if France and Germany remain apart,' he said, 'that would compel an agonising reappraisal of basic United States policy.'[3]

Anthony Eden did not agree. He had delivered a speech at Columbia University in New York in January 1952 on British foreign policy. There was much speculation at the time about the creation of a European Defence Force (an idea later ditched by the French national assembly) and even of a new European federation – an idea being pushed by the Eisenhower administration. Yet in two grandly dismissive sentences Eden ended speculation that British policy under the Conservatives would take a serious European tilt. 'Speaking of the frequent suggestions that the United Kingdom should join a federation on the continent of Europe... this is something which we know, in our bones, we cannot do.'[4] Here he was essentially echoing Churchill's September 1946 Zurich speech in which the war leader had advocated a 'United States of Europe' but one which Britain, though supportive, would not be a part of. What exactly it was within 'the bones' of Eden and Churchill that would not allow them to contemplate Britain being a part of a new European enterprise was never spelt out.

The historian D.R. Thorpe has argued that 'many in Britain felt themselves to be on a different level from the principal continental countries' and that Eden, a 'man of his times' was one of them.[5] This 'different level' was operating when the continentals, pulling themselves up from the failure of the European Defence Treaty, began the negotiations to set up a common market. Invitations were issued to come to Messina. And while other continental states sent full ministers, Eden sent a mid-to-upper level civil servant – a Mr Russell Bretherton. British hauteur was on full display at the time as Eden's deputy, Rab Butler, talked grandly and dismissively, and typically, of Messina as the product of some 'archeological excavations'. These archeological excavations ended up creating the Treaty of Rome – the EEC and the EU.

SUEZ AND HUMILIATION

In the early post-war years Anthony Eden had paid obeisance to, but had not truly ingested, the real role of Britain in the Anglo–American 'special relationship'. The new unspoken rules set by Washington were clear: that Britain could, if it wanted, posture on the world stage, but it could not act – except, that is, in concert or agreement with the new leaders of the Western world in Washington. Anthony Eden was to fall foul of these rules when, as prime minister in 1956, he reverted to an older mode – the leader of an independent imperial power. On 26 July 1956 Egyptian leader Colonel Gamal Nasser nationalised the Suez Canal Company. Eden saw this action as a threat to Britain's security, but after a series of international initiatives no agreement could be secured. In his full pomp and in an extraordinary outburst of suppressed imperialism, the British prime minister decided to invade Egypt.

Having decided to act with France against Nasser, Eden, at a secret meeting outside of Paris, fixed up a deal with the Israelis that they would attack Egypt and thus give Britain and France the excuse to invade the third-world country under the guise of separating the combatants and securing the canal. On 29 October 1956 Israel invaded the Egyptian-controlled Gaza strip and Sinai peninsula.

After an ultimatum to both sides to withdraw, Eden ordered the invasion of Egypt, and 'Operation Musketeer' got underway. A bombing campaign started immediately and was followed up by the invasion itself on 6 November. The invasion bitterly divided British public opinion. It was opposed by many Commonwealth countries. And the USA not only publicly opposed the invasion but also used its economic leverage over Britain to put pressure on the Eden government to withdraw from the canal. This Britain did by December. It was a humiliating retreat for Eden, who resigned from office in January 1957.

Eden's 1956 war seriously offended the Americans on several fronts. He had launched an invasion of a sovereign Arab country without US agreement. He had fixed up a 'secret plan' with the Israelis for the invasion behind Washington's back. He then carried out the Anglo–French–Israeli conspiracy and invaded Egypt without informing the Americans – the US administration first heard about it from a leak by an anti-Eden minister only a few days before. And all this on the very eve of the 'senior partner's' presidential election.

Eden was no novice. He had been at Churchill's side as the wartime leader had assumed the junior-partner role in the transatlantic alliance; he had supported Labour's lopsided post-war 'special relationship', and fully supported Churchill's post-war pro-American line. Yet all the time Eden had had a pent-up hankering after an independent world role – and perhaps a belief that the 'special relationship' could actually allow for real independence of action. Indeed, as one of Eden's biographers put it, Eden throughout his premiership 'found it difficult to adjust to the fact that Britain would inevitably have to play a secondary role alongside America'.[6]

This hankering after independence was one reason for Eden's prickly relations with America's post-war leaders. Reportedly he tended to patronise President Eisenhower – partly because 'Ike' was 'no gentleman' but also because during the war the American president had, technically at least, been below him in the allied hierarchy.[7] He got on even less well with the new American secretary of state, John Foster Dulles. This antipathy was mutual: Dulles disliked what he considered to be Eden's contrived old-world good manners and was also irritated by Eden's 'fey' ways, such as his constant use of the term 'my dear' in addressing men; Eden hated Dulles's new-world tactile over-familiarity.

In any event, Eden's behaviour over Suez was proof positive that the British political establishment had not adjusted to the new power relationships in the Western world, and the American reaction to the

Anglo–French–Israeli invasion – clear, strong and swift – came as a huge shock. In refusing to support sterling unless Britain abandoned the invasion, withdrew its troops from Egypt and handed the problem over to the UN, Washington was laying down the law. And by forcing the British – and the French – to pull back from the canal in such a public manner Washington humiliated the British establishment, and the Tory Party in particular. Later Eden, in retirement, was to ruefully recall a conversation he had had with Enoch Powell some time in the 1940s in which Powell had said to him, 'I want to tell you that in the Middle East our great enemies are the Americans.' Looking back, Eden remarked, 'You know, I had no idea what he meant...I do now.'[8]

The political upshot of the imbroglio was stark. America had shown its opposition to Eden, Eden's policy failed, and after a decent interval Eden resigned. The diplomatic historian David Carlton has argued that by 1956 British dependence on Washington had become so marked – and Eden's burst of independent action so delusional – that the USA was in a position to organise what amounted to a cabinet coup against Eden. He tells the extraordinary story of how the president of the USA ceased to have any direct dealings with the British prime minister and 'set about humiliating him'. He recounts how Eisenhower suggested to his ambassador in London that he go behind Eden's back in a clandestine move to encourage members of what amounted to a pro-American cabal in the British cabinet – Harold Macmillan, Rab Butler and Lord Salisbury – to replace the elected prime minister. So sensitive were these manoeuvres that the president felt he had to talk to his ambassador in code – almost in the manner of a spy novel. Carlton reproduces from US government sources Eisenhower's exact words to the ambassador as he indicates the identity of his potential collaborators. 'Eisenhower: You know who I mean? One has the same name as my predecessor at...university [Rab Butler] the other was with me in the war [Harold Macmillan]'.[9]

To interfere in the politics of a major ally in this way in order to secure a change of prime minister was rather like a Moscow-inspired coup in an Eastern European satellite regime. And it revealed the new power relationship between Washington and London. More surprising perhaps was the willingness of British politicians – in this case Macmillan, Butler and Salisbury – to be part of this palace coup.

The leader of this pro-American cabal, the chancellor of the exchequer, Harold Macmillan, had originally taken a tough line against Nasser, but later softened. He took Eden's place in Downing Street and then immediately sought to restore relations with Eisenhower and Dulles.

During the crisis the Labour opposition leadership was also in league with the Americans. After initially supporting the anti-Nasser rhetoric of Eden, Labour's new leader Hugh Gaitskell not only opposed Eden's invasion but openly campaigned against it in rallies throughout the country. He also, controversially, went on national television at the height of the crisis, while British troops were in action, to denounce the invasion. This extremely contentious move – denounced as 'traitorous' by Tories and the Tory media – was, though, a calculated risk. Gaitskell was extremely close to the Americans and the US embassy, and his position could only have been carried off with the sure knowledge that Britain's great ally in Washington supported it.

With Eden's fall, so fell any notion of an independent British foreign policy. Some Conservatives, not least the aged Churchill himself, continued to believe that had Britain ignored the pressure from Washington and kept its troops at the canal, then the country would have faced down American pressure. 'Who could have got us out?' asked some die-hard Tories. Others in and around the Tory Party – the Suez group of Tory MPs and the supporters of the League of Empire Loyalists – toyed with a break with Washington. But the Macmillan Tory cabinet quickly reasserted the 'special relationship', and within a year it was almost as though no breach with Washington had occurred. All again was sweetness and light across the Atlantic.

British leaders seemed to learn lessons from the Suez humiliation. The country's leadership continued to seek a 'world role' through the junior partnership. But never again – in the half century since the invasion – has Britain taken a foreign-policy action in express opposition to Washington. Joe Garner, a permanent under-secretary at the Commonwealth Office, reflecting later on the Suez affair, spoke for many when he argued that 'I think Suez, more than anything, punctured the Great Power illusion once and for all.'[10] Anthony Nutting, one of two Tory ministers who resigned over the crisis, entitled his book on the crisis *No End of a Lesson*.

Yet was it? Or was it to be, in the other meaning of Nutting's clever double entendre, no lesson learnt?[11] Had Britain's political class still learnt nothing about its real place in the world?

4   MACMILLAN: A 'GREEK' IN THE AMERICAN EMPIRE

We are the Greeks in this American Empire.

Harold Macmillan, North Africa, 1942

Harold Macmillan became prime minister on 10 January 1957 following Anthony Eden's resignation the day before. His 'appointment' – there was no election even among Conservatives – was announced by Buckingham Palace in the afternoon after the Queen had taken the decision to 'appoint' him following private meetings with Winston Churchill and the Marquess of Salisbury. This *emergence* of Macmillan would have been an early lesson to the new Queen – revealing her private role in selecting a prime minister. The BBC news bulletins of the time stated bluntly 'The Queen will *decide* who will become the next Prime Minister.' It was a dark time for Britain's proud elites. Anthony Eden had resigned as prime minister following a great foreign-policy and military failure and a breakdown in relations with the country's main ally. A new prime minister, one willing to accept American leadership, had been installed (without an election). Washington had flexed its muscles, made clear who was boss, and had even engineered Britain's humiliation. A picture of the end of empire could not have been more colourfully drawn. Britain, whether it wanted it or not, was finally confronted with living in a new world, of entering its post-imperial phase.

In one sense the premiership of Harold Macmillan had the potential to represent something of a break. In Tory terms Macmillan came from the commercial, not the aristocratic, class. He was not overly invested in the imperial sensibility, his foreign experience being as an administrator in wartime North Africa, not lordly rulership in India or the colonies. And his defining political objective – overcoming the unemployment of the 1930s which he had witnessed as MP for Stockton-on-Tees – gave him something of a leftist instinct for social change.

Yet Macmillan was, above all, an actor. And he liked treading the boards on the world stage. He was to give many good performances, and one such was on display during his highly publicised visit to Moscow in February 1959 when he tried to act as a go-between for President Eisenhower and Chairman Khrushchev over the question of nuclear weapons. However, the British prime minister – still, just, thought of around the world as one of the 'big three' – made next to no difference on any major international issue during this trip. Yet, wearing a white fur hat as he padded down the aircraft steps in Moscow, he was the picture of a world statesman – and was to be dubbed 'Supermac' by the British cartoonist Vicky.

A global actor, though, needed a global organisation, and during Macmillan's time in Downing Street the British political class began to formulate the idea of an updated and reformed 'British Commonwealth of Nations' as the way forward. Macmillan had argued as late as 1952 for 'the development of the Empire into an economic unit as powerful as the USA and the USSR'.[1] This echo of Joseph Chamberlain's earlier idea of a British superpower based upon imperial preference was not, though, a serious runner in the 1950s – not least because the USA, having dismantled the earlier version, would not tolerate its return. What was possible, though, was a loose – non-economic, non-political and non-military – club of ex-colonial countries which, as the 'British Commonwealth of Nations', would create a forum for discussion and cooperation, and which, crucially, would allow Britain's politicians to head up a world organisation – a kind of mini UN.

Macmillan's Tories, after the Churchill interregnum, restarted Labour's decolonisation programme – with independence for, among others, Ghana (in 1957), Nigeria (in 1960), Sierra Leone (in 1961) and Kenya (in 1963). Alongside this decolonisation, the 1950s saw the arrival of 'non-alignment' and 'the third world', and the idea that any new Commonwealth would need to be multicultural and multiracial. Thus, the Tory government accepted that the unreconstructed apartheid state of South Africa would need to be cut adrift. Macmillan started this process in his famous speech in Cape Town on 3 February 1960 in which he argued that 'the wind of change is blowing through this continent, and, whether we like it or not, this growth of [African] national consciousness is a political fact.'

Macmillan's aim was not the end of the Commonwealth. Quite the opposite: it was to bring into being a reformed, multicultural world body – the British Commonwealth – through which the British political class (headed by Queen Elizabeth) could continue to play a global role.

This aim, needless to say, was warmly supported by the new Queen – who continued to take the 'global' responsibilities inherent in her coronation oath seriously. The journalist Andrew Marr, in a rhapsodic rendering of the Queen's life during these years, shows how she set out to recreate a new global role for herself through the Commonwealth connection. He writes that 'the Queen's first major act after her Coronation was to embark on a gigantic six-month tour of her [sic] wider authority.' She flew across the Atlantic to Bermuda and Jamaica, visited Fiji and Tonga, and then Australia and New Zealand, Ceylon, the Cocos Islands, Uganda and Aden. And, argues the former *Independent* journalist, 'it was an unrepeatable time of triumph for the Queen and the Duke' – for 'Britain's real power might be hollowed out but her post-war prestige was at its peak...she was the newest member of the atomic club, her fighting services had won great victories and across the former Empire there was optimism.'[2] And the unmistakable message from the Queen to her subjects – one that was to be repeated time and again during her reign – was that through the Commonwealth idea it was still right and reasonable for Britain to remain at the top table, a world power with global reach. There was no need for the country to adjust.

'GREECE TO ROME'

The politicians in London, though, were beginning to see things differently – not about the need for a global role, but rather about the way to secure it. The Queen's Commonwealth route to a world role was beginning to appear little more than a fantasy. And for Macmillan, unlike Eden, it was clear that the real road to 'a global role' ran through Washington – and that it was the 'special relationship' with the USA which allowed him truly to tread the world stage.

And the 'special relationship' was becoming more necessary all the time. During the Macmillan premiership the stark facts were that Britain was falling more and more into the American orbit. The full extent of Britain's increasing security dependence on the USA became apparent as problems emerged in the delivery system for the British nuclear deterrent. In February 1960 Britain decided to abandon its own Blue Streak missile and buy instead from the USA the Skybolt missile – which could be fired from an aircraft thus avoiding the problem of fixed launch sites.

This deal was arranged between Macmillan and Eisenhower at Camp David, and the quid pro quo was the controversial decision to allow the Americans to use Gareloch on the Clyde for a new American Polaris base – a base containing nuclear warheads, and therefore subject to Russian targeting – near the large population centre of Glasgow. In a sign of Britain's subservient position within the alliance, Macmillan tried several times to persuade Eisenhower not to push for a nuclear base on the Clyde – he offered instead the more remote base at Loch Linnhe – but Eisenhower insisted, and the president got his way.

Another sign of British dependence was the character of the subsequent Polaris deal between Washington and London concluded in December 1962 at Nassau between Macmillan and President John Kennedy. Macmillan sold himself as the youthful Kennedy's wise old uncle, but in reality he was a supplicant.

Britain's own nuclear bomb had been built by the post-war Labour cabinet in an attempt to retain some independent influence and to keep a seat at the geopolitical 'top table'. There was considerable opposition in Washington to Britain retaining a nuclear force, partly because – an argument that might have been disingenuous – of the problems it would cause for the French. The Americans also balked at anything 'independent', offering initially to provide the British with the missiles on condition they were 'assigned' to a NATO multilateral force. Macmillan finally got an agreement that stated that the British Polaris system would indeed be assigned to NATO except in a 'dire national emergency'. Yet, the truth was that the delivery system for British nuclear weapons became progressively dependent upon American technology and goodwill (Polaris needed an American guidance system and regular upgrading in the USA). If nuclear independence was a test of national independence, then France – which under De Gaulle insisted upon a genuinely independent and self-sufficient nuclear system – remained an independent nation much longer than Britain.

This Nassau agreement was yet another piece of British vainglory – and counter-productive at that. For, far from retaining the ostensible prize of an independent nuclear deterrent, the British government remained dependent on the USA and at the same time managed to sour relations with the French, the result of which may well have led to De Gaulle's veto – one month after Nassau – of British membership of the EEC.[3]

The idea of Britain as 'junior partner' to the USA in the Atlantic alliance was, though, still difficult for many Conservatives to swallow. And to appease these sensibilities, and indeed Macmillan's pride, a new line of reasoning entered into the discourse. It amounted to an argument that Britain, if not strong and powerful, was 'wise' and 'prescient'. The comforting image was drawn of Britain as 'Greece' to America's 'Rome'. Macmillan himself had suggested this role when, in North Africa during the war, he had written to Richard Crossman. 'We are Greeks in this American Empire,' he had argued, and 'we must run the Allied Forces HQ as the Greeks ran the operations of the Emperor Claudius.'[4]

Peter Riddell, in his excellent account of the Anglo–American 'special relationship', reports Macmillan as understandably irritating some American policymakers with this 'Greeks and Romans' comparison. Riddell calls it a 'patronising implication that the wise and experienced British could guide and educate the crude, though powerful, Americans' and suggests that 'while not expressed publicly after the 1960s, this thought still persisted in the minds of some British politicians and diplomats for a long time afterwards.'[5]

MACMILLAN: A SWITCH OF ROLE?

Yet, amid all this anxious searching for 'a global role' at the side of the Americans, Macmillan's, and the Conservative cabinet's, decision in 1961 to apply for entry into the EEC was a surprising sign of change – perhaps a new clear-eyed appreciation of reduced power and a willingness to abandon global illusions? And questions still remain about why this generation of post-Suez Tories made the application.

One answer was that the British political class, still reeling from Suez, had taken the big decision to abandon its obsessive search for a global role and instead settle for becoming a European power. But the contemporary historian and acute observer of prime ministers, Peter Hennessey, sees the application in a different light. Hennessey believes that Macmillan had not given up on the 'world role' – and that he sold the idea of EEC entry to the cabinet as a way of harnessing the economic dynamism of the EEC to Britain's still global aims.[6] And the 'Eurosceptic' historian Martin Holmes agrees – that rather than a change of course based upon a new realism, it was the same old tune: 'he and his generation of Conservatives wanted to find a way in which British power could be rekindled, a way in which our influence could continue to spread beneficially beyond Britain's borders.' Holmes argues that Europe was seen by Macmillan and his circle as nothing more than a 'substitute for empire'. He suggests that they said to themselves, 'why not join the European Community?' 'If Britain could join Europe then our diplomatic experience, our skills in negotiation, and our special relationship with the United States...could provide the Europeans with political leadership.'[7]

If Holmes is right in this, Macmillan's application was certainly not wholehearted. It was a contrivance. The longing for a world role – albeit at the side of the Americans – still dominated. The three most influential political figures of the immediate post-Suez era – Harold Macmillan (prime minister from 1956 to 1963), Alec Douglas-Home – (prime minister from 1963 to 1964) and Queen Elizabeth – saw themselves as worldly wise, realistic statesmen and women; yet none of them, even in the aftermath of the Suez humiliation, truly sought to adjust policy and abandon the 'world role' and the 'special relationship' in favour of a more realistic and modest foreign policy in Europe. In any event, President De Gaulle vetoed Macmillan's application in 1963 – he believed that if Britain joined it would become an 'American Trojan horse' inside the Community.

HUGH GAITSKELL AND THE AMERICAN CONNECTION

During the Macmillan years, the cause of the American 'special relationship' in Britain was greatly enhanced by the leader of the Labour opposition, Hugh Gaitskell. Gaitskell had shot to prominence as a fierce opponent of Eden's attack on Suez in 1956, and his eloquence at this time had burnished his radical, anti-establishment credentials. Yet at the same time many in the Labour Party saw him in a different light – as an upper-crust, public-school-educated Tory. Indeed, like many Tories of the time, he was a son of empire – literally so, as he was born in India into a colonial civil-service family during the imperial Raj. He went on to public school in England and thence to Oxford.

This imperial background was hard to slough off, and it led him naturally to the kind of 'world role' thinking of his class; indeed Gaitskell believed the Commonwealth to be hugely important for Britain's future, and saw EEC restrictions on imported goods from the Commonwealth as a major reason to oppose British entry. And in his emotional conference speech against British entry in 1962 he sounded as 'imperial' as any traditionalist as he rhapsodised about Britain's world role, evoking 'a thousand years of history' and imperial Anzac connections of 'Vimy Ridge and Gallipoli'.

Yet, appearances to the contrary, Gaitskell was no traditionalist. He was an atheist and a republican (who, for reasons of prudence, as leader of Her Majesty's loyal opposition kept his republicanism quiet). He was a 'Wykemist' (a term for those who attended the intellectual and upmarket public school Winchester) and, like many on the left, was guided by reason rather than tradition. He was in essence a European social democrat with cosmopolitan tastes. And he wanted to change Britain. He believed the country's still strong class system – and sense of class – disfigured society, and he disliked the still strong racist attitudes permeating society, not least the upper-class English. His campaigning organisation, the Campaign for Democratic Socialism (CDS), openly confronted bigotry and anti-foreigner sentiment, arguing that 'an inward looking re-orientation would encourage the conservative and not the progressive forces in Britain. Those who are most suspicious of foreigners are most nervous of change.'[8] He married a German Jewess and took his holidays in Yugoslavia (often as a guest of Marshall Tito). All this was hardly the stuff of Tory imperial traditionalism.

Whereas many in Britain's traditional ruling class were resentful and hostile to America, and used the 'special relationship' as a cover for pursuing a world role, Gaitskell, on the other hand, was a true believer. He was, literally and lavishly, pro-American – an ideological fellow-traveller. Britain's 1960s Labour social democrats saw America, then the land of Kennedy, Johnson and Martin Luther King, as 'the new frontier', 'the great society', and the civil-rights movement. They saw the American republic as more classless and egalitarian – socially if not economically – than stuffy old Britain, and, as meritocrats, they warmed to the more open and democratic atmosphere of the USA. Also, Labour leaders had few imperial hang-ups and, unlike many of their Tory counterparts, did not suffer from nostalgia for empire. Many of them positively welcomed American power in the world, and America's supplanting of the British imperial influence.

The late 1950s and early 1960s was the height of the Cold War, and Gaitskell was the archetypal cold warrior – what Americans would call a 'liberal cold warrior'. Though often difficult to comprehend today, the atmosphere of the times was dominated by the East–West conflict, and for many in the Labour Party a deep political commitment to social change at home went hand in hand with seeking to defend the West against the spread of communism. Gaitskell saw the USA as the undisputed leader of the Western system, and opposed any weakening of the relationship with Washington. He supported NATO against the left in the late 1950s, a campaign that culminated in his famous 'fight, fight and fight again' speech opposing unilateral nuclear disarmament at the party conference in 1960. Interestingly, he was undogmatic about keeping the British bomb – and was determined primarily to keep NATO nuclear.

Hugh Gaitskell liked Americans, so much so that he formed close American friendships. As with many genuine social egalitarians, Gaitskell was fond of the American way of life, which he saw as refreshing and enterprising. Roy Jenkins, a completely different political character with quite different ambitions and tastes, reported of Gaitskell that 'he became strongly pro-American, not uncritically, nor to the exclusion of some tough bargaining with them, but deeply because multi-dimensionally so, liking the country, the life, the intellectual style. He always, I am afraid, much preferred Americans to continental Europeans.'[9] One such American was the CIA's Joe Godson. Godson was a US embassy official in Yugoslavia where he met Gaitskell during the opposition leader's many visits to the country. Godson was a bright and funny life-force, and Gaitskell took to him. Over the years he became a more than welcome guest in Gaitskell's circle and was in and out of Gaitskell's office, so much so that Gaitskell was warned by political friends that it would be judicious to lower Godson's profile.

Hugh Gaitskell died prematurely in January 1963 aged 59, and subsequently came to symbolise British social democracy for a whole generation. Yet he was to leave a discordant note among his band of loyal followers when, in 1961–62, during the last year of his life, he opposed British entry into the EEC – and in such a high-profile manner. Many of his younger supporters, like Roy Jenkins and Bill Rodgers, were wounded by his visceral opposition to entry, and even years later could not fully understand the reasons for it. Yet, like many surprising political moves, there were a number of contributing factors all coalescing at the same time. One was that in these years Gaitskell had just come through a bruising contest with his left wing over unilateral nuclear disarmament – and opposing the EEC was one way of restoring party unity – as well, that is, as out-manoeuvring Macmillan – ahead of a general election. Another reason may well have been purely personal: Gaitskell's wife Dora was bitterly hostile to Germany.

Attitudes to America are, in a sense, one of the great unspoken dividing points in British political life. British politicians are rarely neutral on the issue; and Gaitskell (like Margaret Thatcher, but unlike Edward Heath and Roy Jenkins) was very decidedly on the American side.

A son of the establishment, Gaitskell was nevertheless an anti-establishment figure. Born into a family of the Raj, he rejected imperialism as his social vision for Britain and turned westwards to egalitarian America not eastwards to the hierarchy of India. An atheist, a robust intellect, both non-conformist and confrontational: these attributes rebuked the honed-down and careful upper-class English habits of mind of his day. He was incapable of the flamboyant posturing of Welsh radicals like David Lloyd George or Aneurin Bevan, but that made him all the more serious, and potentially deadly (had he lived beyond 1963).

SATIRE AND DEFERENCE?

The Macmillan–Gaitskell era, which started with such a bitter falling out between the British Tory leadership class and the Americans, ended though with a rapprochement. However, Britain's humiliation in the Suez crisis and the continuing suspicion of British official lying (about the British–French–Israeli collusion) destroyed the legitimacy of the country's traditional rulership class – a defeat from which it never fully recovered. And this defeat also helped forward the beginnings of a more democratic, less deferential culture. The consumer boom, the spread of post-war affluence, and full employment all conspired to modernise British society, to give it some of the flavour of the more rapid middle-class development proceeding in North America and on the European continent. A more 'classless' and socially mobile British way of life was revealing itself. The 1950s and early 1960s were to see the emergence of the mass consumer market, suburban development, and increased foreign travel. Perhaps the most impressive of all the early signs of bourgeois modernity was the mass popularity of the Beatles, with their vibrant, classless, provincial (from a British perspective) but international appeal.

The early 1960s witnessed the first 'irreverent' anti-establishment entertainment, *That Was the Week That Was*. Week after week a mass audience was presented with the spectacle of traditional authority being ridiculed. David Frost, a classless and cosmopolitan Englishman if ever there was one, became (through the power of the television medium) the nation's grand inquisitor, wielding a cultural influence potentially even more powerful than that of the scions of paternalism in the upper reaches of the British media. The new meritocratic militancy was also to mock the backward restrictive practices of traditional 'working-class life', as in the film *I'm All Right Jack*.

Politically, it was the Conservative Party which presided over the consumer boom; and, as the Tories were still drawn from a very narrow social stratum, this ensured that the country's first-ever taste of mass affluence would run its course under the political tutelage of paternalists. The post-war Tory leadership – Churchill, Eden, Macmillan, Douglas-Home – tended to view the onset of mass prosperity in traditional paternalist terms, as though this new consumer affluence was a kind of 'grace and favour' reward to the workers for their war efforts and then for voting Conservative in 1951 and 1955. Harold Macmillan's throwaway remark that 'You've never had it so good' ('You', not 'We') was typical of this paternalist mentality, as was Douglas-Home's depiction of old-age pensions as 'donations'.

Whereas the Tories (still largely landed, public school and Oxbridge in their recruitment system) remained untouched by notions of a more mobile society, ideas of social egalitarianism were to express themselves politically among left-of-centre types. Labour revisionists, like Gaitskell, Anthony Crosland and John Strachey, were becoming increasingly attracted by American-style social and cultural openness.[10]

Crosland's pioneering book *The Future of Socialism*, published in 1956, placed equality as the highest political value of all, saw British society as deeply unequal, and by contrast saw great merit in American openness and egalitarianism. Indeed by the early-to-mid-1960s many believed that Britain was witnessing a subtle but decided 'embourgeoisement', a dry term for the creation of a genuine, assertive and dynamic middle class – the kind of middle class which had developed earlier in the post-war USA. Sociologists and political scientists discovered the 'affluent worker' – an elector who voted instrumentally – that is as a discriminating individual in his or her own interest – as opposed to traditionally (for Labour) or deferentially (for the Conservatives).

Yet this emergence of Britain as a more modern (middle-class) society was somewhat overdrawn – certainly by the early 1960s. A major survey of Luton, north of London (picked because it was an archetypal 'affluent worker' town of the era), concluded that Britain's 'affluent workers' were not becoming as 'embourgeousified' as their 'blue collar' American counterparts. Most of them, although better off, were retaining their 'working class' cultural identity. It was a case of proletarians with wall-to-wall carpeting, but proletarians nonetheless.[11] And among the middle classes too, deference to 'betters' and to traditional symbols of authority and aristocracy was still deeply entrenched. Evidently the British people still knew their place. In the media of the time there was next to no criticism of the monarchy, the established Church of England or the hereditary-based House of Lords; and there was little outrage at the fact that the prime minister of a democratic country, Harold Macmillan, had been 'appointed' by an unelected head of state without an election of any sort.

Indeed, almost as a mark of the strength of continuing deference, in October 1963 it was to happen all over again.

5 DOUGLAS-HOME: THE QUEEN PICKS 'HER' SECOND PRIME MINISTER

Six-and-a-half years after picking one prime minister, Queen Elizabeth was to select a second. Harold Macmillan was succeeded as prime minister in October 1963 by Sir Alec Douglas-Home – whose full name and title was Alexander Frederick Douglas-Home, Baron Home and the Hirsel, KT, PC. Douglas-Home was an unelected, hereditary peer, and unlike Macmillan was the Tory real McCoy – a landowning aristocrat from the Scottish borders. A classic imperialist in his younger days, he had supported Neville Chamberlain's geopolitics aimed at all costs towards maintaining the British empire.

And he had come to power in a very imperial and aristocratic way, by 'emerging'. In 1963 the Tory Party still did not elect its leaders. And when Macmillan resigned there were no procedures in place to hold an election for his successor. Instead, a Ruritanian system of 'soundings' of opinion among Tory MPs, peers and activists took place. In full view of the new democracy of the media age a small cabal of senior Tory leaders, together with the Queen, held discussions following these 'soundings'. The Queen's role in this process was pivotal. For, in essence, she, no doubt aided by her private secretary, was the final decision-maker in the process: expected to choose the new prime minister on the secret 'advice' given to her by the self-selected senior Tories. To untutored minds watching from the outside it may well have looked as though the Queen had picked the prime minister.

As in the manner of a papal cabal – though with no formal voting as in the Vatican – the new British prime minister, the new leader of a democratic nation, was suddenly announced to a waiting world. This largely unknown politician, a member of the House of Lords, suddenly appeared waving on the steps of Downing Street having been 'commissioned by the Queen' to form a government. The manner of his elevation was a procedure worthy of Gilbert and Sullivan – and it was to be bitterly denounced by Tory MPs Iain Macleod and Enoch Powell. When Macleod, who was leader of the House of Commons, complained in public about a Tory 'magic circle' that with effortless superiority, and not bothering about modern conceptions of democracy, had hand-picked the new prime minister, he was denounced in the *Sunday Telegraph* by journalist Peregrine Worsthorne. 'What is boring and irrelevant,' announced Worsthorne, 'is the suspicion that there was an upper class conspiracy.'[1]

What Britain's allies in Washington or in the democracies of continental Europe felt about this method of selecting a British prime minister in the early 1960s was not reported in the British press.

Alec Home – as he came to be known – was an almost perfect example of how official Britain, no matter all the reforms of 1945–51 and the social changes underway in the 1950s, had simply not moved on. Home, in personal terms, was a charming, friendly and courteous man, but was also the classic aristocrat whose understanding of, and relationship to, the bulk of the population was minimal. While prime minister he would refer to welfare payments as 'donations'.

His experience in government, though, was primarily in foreign policy. And he followed a fairly coherent 'great power' policy. As Neville Chamberlain's parliamentary private secretary before the war he had supported Chamberlain's forlorn attempt to maintain Britain's empire through the policy of appeasement of Hitler. And in the Cold War years he supported the new foreign-policy line of Britain's establishment – for Britain to remain a global player through junior partnership with the USA. Home became, like so many of his class, very pro-NATO and seemingly pro-American in the 'Greece to Rome' manner, coming loyally to accept British subordination to US leadership.

Home was clear proof of the British political class's continuing attachment to a grandiose global role. The defeat and humiliation of the Suez affair had dented, but not destroyed, this attachment. And the idea that Britain could remain a great power had been reinforced during the Conservative years by a general sense that the country was doing well. Britain's living standards had slowly improved, and the country was experiencing something approaching full employment and a consumer-durables revolution.

It was a time, though, of growing competition from Japan and European neighbours – principally Germany; and Britain was beginning to fall down the economic league tables as its economy remained largely unreconstructed. As did its political and constitutional system – as testified to by the Byzantine 'selection' of Home as prime minister in 1963. In the early 1960s a small head of steam was building up on the left around ideas of modernisation – many of them linked to Europe – but the predominant ethos was one of complacency. Britain's security rested under the American defence umbrella, and the American-led consumer boom put off thoughts of change and adjustment. It was a period in which, ultimately, long-held illusions about the British way of life and British power were simply reinforced.

IMPERIAL MENTALITY

It all came down to the continuing hold on Britain's leaders – from the Queen and the politicians to the opinion-formers – of the old late-Victorian ruling-class imperial mentality. At the heart of this mentality was a reverence for the empire and past greatness, and for ideas of rulership that went with empire, rulership based upon inherited privilege and a sense of superiority. It was reactionary, traditionalist and insular.

As the sociologist Michael Young argued in his famous book *The Rise of the Meritocracy* in 1958,

> by the middle of the twentieth century, tradition was over-valued, continuity too much revered…Britain, in other words, remained rural-minded long after eighty per cent of its population were collected in towns – altogether as strange an example of cultural lag on a mass scale as China before the Mao Dynasty…Ancestor worship took the form of reverence for old houses and churches, the most amazing coinage, the quaintest weights and measures, Guards regiments, public houses, old cars, cricket, above all the hereditary monarchy, namely the aristocracy, which could trace its descent from a more splendid past.[2]

AN 'ESTABLISHMENT': THE PUBLIC SCHOOLS

It was a mindset and culture that survived well into the twentieth century (and beyond, as we shall see) because it was carried over into Britain's newly emerging groups – in business, in the growing public sector and in the political class. But it also survived – virtually in unreconstructed form – because the English public schools had survived, and prospered.

In the late 1950s a body of elite opinion was becoming highly critical of the social effects of the public schools. John Vaizey argued that the public schools 'stick out like a sore thumb in an otherwise democratic society – or a society that likes to pretend it is democratic'.[3] The historian Hugh Thomas (now Lord Thomas of Swynnerton) could write in very sharp terms about them:

> To those who desire to see the resources and talents of Britain fully developed and extended, there is no doubt that the fusty Establishment, with its Victorian views and standards of judgement, must be destroyed ... the editor, however, cannot refrain from pointing out that it is in childhood that the men who make the present Establishment are trained; and that therefore we shall not be free of the Establishment frame of mind, permeating all aspects of life and society, and constantly reappearing even when apparently uprooted, until the public schools are completely swept away, at whatever cost to the temporary peace of the country.[4]

These public schools were not, in themselves, the issue. The real problem was that they had a wider and deeper social effect. They – particularly the leading ones, such as Eton, Harrow, Westminster and Winchester – continued to produce, long after it was needed, a governing class. They provided 'a continuous stream of socially gifted and athletic amateurs to act as proconsuls in, however, an empire than no longer exists'.[5]

These schools reached into every facet of British institutional life: the officer corps in the army, parliament, the civil service and the upper echelons of the City and the BBC. Public schools and the old medieval universities populated the higher reaches of the civil service, producing, according to one critic, 'an ethos totally out of keeping with the times'. Top civil servants, it was argued, were moulded by these schools and the unchanged 'Arnoldesque' Christianity and 'effortless superiority – in other words lack of specialist knowledge'.[6] It was a culture that produced the type of civil servant that was later caricatured by Anthony Jay in the TV sitcom *Yes Prime Minister* as 'Sir Humphrey'.

These schools also reached into the higher reaches of the BBC, by far the most powerful moulder of opinion in the country during the 1950s and 1960s. The liberal Tory columnist and author Henry Fairlie is credited with introducing the term 'the establishment' into British politics in 1955. And later, he developed the idea as part of a critique of the paternalist character of the BBC in the era of its first director general, Lord Reith. Fairlie's argument against the influence of the BBC was that it was patronising in its attempt to impose an elite culture on the public. And Fairlie went so far as to suggest that it 'brainwashes' the British. 'It would turn up its nose at subliminal advertising. But it is guilty, day in and day out, of subliminal advocacy, slipping in, through the apparent innocuous words of the chairman, a whole attitude to life and thought.'[7] And the 'attitude to life and thought' was that of Britain's mid-century 'establishment'.

Also, the schools (and the old universities) were populating the higher reaches (and better-paid jobs) of the City of London. The attraction of 'the City' for the families who had sent their children to public schools was obvious. The rural, indeed arcadian, country and 'county' culture at the time – one very much associated with the new Queen and the royal family – saw careers in the army, the church (of England only) and 'the City' as socially acceptable. Industry, commerce, engineering and science were generally somewhat disdained, either as 'trade' or as 'technical', needing expertise and professionalism. However, the army and the clergy were badly paid. So 'the City' it was. And the City had other advantages as well. London's financial centre was beginning to finance a worldwide post-war boom, and British global financial influence was becoming a nice substitute for the empire – which, as it happens, the schools had trained the young men to run.

Indeed so popular was the City among England's upper classes that the educational and social origins of the top inhabitants of London's financial district in the late 1950s had hardly changed in a century. A roll call in 1958 of the Court of the Bank of England would show: the governor of the Bank of England was educated at Eton and King's College, Cambridge; two other members were educated at Marlborough and Corpus Christi, Cambridge; another was educated at Eton and Sandhurst; two others at Eton and Trinity, Cambridge; another at Eton; another at Wellington; another at Winchester and Trinity, Cambridge; another at Eton and Trinity, Oxford; another at Rugby and Magdalene, Cambridge; another at Rugby and Trinity, Oxford; another at Winchester.

The 1944 Education Act, introduced by the wartime coalition government and piloted through parliament by the Conservative Rab Butler, promised a free, common and universal system of education for students up to 18 and proclaimed the principle that 'the nature of a child's education should be based on his capacity to promise and not by the circumstances of his parent.' But it did not resolve the problem of private education (or church schools) even though the 1944 Fleming Committee had explained how these private schools could be integrated into the state system.

The post-war Labour government presided over the emergence of three types of state school: grammar schools, secondary moderns, and a small number of technical schools. And during Labour's opposition years in the 1950s and 1960s, the great educational debate became increasingly dominated by the merits of selection in the state sector; the issue of fee-paying public schools remained largely ignored – an 'elephant in the room'. By 1958 over half the entrants to Oxford and Cambridge came from public schools, as did all High Court judges but one, all the bishops but one, almost all Tory MPs and, intriguingly, a third of Labour MPs.

In a sense, it is not surprising that even in the post-war era, when left-of-centre ideas about society and education dominated the polity, Britain could still not bring itself to reconstruct (through tax or charitable reforms), let alone abolish, its private-school sector. One reason was obvious: that in the post-war decades too many of Britain's top people – including Labour politicians – were themselves privately educated and had sent, or were sending, their own children to the same kind of school. The Queen, who continued to set the tone for many families in the country, sent all her children to private schools. Charles, Andrew and Edward went to Gordonstoun after their prep schools, Anne went to Benenden.

The social composition of the leadership of Britain's post-war cabinets tells the same story. Tory cabinets were the most narrowly drawn socially. By 1963, at the very end of the post-war Conservative years, and almost two decades into the universal welfare state, the social composition of the Home-led Conservative cabinet spoke volumes. Of the 23 members of the final Home cabinet, only three had received state education. Oxford and Cambridge were the only universities represented, attended by, between them, sixteen cabinet members (thirteen Oxford, three Cambridge). Ten went to Eton; six went to Eton and Oxford. Of the seven who did not attend university, three had had military training at Sandhurst (two) or Woolwich (one). Only one, Ernest Marples, went neither to a fee-paying school nor a university, making his way professionally as an accountant.

Harold Wilson's first cabinet in 1964 was to have the same number as Home's outgoing cabinet. There was a significant shift towards former 'day' – as opposed to boarding – students: fifteen, as compared with three under Home. But Eton, Harrow, St Paul's, Wellington, Christ's Hospital and Winchester were all represented. The Oxford flavour remained strong. Of the thirteen who attended university, three fewer than under Home, eleven went to Oxford, none to Cambridge, and one each to Durham and Glasgow. Eight went neither to fee-paying schools nor universities. Interestingly, the secretaries of state responsible for education under both Home and Wilson attended public school and Oxford.

Labour in the 1960s began to experience the 'gentrification' problem, for as trade-union influence within the party started to wane, the number of Labour MPs from Oxbridge (and other university) backgrounds was growing – and many of them were sending their own children to fee-paying schools. In a satirical dig at the public-school-educated Labour MP Richard Crossman, one commentator quoted from the young idealist in Ernest Raymond's novel *Tell England*: 'I think I'm a socialist... And I think it's up to us public schoolboys to lead the great mass of uneducated people who can't articulate their needs.' It was a case of 'Move over Kier Hardie, Crossman is here'.[8] Labour was to continue avoiding the issue for the rest of the twentieth century – and beyond. In 1964 the party's manifesto promised a trust 'to advise' on the best way of integrating the public schools into the state system.

I was a young Labour candidate at the time of the 1966 general election, and continually asked influential Labour politicians why they would not grapple with the public-school issue. I was told that it was a question of 'freedom of choice' for the parents, and although it was conceded that something might be done about tax relief for the schools, there was never much passion about it. By 1974, in both elections that year, the promise was to abolish tax relief and charitable status for public schools, a promise that was repeated in 1983. In 1992 the whole issue was ignored. And by 1997 New Labour abandoned even any criticism and gave a guarantee to public schools: 'Labour will never force the abolition of good schools whether in the private or state sector' as well as pledging to retain 'church schools'.

'THIRTEEN WASTED YEARS'

So the story of Britain ten years into the reign of Elizabeth is of a very old-fashioned 'establishment' still warming itself in the afterglow of empire, with all the pretensions and ambitions of an imperial elite – determined to sustain a world role as well, now, as the universal welfare state. This grandiose ambition, though, rested on the slenderest of shoulders: the strength of the British economy.

In the aftermath of the war Britain's economy was the strongest in Europe and for a time looked set to remain so. 'Manufacturing capacity [was] largely intact [and] British firms seemed to be in a strong position to make permanent gains in world markets at the expense of their pre-war competitors.'[9]

However, the country's underlying economic weaknesses, hidden by the general Western post-war boom, soon surfaced. And by the mid-1960s it was clear that Britain had fallen behind its main competitors – particularly Germany and Japan. Britain's comparative decline was stark. A key indicator – share of world exports of manufactures – tells the story. In 1950 the percentage figure for Britain was 24.6, West Germany 7.0, Italy 3.6, France 9.6, USA 26.6 and Japan 3.4. By 1964 it was Britain 14.0, Germany 19.5, Italy 6.2, France 8.5, USA 20.1 and Japan 8.3 (and by 1973 Britain's 14 had fallen even further to 9.1).[10]

By the mid-1960s Britain's comparative decline was the central narrative of serious analysts. And the Labour opposition leader Harold Wilson made 'the decline' of 'thirteen wasted years' (1951–64) the centrepiece of his campaign for the 1964 general election (together with attacks upon the outdated social system that he argued had refused to reform and change).

But as well as comparative economic decline, the 1950s and 1960s saw Britain's historic class divisions and inequalities derived from the industrial revolution begin to harden rather than dissolve. And for many commentators at the time – people like Michael Shanks, the Labour MP Austen Albu, the economist Andrew Shonfield and Tony Crosland – these class problems – the entrenched attitudes of both labour and management, set to become even sharper in the 1970s – remained at the heart of the British problem. One of the most influential books at the time was the Penguin Special *The Stagnant Society* by *Financial Times* journalist Michael Shanks. He argued, developing an increasingly influential theme, that Britain's poor economic performance was primarily down to 'our whole system of industrial and class relations' and that 'it is class divisions which above all inhibit economic efficiency and growth.'[11] Shanks's call, like that of many other commentators at the time, was for a 'meritocracy' – not equality of incomes or wealth, but rather equality of 'status, power and opportunity'. It developed the idea of 'the opportunity society' that was going to become a mantra, promoted (though not secured) later in the century.

Among the host of explanations for Britain's 'stagnant' society and economy one other – fatalistic – argument stood out. The whole British system (political, economic and social) was certainly too old-fashioned, yet we could not properly break with these past ways of doing things because we had not been defeated in war. Unlike the French and the Germans, the shock to our industrial and social infrastructure was less total and thus our break with the past less complete.

In any event, during the 1960s, particularly in the later years of the decade, Britain's unreconstructed class problems were beginning to morph into industrial trench warfare. Polarisation in the workplace – entrenched bloody-mindedness by employees on the one hand and management snobbery and inefficiency on the other – began to feed off each other. Yet Britain's politicians refused to reform industrial practices, turning their backs on new ideas about industrial democracy because trade unions and business were against any change. So the country, unlike modernising Germany, said no to new governance in industry, no to stakeholding, no to trade unions on boards, and refused to encourage real cooperatives and mutuals.

It was an environment in which trade unions were allowed by both Labour and the Conservatives to increase their power. And British business and management, still infused with languid habits of empire, were simply not commercially ambitious enough – resting on laurels, assuming British products would sell abroad simply because they were British.

It was a time when the seeds of the country's later economic imbalance were sown when Britain's elites increasingly simply turned away from industry. The industrial world, with its science and engineering culture, had anyway never appealed to England's social and political elites in the landowning classes. As Martin Weiner was later to suggest

> ...In the world's first industrial nation, industrialism did not seem quite at home...Having pioneered urbanisation, the English ignored or disparaged cities...The more I explored these incongruities, the more important they seemed to become...Taken together they bore witness to a cultural cordon sanitaire encircling the forces of economic development – technology, industry and commerce.[12]

Industry was distasteful, and anyway there was an easier way of making money – the City. Added to this arcadian bias was another growing bias – in favour of investing abroad rather than at home in British industry, as the fear of nationalisation was still rife. Unlike the German banks, which were investing in German industry, Britain's banks and financiers had their eyes on profits in the wider world. The empire still beckoned.

PART 2
Tumult, and change?

6 WILSON: THE 'WHITE HEAT' OF CHANGE?

'WHITE HEAT'

Harold Wilson was elected leader of the Labour Party in early 1963 following the death of Hugh Gaitskell. Wilson was a grammar-school boy from Huddersfield in Yorkshire with a first-class degree from Oxford and was the epitomy of the meritocrat. To many commentators at the time Wilson represented change, serious change – at least among the elites. The new meritocracy for which he stood – of men, and some women, who were state educated, often with a scientific, technological and industrial bent – would increasingly replace the old public-school and landed network, 'the establishment', which had run the politics of Britain even after 1945. And this change would, over time, affect more than domestic policy. As new leadership groups, from new educational and social backgrounds, started to emerge they would bring with them a new more modest and realistic view of ourselves as a country, and a new view of its place in the world. While the traditional upper classes retained their dominance, a full break with post-imperial nostalgia – what R.H. Tawney described as 'warming ourselves over the embers of empire' – would never be possible. Yet Harold Wilson's generation, less steeped in colonial rulership, and less romantic about empire, and might well serve at least to puncture 'the grand delusion'.

Wilson's election as Labour leader coincided with a certain radical sentiment in the air, an irritation with stuffy manners and ancient hierarchies. It was the age of 'swinging London'. A flavour of these 'reforming' times can be captured by reading a little-known but highly influential book of essays published in 1959. Called *The Establishment*, it was edited by the historian Hugh Thomas (later to be made a peer by Margaret Thatcher) and included essays from both Labour and Tory contributors. It was written with a radical verve and passion, and included ideas and sentiments (for instance, about the public schools and the army) that, for their times, were revolutionary. Almost every British institution – bar the monarchy – was savaged. Thomas himself declared that 'to those who desire to see the resources and talents of Britain fully developed and extended, there is no doubt that the fusty establishment, with its Victorian views and standards of judgment, must be destroyed.'[1]

In this book Simon Raven (army captain and book critic for the *Spectator*) attacked the officer corps in the British army. 'I found a caste rooted in its own conception of superior, God-given status,' he wrote. John Vaizey (later to advise Labour minister Tony Crosland while he was education secretary) argued that the public schools which 'lie at the root of the establishment...[stand] condemned'. Thomas Balogh, Oxford economist, later to be the most influential policy advisor in Harold Wilson's inner circle, made a systematic critique of the amateur in Whitehall in 'The Apotheosis of the Dilettante'. The stockbroker Victor Sandelson wanted the City of London open to 'talent from whatever class or education'. Former Tory MP and assistant editor of Punch, Christopher Hollis, pointed to the way in which 'the establishment' had neutered parliament through the two-party system. And *Daily Mail* columnist Henry Fairlie, who may well have been the first person to introduce the term 'the establishment' into the political discourse, made a searing attack on the 'baleful' influence on British life of the BBC for its patronising 'attitude to life and thought'.[2]

In the early 1960s these egalitarian ideas had broken through into the developing mass media, and formed part of what became known as the 'satire boom'. Prominent in all this was the satirical television show *That Was the Week That Was* that ran for two years from 1962 to 1963 and included sketches and biting criticism, of a kind never exhibited before on radio and television, of authority figures and established institutions. The targets included the Tory prime ministers Macmillan and Home, the monarchy, sexual hypocrisy, Britain's class system and the country's global role.

It was against this background that Wilson built his campaign for the general election of 1964. The theme was social 'modernisation', and he made his early mark with a speech that established Wilson's reputation as a classless technocrat from the traditional class system. In what became a famous phrase, he proclaimed in his first speech to the Labour Party conference as leader that 'the Britain that is going to be forged in the white heat of the [technological] revolution will be no place for restrictive practices or for outdated measures on either side of industry.'

He attacked what he called the 'gentlemen and players' society, and savagely ridiculed Douglas-Home, as but a 'fourteenth earl'. His modernising rhetoric, often evoking Lloyd George and Joseph Chamberlain, was used to devastating political effect. Wilson himself (a meritocrat from the north, in his classless Gannex raincoat) represented both in his media persona (1964 was a television election) and his political rhetoric the hope of creating a more classless, more modern nation that would finally put to rest Britain's ancient social forms and values.

Indeed Wilson was an almost perfect British embodiment of the confident 'mid-Atlanticism' that the young president John Kennedy had established as a political genre on the other side of the Atlantic. It seemed to some that a 'New Britain' (Labour's slogan for the 1964 election campaign) was indeed about to dawn, and that it would bring with it the 'unleashing of talents' (much talked of at the time) through a social and economic system which would reward efficiency, merit and enterprise.

Harold Wilson's government, elected in 1964, initially saw itself as a modernising administration, set to sweep out the dead wood of 'the establishment'. The Tories were painted as out-of-touch traditionalists from another age. Britain's 'upstairs–downstairs' class system was singled out for attack. Wilson's rhetoric was all about the need for sweeping reforms; and he pledged that Labour would modernise Britain by embracing the technological revolution which had been the subject of his 'white heat' speech.

This modernising impulse had its effect on the foreign policy of Wilson's new government – for it reinforced the 'special relationship'. The USA was seen – socially and technologically – as the fount of modernisation. Wilson came to Downing Street after John Kennedy had been assassinated but had made a point, while leader of the opposition, of modelling his style – progressive, young, modernising – on that of the president's.

Labour saw the US Democrats as a progressive force to copy, and Wilson borrowed from Kennedy the idea of using 'the first 100 days' to set the agenda for reform. For many of the incoming Labour MPs in the class of '64, America's classlessness and 'go-ahead' attitudes were going to replace those of fusty old Britain. Labour was going to arrest Britain's decline by becoming more like America – or at least its cultural egalitarian aspects. Indeed the connections across the Atlantic between some of the coming influential Labour politicians and the USA were strong: Denis Healey had spent time in the Rand Corporation, and Tony Crosland, Tony Benn and the young David Owen, who stood as a candidate in 1964 and entered parliament in 1966, had married American women.

NO END OF GRAND ILLUSIONS

However, this 'modernising' influence on some of Labour's coming young men did not cut much ice with the broader Labour party and movement. In fact, one of the fascinating features of the Labour Party at this time was how 'conservative' and traditionalist it was. Labour was still dominated by the trade unions, and its MPs were still primarily drawn from these union backgrounds. Many working-class Labour MPs were cultural conservatives who prided themselves on their patriotism and supported the same myths about Britain and its history as did the Tory aristocracy. Many were stoutly for traditional institutions like the monarchy, supported big defence expenditure, and were mildly racist and disdainful of foreigners, particularly southern Europeans. They were simply not the stuff of 'modernisation'.

Thus, for them, a more modest foreign policy based upon a new more modern and realistic vision of Britain's role in the world was a non-starter. In fact, once in power Labour conducted itself as though the country was still a 'great power', that the Second World War had not reduced its strength and status, and that the Suez fiasco of 1956 had been a Tory failure rather than a sign of British global decline.

Labour's 'New Britain' manifesto for the 1964 election was revealing. It argued that the 13 years of Tory rule had weakened Britain's role in the world, and that under Labour 'Britain would play its proper part in the world.' And there was no criticism of over-extension around the world, and no plans to withdraw British troops 'east of Suez' in Aden or the Trucial States (a debate about this 'east of Suez' role was only forced on a reluctant party by the economic crisis of 1967).

Labour's programme in 1964 did recognise that the colonial times were over, indeed it made great play of the point that previous Conservative governments had been 'churlish' in accepting the fact; but it insisted that Britain would continue to play a global role through the Commonwealth. In fact in 1964 Harold Wilson's party and government placed the

Commonwealth, with the Queen at its head, as the very centrepiece of their foreign policy. 'The first responsibility of a British government is still to the Commonwealth,' asserted the Labour manifesto (which also attacked the Conservatives for 'being prepared to accept humiliating terms for entry into the European Common Market'). Indeed it went further, praising British global moral leadership. It rhapsodised: 'no nobler transformation [from empire to Commonwealth] is recorded in the story of the human race.' Even on the left the 'grand delusion' was still very much alive.

And it remained alive. The Wilson Labour government still sought a great-power role. Wilson's biographer Philip Zeigler has shed a fascinating light on Wilson's own entrapment in this delusion of British power and importance.

> As far as he was concerned, he argues the 'great' was still in Great Britain and ever more would be so. When [realists] in his party suggested that it was folly to waste vital resources keeping forces in such far flung places as Singapore or Hong Kong he retorted that such people would like to contract out and leave it to the Americans and Chinese [to confront each other].

Ziegler reports that Harold Wilson was often ridiculed for absurdly overstating Britain's influence in the world. And he also reports the prime minister as grandiloquently proclaiming that 'Britain's frontier is on the Himalayas.'[3]

During the late 1950s and early 1960s the Labour Party had been riven by the issue of nuclear weapons, but in government Wilson remained determined to keep Britain at the 'top table' in the nuclear business. His government remained a resolute defender of NATO's nuclear posture, and of its 'first strike' capability and doctrine, and it supported American nuclear bases in Britain. But it went further. Wilson and the Labour cabinet were determined to keep Britain's own nuclear weapons as well, and he signed the Polaris deal with the USA which secured the delivery system that allowed the country to retain an 'independent deterrent' which could, theoretically, be launched by London alone against the Soviet Union.

Wilson, like so many upwardly mobile Britons of that immediate post-war generation of leaders, ultimately fell in with the myth of the traditional upper classes: the virtues of empire and the continuing reality and beneficence of British power.

Yet, Wilson's attachment to the habits of the past in foreign policy was not surprising – for, apart from the radical rhetoric, the whole 'New Britain' project was, in reality, rather tame. It represented a broader failure.

From day one, what 'New Britain' really amounted to was an attempt to achieve social goals through greater economic growth than under the Tories. This growth was to be achieved by a greater measure of planning – induced by a Department of Economic Affairs which would restrict the authority of the Treasury. Despite the rhetoric, attacking the deep-seated class structure and rigidities of Britain was not really on the agenda.

Perhaps it never was. Once in office Wilson was very accepting of the traditional trappings of authority and power, and was personally very deferential to the Queen. During his period as prime minister he colluded with the palace to undermine Tony Benn's attempt to create new stamps without the Queen's head on them; he refused to give full support to his truly radical cabinet colleague, and lord president, Richard Crossman, who wished to reform what he called the 'mumbo jumbo' of the Privy Council system; and he privately sided with the Queen to stop a debate on a bill to abolish titles. More importantly, Wilson – again against the sentiments of many of his cabinet colleagues – and again in cahoots with a very engaged and concerned Queen, defended against attacks on the Queen's finances, and ended up in 1969 doubling the Queen's state income to just shy of a million pounds.

Harold Wilson was reportedly 'devoted to the Queen and [was] very proud that she like[d] his visits to her'. And when he resigned, the Queen, in appreciation of his service, gave him a photograph of them in the rain together which he reportedly kept by him for the rest of his life.[4] The Yorkshire meritocrat from Huddersfield, the scourge of the establishment dedicated to a 'classless society', had somehow managed to exempt the Queen and all she stood for from any responsibility for the traditional social 'rigidities' he supposedly so despised.

Indeed the Wilson government was to end up giving traditional wealth and authority a clear pass. The new government had no serious programme for any real redistribution of income and wealth. Ideas about a wealth tax were taken seriously when the party was in opposition, but were quickly shelved in power. The government did try to address the problem of 'poverty', but only by weakening the middle-income sector, and not the very wealthy (land taxes did not appeal to Labour). Nor, and importantly, was Labour in the business of eroding the deep-seated class divisions maintained by the flourishing private education sector, principally the public schools. Securing the long-term health of state education in Britain by causing the private sector to wither on the vine (as happened in the health sector) would have been a natural step for a real progressive party in the 1960s. But Labour's leadership not only rejected abolition of fee-paying, they even refused to tax these schools or alter their privileged charitable status.

As with traditional wealth, so with ancient institutions. Labour – under Richard Crossman's leadership of the House – failed to 'reform' the House of Lords, and there were to be no further plans for constitutional modernisation: no attempt to reform the 'olde English' institutions such as the established church or the Privy Council (indeed such ideas would have been anathema). The Labour MP John Mcintosh campaigned for the need to reform parliament (particularly via the select-committee system, giving committees teeth, as in the US congress), but his ideas were largely ignored. And the anti-monarchy views of Labour MP Willie Hamilton (no firebreathing Marxist) were considered eccentric. It was thus fitting that Harold Wilson, Britain's 1960s 'new man', was, at the end of his long parliamentary career, to end up with the Order of the Garter, bestowed by a grateful Queen, and as Lord Wilson of Rievaulx.

During Wilson's premiership a body of moderate Labour MPs – social-democrat Gaitskellites – were insistently critical of this conservative leadership of the party (Jim Callaghan was considered worse than Wilson and an out and out 'reactionary'). These social democrats were social modernisers in the sense that they opposed what they saw as the stuffy conventions and institutions of conservative Britain. Their leader Roy Jenkins as home secretary had legalised abortion, abolished theatre censorship and decriminalised homosexuality. Jenkins became a hate figure on the right.

However, these progressives, like all the politicians of the era, were unable even to begin to tackle the country's deep-seated class problem. Like many in the Labour Party of that time they saw the state as the instrument for change, even while the state was controlled by a paternalistic establishment they claimed to despise. One problem with Labour during the Wilson years was its inherent paternalism – no axe was wielded to wealth and tradition and no change demanded of the conservative 'working classes'. This problem was superbly diagnosed by the Canadian-born economist Harry Johnson. He suggested that in Britain there were social values underlying Keynes's approach to economic questions which were typical of the British academic milieu, particularly that of Oxford and Cambridge. Martin Weiner described his views as 'centered around the colleges, which' to him

> remained in spirit feudal institutions, a way of life [that]…encouraged a paternalistic and static attitude towards the working class. The main social obligation of the authorities (like the college fellows vis-à-vis the college servants) tended to be seen as that of guaranteeing employment. The 'social problem' was fundamentally that of providing security for the masses.[5]

Whatever its merits, it was hardly the stuff of social modernisation. And during Wilson's years Labour's left wing were just as tame. Drawing their Bevanite ideas from John Ruskin, Charles Dickens and William Morris, they were as much in sympathy with the late Victorian revulsion against industrial capitalism as any high Tory. Like their Conservative opponents they had little interest in setting 'the workers' free from their lifetime ghettos in council estates or trade-union clubs. And the trade unions of the 1960s were no more radical. They sought trade-union power and collective advancement, not individual development through embourgeoisement. And they were often led, by today's standards, by extremely reactionary and sometimes corrupt leaders. They were a conservative force.

DEVALUATION AND DELUSION

As the 1960s progressed whatever small instinct for change existed in Wilson's Labour government was soon to dissolve amid the economic crises and social instability which engulfed the government and country from 1967 onwards. It was an atmosphere in which economics, not reform, would dominate.

The original overall economic strategy of the Wilson government as it took office in 1964 was to achieve growth through the new Department of Economic Affairs, which would end the restrictive, orthodox approach of the Treasury. Indicative planning and an industrial policy of picking winners was central to this new approach. Inflation would be dealt with by an incomes policy (wage and price controls). The welfare state would be supported by relatively high rates of tax – by today's standards – on incomes and corporations. In essence Wilson sought to continue the post-war consensus behind the mixed economy, but make it more efficient.

But the economic policy was dogged from the start by the attempt to stave off the devaluation of the pound. At the time the pound sterling was seen as a national virility symbol (the earlier devaluation of 1949 was still considered a humiliation). With the Queen's head on one side of the notes, there was national honour, as well as money, involved; and the Wilson government put off for almost three years what in the days before the current system of variable exchange rates many considered a perfectly rational and inevitable devaluation. It was another case of national *braggadoccio* based upon the illusion of power, but as the balance-of-trade problem got worse the government finally yielded and sterling was devalued in 1967 from 2.80 to 2.40 dollars to the pound.

Britain's ailing economy had been falling behind its European and American competitors for decades – in large part because of the loss of wealth and power in two world wars. Yet by the 1960s it was becoming clear that this 'structural' decline was compounded by endemic British problems which no party had been able to sort out – the country's stubborn out-of-date management systems, class antagonisms and industrial trench warfare, all of which continued to disfigure British industry.

As the economy increasingly failed to deliver, industrial militancy grew as old-fashioned management fought it out with an unreconstructed trade-union movement (and increasingly too with militant shop stewards). 'Wild cat' strikes grew in number, and a six-week strike in the docks by the communist-inspired National Union of Seamen, dubbed by Wilson 'politically motivated men', finally led Wilson to act. His secretary of state for employment, Barbara Castle, introduced a white paper called 'In Place of Strife' aimed at taming the unions. But under pressure from the unions and the wider Labour movement Wilson eventually backed down, and withdrew the white paper. It was a humiliation, and lost Wilson any reforming credibility he may still have possessed.

Yet some Labour politicians, not all of them on the left, thought that the workers, and their unions, had a point. As Tony Crosland later argued while opposition spokesman, 'the growth in industrial unrest has two even more elemental causes: the fear of inflation and the fear of losing a job.' And he argued that 'the level of aspiration and the pattern of consumption (with hire-purchase and, increasingly, even mortgage commitments) now make a break in income flow exceptionally painful.'[6] But Wilson's government had made its choice. In the Britain they tried to govern, the unions could be reformed more easily than could the old-fashioned practices in the boardroom.

HEATH: FAILURE OF A RADICAL?

Edward Heath entered Downing Street in June 1970 and, like Wilson before him, was an instinctive moderniser. And, again like Wilson, he was classless. A grammar-school boy from Kent (his father was a carpenter), he was the first Tory leader not to go to a public school; and, incredibly, the first to be elected (in a formal ballot of MPs) thereby freeing the Queen from involving herself in the picking of a Prime Minister. His lack of interest in (if not disdain for) old-fashioned English privilege was displayed when he took the historic step of discontinuing hereditary peerages. His classlessness also showed in his attitude to industry and commerce – for although his government was marked by hostility to the trade unions he was also a fierce opponent of its mirror image, the outdated 'old-boy network' in British management. And his instincts were not those of the traditional rural Tory. He once proclaimed, much to the annoyance of the rural lobby, that 'the alternative to economic expansion is not, as some occasionally seem to suppose, an England of quiet market towns linked only by trains puffing slowly and peacefully through green meadows. The alternative is slums, dangerous roads, old factories, cramped schools, stunted lives.'[1]

Heath was a meritocrat; and his reaction against Britain's decline took a visceral technocratic and modernising form. He once described Britain as a 'Luddite's paradise...a society dedicated to the prevention of progress and the preservation of the status-quo'.[2] As leader of the opposition during the 1960s Heath had presided over a Conservative Party policy review which had culminated in the 'Selsdon Park manifesto', a radical quasi-neo-liberal prospectus which broke with over twenty years of Conservative support for the post-war consensus. During January and February of 1970, just ahead of the election, Heath's shadow cabinet, in order to prepare the ground for what he called his 'quiet revolution', engaged in a series of speeches clearly signalling that a Heath government would make a clean break from the post-war social-democratic consensus. In one such speech, Sir Keith Joseph spoke of the need for a new national economic strategy which would involve no automatic partnership between government and industry; each, he argued, had a distinctive role, and the government's was to create a background in which the free-enterprise system could work more effectively through changes in company and taxation law. Another speech by David Howell (a former director of the Conservative Political Centre) reflected Heath's views on how the quality of government could be improved by specifying areas and activities from which the government would distance itself. He promoted Heath's view that new administrative techniques developed in America and designed to test and evaluate government accountability and to streamline its structure were needed in Britain.

By the time of his first party conference as prime minister (in Brighton in October 1970) Heath had re-formulated the 'quiet revolution'. His theme for the conference was the need to create a more self-reliant society, a pointed rejection of traditional Tory paternalism. He argued that his 'revolution' amounted to 'less government, and of a better quality'. And he outlined a daring programme of governmental disengagement whereby individuals were to be encouraged to be more responsible for themselves and their families, free to make their own decisions, if they wished to, rather than having them imposed by bureaucracies. Disengagement was to extend to private industry as well: 'lame ducks' would no longer be rescued. Heath's 1970 prospectus amounted to Thatcherism without privatisation.

After a major review of public expenditure in October 1970 Heath's chancellor of the exchequer, Anthony Barber, outlined his budget proposals for 1971, which included cuts in the defence budget (while honouring commitments in the Far East and the Gulf states), a cut in income tax for most wage earners and a reduction in corporation tax. The new government was firmly opposed to an incomes policy. The details of Heath's economic policies remained, for the moment, consistent with the theme and strategy of radical neo-liberal disengagement.

HEATH'S U-TURN

Yet the course of Heath's 'quiet revolution' was to run for only a few more months. Over the next three years its central planks were to be dismantled, one by one. First, there were the early economic policy reversals (in the first six months of 1971) which brought the monetarist and free-market economic strategy to a shuddering halt. Then followed a group of further statist measures (enacted in the first few months of 1972) which formed the sharp curve of the 'U-turn.' Then came the greatest reversal of all, the introduction of a compulsory incomes policy (announced in November 1972) which completed the manoeuvre.

The 'dash for freedom' was therefore virtually over before it had begun. This 'U-turn' amounted to the sharpest reversal of declared domestic political strategy seen in a lifetime – and it stoked up considerable resentment within the Conservative Party, causing bitter opposition to Heath that would surface during Margaret Thatcher's later successful leadership campaign.

The fact was that Heath, and those around him, balked at the unemployment consequences of his free-market economic strategy. When in 1971 his 'lame ducks' policy – no subsidies for unsuccessful industries – was put to the test by the Upper Clyde Shipbuilders sit-in, and the Chief Constable of Glasgow told him that he could not guarantee public order, Heath backed off. And then when the unemployment figures topped the million mark the prime minister took fright – and reversed engines. And from 1971 onwards Heath presided over what amounted not just to a U-turn but to a fully fledged social-democratic programme that any left-of-centre government would have been proud of. He kept public expenditure high, he attempted a 'dash for growth', and he sought to fight inflation by an incomes policy – a strategy which would bring him into direct conflict with militants in the trade-union movement. And increasingly, also like the social democrats in the Labour Party, he saw Britain's integration into the EEC as the last, best hope of national renewal. For him the cause of modernisation was becoming best served by the cause of Europe.

DECLINE, AND 'DECLINISM'

Heath's spectacular 1971 U-turn, following the failures of the 1964 – 70 Wilson government, set alarm bells ringing and ushered in a new mood. The idea of decline – of irreversible national decline – was beginning to set in. Indeed such a sense of decline had been building ever since Britain began to slip down the economic league tables in the late 1950s, a slippage that had become a theme of the politics of the late 1950s and early 1960s. Harold Wilson had made vivid this theme by constantly reciting the figures of Britain's low economic performance in his attacks on what he described as the 'complacent' Tories. For some, this idea of decline was powerfully reinforced by the fallout from the Suez affair – clearly proving to some that Britain was no longer the power, domestically and internationally, that she had been earlier in the century.

Cecil King's diaries covering the period 1965 – 70, and published in 1972 revealed the sheer alarm at the country's position held by many top people in Britain following the failure of Wilson.[3] And this sense of alarm was to grow even stronger during the early 1970s when the country was engulfed in the 'three-day week' and the bitter disputes between government and miners – bringing home the acute nature of Britain's crisis. In December 1973 the chancellor of the exchequer, Anthony Barber, could state that 'over the past week or so many have described the situation which we as a nation now face as by far the gravest since the end of the war. They did not exaggerate.'[4] In 1976, just before the IMF was to visit London, Alistair Buchan, in an essay in the *Times* in January 1976 could write, 'one of the preoccupations of reasonable men and women across the world – in Washington, in the Commonwealth countries, in the European capitals – is the question "Will Britain flounder?",' and went on to suggest that the British, unlike intelligent observers abroad, 'hold their peace because they are afraid'.[5]

This sense of heightened or acute crisis pushed to the fore a lively debate about British decline, the reasons for it, and how to recover from it. It was so pervasive a debate that it was dubbed 'declinism'. And the mid- to late 1970s became a period of 'high declinism'. In 1972, the same year as the publication of *The Cecil King Diary*, one of the classic so-called 'declinist' books of the period, Correlli Barnett's *The Collapse of British Power* was published. It was a poignant and powerful analysis in which Barnett argued that Britain's decline could be traced back to the late nineteenth and early twentieth centuries – with 'the decay of British power between 1918 and 1940' and 'its collapse between 1940 and 1945'.[6] And he also argued that the decline was caused by a fatal combination of 'imperial overstretch, moral pretensions and inadequate education, particularly technical' – attitudes fostered in establishment minds by the ruling culture of the late-nineteenth-century public schools (he singled out the Rugby of Dr Arnold for particular analysis, and scorn.) By educating England's future elites in the wrong way – attempting to create moral character and benign rulership, 'all that was noble and good', rather than hard-headed realism – a whole generation of twentieth-century leaders were infused with the wrong values. It was a withering critique that could at least help explain why so many of Britain's post-war leaders were to lack strategic vision and grasp, and could not properly identify Britain's real position and place in the world, constantly overstating and overselling the power of the country.

Barnett put it all down to hubris, moralism and complacent 'overstretch' among England's elites during the height of empire in the late mid-nineteenth century. He argued that 'just at the time when we were beginning to congratulate ourselves – "we have the secret, we are absolutely tremendous" – other nations were thinking hard how to catch up with us.'[7] Barnett was educated in a state school in Croydon and went to Oxford in the late 1940s, where he developed his critique of the educational system, specifically of 'Britain's unquestionable backwardness in education generally, and particularly technical education'.[8]

It was a time of feverish introspection, but also one – unusual for the post-war British – that was largely lacking in complacency. Andrew Gamble has suggested that 'it is hard to think of a major public intellectual who has not contributed to the decline debate.' And in 1974 he himself argued that 'if capitalism is to survive some new relationship has to be worked out with the trade unions.'[9]

All kinds of explanations for decline were bubbling, some of them under the surface, only reaching the light of day in later books and articles. There were those who put decline down to cultural factors (like Martin Weiner, whose 1981 book *English Culture and the Decline of the Industrial Spirit* became a vogue work: he put Britain's decline down to anti-industrial values of a people in love with England as a rural arcadia). Others suggested it was primarily to do with the predominance of the City of London and finance over manufacturing (a key part of the analysis of Labour MP Stuart Holland and of futurologist James Bellini). Others yet placed the blame on institutional failures such as the lack of constitutional modernisation (a view of the politician and writer David Marquand). Yet underlying all these explanations was a fundamental geopolitical analysis: how imperial overstretch, cultural complacency, and two wars, had decisively diminished the nation's power.[10]

DECLINE THE SOLUTION?

So dominating did the debate about decline become that a 'defeatist' aphorism did the rounds in Westminster and Whitehall. It went something like this: 'Britain's decline is not the problem, decline is the solution'. Yet, 'defeatist' or not, such thinking introduced an unusual and needed note of realism into the British political debate. And this acceptance (albeit grudgingly) of the country's reduced role was beginning to further the idea that the country's future would best be managed by reorientating its view of itself away from a grandiose 'world role' towards a more modest European one.

In the 1970s this declinist analysis, with its more realistic new role for Britain (as a European, as opposed to a 'world' power), was to take hold in the centre of British politics – on the Labour right and the Conservative left. However, Britain's then insurgent political extremes – the Bennite left of the Labour Party and the Thatcherite right of the Tory Party – rejected the 'unpatriotic' idea of decline as the solution.

On the socialist left there was a view that Britain had a unique capitalist crisis – an analysis outlined most cogently in a host of articles and essays in the *New Left Review* in the early and mid-1970s. The *New Left Review* was edited and written by neo-marxist socialist writers such as Perry Anderson, Robin Blackburn, Tom Nairn and Peter Gowan, and the thrust of their argument was that there was nothing inevitable about decline, and nothing that could not be put right by an 'alternative strategy'. This alternative would transform Britain by transforming the capitalist economy into a socialist one, directing investment to home industries, increasing trade-union power and industrial democracy, thus causing what Labour's Programme 1976 described as an 'irreversible shift of power to working peoples and their families'.

The leading thinkers and strategists of the British broad left certainly rejected the 'world role' afterglow of imperialism represented by the Commonwealth and the Queen; but, rather like the established political class, they still saw a world leadership role for the country. They rejected American 'capitalism' and Soviet 'state capitalism' but also rejected the European welfare-state model – they were opposed to entry into the EEC, which they saw as a 'capitalist club'. Their heroes were anti-colonialists like Che Guevara and Ben Bella. In essence, their view was that Britain should lead by example, become a non-aligned country, and take itself out of the Western system, without joining the communist bloc. Britain would continue to have a 'world role' – as leader of a non-aligned movement – rather than the more modest, European, role being offered by the declinists.

The Tory right too rejected the idea that 'decline was inevitable.' During the 1970s Tory economic thought was becoming increasingly 'dry', a term introduced to distinguish those on the right from the more left-wing Tory 'wets'. And Tory politicians were falling under the influence of neo-liberal economists from the USA, Milton Friedman and the Chicago School chief among them. These Tory 'dries' believed that the rigours of the market would solve the problem of decline and lead to a rebirth of Britain. Indeed Margaret Thatcher herself, when leader of the opposition and prime minister, made a point of attacking the notion that decline was inevitable. She turned what she saw as the cynicism of the decline debate into a powerful political weapon. 'At the heart of a new mood in the nation,' she argued, 'must be a recovery of our self-confidence and our self-respect. Decline is not inevitable.' Rather than accepting it she sought to reverse it. And Winston Churchill was called in aid: 'it is given to us to demand an end to decline,' she said, 'and to make a stand against what Churchill described as the long dismal drawling tides of drift and surrender.'[11]

DECLINISTS FOR EUROPE: IAN GILMOUR

To these Tory right-wingers the chief 'declinist' and 'capitulationist' – and mortal political enemy – was Ian Gilmour. Gilmour was Edward Heath's minister of defence and later became lord privy seal in Thatcher's first administration. Many of the younger Thatcherites saw him as a shadowy and dangerous character, the *eminence grise* of defeatism and 'declinism' and the advocate of a European future. On the face of it Gilmour was an almost perfect caricature of the old English pre-war political establishment. A scion of wealth and land, this thin, tall, languid, 'wet' Tory was not, though, quite what, at first blush, he might have seemed. A member of the gentleman's club White's, he was seemingly at home among the county 'hunting, shooting and fishing' rural, shire fraternity. Yet he was, in fact, not at home at all. An intellectual in a philistine culture, he possessed a detached wry humour, wide sympathies, and a very un-Tory-like politically serious disposition.

He was dismissive, almost contemptuous, of Thatcher's proposed free-market solutions – they were, for his taste, far too extreme, or, as he called them, 'ideological' and 'dogmatic'. His fear was that the developing Thatcherism he saw around him would, if implemented, weaken the social fabric of the country and lead to another extreme, this time socialist or worse, counter-reaction.[12]

Gilmour's 'declinist' school of thought served to introduce into British politics a new factor – a sober and realistic assessment of Britain's new place in the world. The charge that 'declinists' were in some sense cynically seeking or wanting national decline for its own sake was an unfair depiction. Rather, their view was that the country should accept, and work within, the limitations which decline placed on British power. And that, in turn, meant that a difficult truth needed to be faced – that there was in fact no '*national* road to recovery' available. Academics Elizabeth Meehan and Marie-Therese Fay were later to argue in a perceptive analysis in 1981 that a 'national road to recovery' might not exist because, in reality, there was no longer any such thing as a singular British economy. They argued that 'it may not be valid to speak of a national road to recovery in the British context' because both 'sub-national features' as well as 'trans-national sectors could invalidate discourses of national economies (and therefore much of the debate on British national decline)'. They set the whole thing in a European, not British, context.[13]

For Gilmour and many in the mainstream centre of British politics the only real solution was not a British one at all, but lay in Britain's full integration into Europe. Whatever was wrong with Britain could not be solved by Britain alone. And trying to solve Britain's problems in isolation – outside the European context – would be a hopeless venture and only lead to further devaluations, division, trouble and poverty. The only way forward was amounted to a strategy of 'ever-closer union' – or bust!

This radical approach often 'dared not speak its name': for by arguing that Britain could not solve its problems alone – through a 'sovereign solution' it would lay itself open to charges of being unpatriotic, even undemocratic. But even so the idea that Britain needed to integrate with others in order to save itself remained the guts and soul of the drive in the 1970s for Britain to join the EEC.

By contrast, the growing voice of the radical right, or 'early Thatcherism', saw Britain as able to solve her own problems. Thatcher, like her left-wing socialist opponents, believed fervently in the *national* road to survival and recovery. The irony here was that these neo-liberal, market solutions were also solutions that could only be effected through an international context – through, as it turned out, merging Britain into the increasingly globalised economy and in close, 'ever-closer', association with the USA. Thus it was that in the depths and fog of the national crisis of the 1970s the two alternative geopolitical futures for Britain – 'ever-closer' relations with Europe, or alternatively an 'ever-closer' 'special relationship' with America – began to emerge and clarify themselves.

HEATH'S DASH FOR EUROPE

Edward Heath chose Europe. He was the first truly post-imperial prime minister, and by the time he came to office the last serious British imperial military presence – the forces east of Suez in the Gulf – had been abandoned. And, crucially, Heath shared none of the nostalgia or pretensions for a 'world role' that had infected every one of his post-war predecessors. He was simply uninterested in a grand role on the world stage, and consequently playing junior partner to Washington also left him cold. He had been Tory chief whip during the traumatic months – for the British establishment – of the Suez affair, and that searing experience had led him to a clear-eyed understanding of Britain's true position in the world – and in the world according to Washington! For Heath, Britain's 'glorious past' was just that. Its present and future was that of a medium-sized country off the coast of mainland Europe desperately in need of social and economic modernisation.

Heath's original fervour for European unity may, like that of many of his generation, have come from his experiences during the Second World War – leading him to view European unity as the only way to avoid future European wars. But during the 1960s, as he witnessed governments grappling with the British disease of union militancy and backward management, he came to the conclusion that the much-needed modernisation could only be made by an irreversible immersing of the country in the new Europe.

But a European future for Britain was a revolutionary idea – particularly for Conservatives. Heath had initially largely avoided the European issue by launching his premiership on the back of a domestic programme of free-market change – the famous 'Selsdon Park manifesto', named after the hotel at which the plan had been drawn up. He had called for a 'silent revolution'. And although he was known as a keen European, Heath had not stressed Europe in the 1970 general-election campaign. Yet chance now took a hand, and only days after Heath had taken over in London the new French president Georges Pompidou made it known that he was prepared to lift De Gaulle's veto on Britain's

EEC application. Heath immediately headed off to Paris, and a deal was done: negotiations for Britain to join the EEC started on 30 June 1970, just 12 days after Edward Heath entered Downing Street.

Heath signed the Accession Treaty at the Egmont Palace in Brussels, and Britain entered the EEC – together with Ireland and Denmark – as a full member on 1 January 1973. This historic and revolutionary act had, though, been achieved very much against the grain of British politics and tradition. Indeed in securing British entry Heath had taken few prisoners. He forced a parliamentary vote on a three-line whip, using all the resources of persuasion at a prime minister's command. And even then his victory was only secured because 69 Labour MPs defied their own party whip to vote with the pro-European Tories.

It was this revolution that led Heath towards yet another revolution – for it soon became clear that as prime minister he would be placing the European connection – and future – ahead of the 'special relationship' with the USA. To this day he remains the only post-war British prime minister to do so. In 1970 the European Council had established the European Political Cooperation procedures for foreign policy; it was an unprecedented step and was hailed at the time as the beginning of a European foreign policy – and Heath took it seriously. Whenever possible he tried to side with his major European colleagues. At Heath's December 1971 summit with President Nixon, Henry Kissinger recorded that 'Heath pursued his favourite theme of European unity and assured the president that it would be competitive not confrontational. It was an interesting and not entirely reassuring formulation, a considerable step away from the automatic cooperation taken for granted by our own twin-pillar Atlanticists in the 1960s and by all of Heath's predecessors.'[14]

This new alignment in Britain's foreign policy was on display in British policy in the Middle East. During the Middle East war in October 1973 President Nixon decided to provide Israel with military equipment and asked the British government for over-flying rights so that the Jewish state could be resupplied from North America. Heath refused, and the USA was forced to use the Azores instead. Criticised for supporting the French in calling for Israel to implement UN Security Council Resolution 242, Heath bluntly stated, in words unthinkable from a British prime minister before or since, 'The day when the voice of the United States automatically prevailed over each of its individual partners has passed.'[15] At the Tory conference he called, again in terms unusual for a British prime minister, for a 'common European policy towards our principal ally, the United States'.[16]

Henry Kissinger said of Edward Heath that 'of all the British leaders Heath was probably the least committed emotionally to the United States. It was not that he was anti-American...[but he believed] that the "special relationship" was an obstacle to the British vocation in Europe.'[17] This did not stop Heath getting on with America's leaders. He and Nixon, however, did not hit it off personally. 'Like a couple who had been told by everyone that they should be in love and who might try mightily but futilely to justify these expectations...the relationship never flourished'. Heath, like Nixon, was shy and awkward. In his biography *The White House Years* Kissinger, who witnessed the Nixon–Heath get-togethers, offered a shrewd assessment of Heath, proof of his negotiator's eye for an opponent: he wrote that Heath

> rose from modest beginnings to lead a party imbued with Britain's aristocratic tradition. The ruthlessness necessary to achieve the ambition did not come naturally...he was a warm and gentle person who anticipated rejection and fended it off with a formal politeness...He had a theoretical bent closer than the rest [other prime ministers] to that of the continental Europeans.[18]

Nixon outlasted Heath in office by a few months. Heath lost the general election of February 1974 after a year of bitter industrial disputes exacerbated by the sheer bad luck of the huge oil-price inflation set off by the 1973 Middle East war. He was to lose, just, the subsequent general election held in October 1974; and a year later he lost out to Margaret Thatcher as leader of the Conservative Party.

Heath's short-lived and turbulent administration represented a real break with Britain's 'world role' fixation and hence with the 'special relationship'. To attempt to solve Britain's problems in a European context, and to secure the country's future as part of Europe, was radical stuff. Ultimately it was too ambitious. It went against several grains. It challenged the post-imperial 'Atlanticist' foreign-policy consensus that placed the USA at its heart – and it did so, in the 1970s, at a time when the Cold War dictated American leadership of Europe. Also, it went right up against 'Queen and country' nationalist culture – with its myths of 'independence' and national 'greatness' that were still well embedded.

Heath won the battle over Europe: Britain became a full member of the EEC. But he may well have lost the long-term war. For the bruising nature of the campaign to secure this radical break with British tradition and culture still resonates. Heath and the Europeans were, after all, challenging some basic myths and a deep-felt identity.

ROY JENKINS AND LABOUR'S EUROPEANS

Heath could not have secured his pro-European mission without decisive help from Labour's pro-Europeans, those 69 Labour MPs who voted against their own leadership on a three-line whip. The vote – historic by any standards – represented a deep schism within the Labour Party – a split that was never truly healed. In one sense this split led directly to the overhaul of the British party system which occurred some eight years later when Labour broke up, and the SDP was formed (by the 'gang of four' all of whom were numbered among 'the 69') – a split on the left that wounded Labour for fifteen years. It was this division that was crucial in allowing the Thatcherite revolution to get underway.

This historic revolt was led by Roy Jenkins, and it remains his great 'moment' in British parliamentary history – arguably much more important than his earlier role as a liberal home secretary. Jenkins was a convinced European. He first came to prominence as a young Gaitskellite MP when he went to the rostrum at the Labour Party conference in 1962 and broke with his mentor and hero, following Gaitskell's anti-EEC 'Vimy Ridge' speech. And after he became chancellor of the exchequer in 1967 he became Labour's leading pro-European, and during the debates on Europe in the 1970–72 period he formed an unspoken alliance with Heath. In 1975 he joined with Heath as the effective co-leader of the 'Yes' campaign in the referendum on the EEC in June 1975, which was won by a 2-to-1 vote majority on a 67 per cent turnout.

The origins of Roy Jenkins's Europeanism were in no way anti-American. Like many Labour right-wingers (particularly Hugh Gaitskell, Tony Crosland, Roy Hattersley and David Owen) he was fascinated by American politics. He wrote a book about Harry Truman and, with Arthur Schlesinger, wrote one on Franklin Roosevelt, and he also penned short biographies of Joe McCarthy, Adlai Stevenson and Robert Kennedy. But he became convinced – partly due to wishful thinking while active in the European cause in the 1960s during the Vietnam imbroglio – that American power was waning, and he wrote an essay poignantly entitled 'Twilight on the Potomac' to make the point.

Jenkins was, unusually for a top-rank politician, an historian – a student of contemporary history and a biographer whose subjects, as well as Roosevelt and Truman, ranged from Herbert Asquith to Churchill. This historical bent equipped him with a detachment from everyday politics that allowed him to set the country's problems in a wide context. And his cosmopolitan habits, and his contacts and friends abroad, particularly continental ones and those among the Kennedy generation of Democrats in the USA, added to his ability to view his country from outside the narrow perspectives of Westminster.

He was in fact the only major politician, other than Heath, of this crucial generation which came to power in the 1970s, who had truly ingested Britain's reduced role in the world, and thus saw clearly the continuing global pretensions of many of its leaders. And he could laugh in support of the depiction of the middle-class Britain of his day as being 'smug with not much to be smug about'. It was in large part this recognition that led him so early in the post-war years to embrace the cause of Britain in Europe.

Of course although Edward Heath and Roy Jenkins took Britain into Europe, it was Harold Wilson who kept her there. Wilson had surprisingly won the February 1974 general election, but had come to power on a pledge to renegotiate Heath's terms of entry into the EEC and then hold a referendum on the issue. Holding a referendum was the only way that Wilson could keep his deeply divided party united on the issue – as both sides pledged to accept the result.

Wilson may have successfully secured Britain in the EEC – outmanoeuvring his opponents by calling a referendum, and then winning it – but he had done so at a huge long-term cost to the European cause in Britain. Wilson himself had been half-hearted about the whole thing – 'I am not throwing my hat in the air about it,' he had said – and he gave Britain's European future no vision or colour, and set out none of the big arguments for Europe. In the campaign the issues got bogged down – to the long-term disadvantage of Britain's pro-Europeans – in small, niggly, issues of trade standardisation and Commission incompetence and bureaucracy. The fact was that Wilson was un-engaged with Europe. His eyes, and his horizons, were still on the Himalayas.

8 CALLAGHAN: END OF AN ERA

Edward Heath's government was brought to an end in February 1974 by the National Union of Mineworkers (NUM). In 1973 the NUM had started a 'work-to-rule' as it tried to exert pressure to keep wages up, in line with rising prices – an action which ran directly counter to the government's wage controls. Coal stocks dwindled and Heath and the NUM could not come to an agreement.

As a result Heath, in order to save electricity for essential services and businesses, went into emergency mode and placed the country on a 'three-day (working) week' from 31 December 1973. This emergency atmosphere was nothing new for the people, as earlier strikes during his premiership had caused major disruptions, including scheduled electricity outages and even the closing down of television services at 10 p.m.

Heath, finding it increasingly difficult to govern, decided to call a snap general election under the slogan 'Who governs Britain?'. Heath and others in the Conservative government felt they were being confronted by a radicalised left-wing movement set not just against the government but the whole capitalist system, an insurgency that had been building for some time – and one that could only be defeated by a vote of the people. Within the trade unions there were certainly some very radical voices, many of them associated with extreme-left organisations. A whole generation of shop stewards had been influenced by the successful sit-in of workers at Upper Clyde Shipbuilders in 1971, and their leader, the communist Jimmy Reid, had become a folk hero to many. The Labour MP and cabinet minister Tony Benn had lent his support to these shop stewards. Also, large-scale violent picketing had won the day during an NUM dispute in 1972. As well as this growth in militancy on the shop floor there had been a sharp move leftwards in the major trade unions, such as the TGWU (now led by Jack Jones) and the AEU (now led by Hugh Scanlon). Mick McGahey, the vice president of the NUM, had made clear the objectives of some trade unionists: 'it is not negotiation in Downing Street we want, but agitation in the streets of this country to remove the government.'[1]

The result of the election was a hung parliament with the small Liberal Party, led by Jeremy Thorpe, holding the balance. Heath, though, had lost. He had appealed to the people to back him, and they had refused to do so – at least unequivocally. In effect the NUM had won, for they had been the reason for the election being called by the government in the first place – and the government had not been returned. The scene was set for Harold Wilson to return to Downing Street.

THE SOCIAL CONTRACT

Harold Wilson had not expected to become prime minister again. It was no doubt a pleasing shock to find himself standing on the steps of 10 Downing Street waving to the crowds. But this time the thrill of office must have been tempered somewhat by a sinking realisation of what had fallen to him: the management of a nation in severe crisis, one in which, in the middle of an energy crisis and growing industrial trouble, an elected government had been brought low by militant trade unions.

Political 'management' was to become Wilson's watchword. And it soon became clear that he saw his role as prime minister as a holding operation. Labour, with its special relationship with the victorious trade unions, could save the country from social upheaval. His private boast was that if as prime minister he was able to 'get everybody in the Kingdom back to bed at night without too many heads being broken' then he would consider himself a success. And he saw himself also as 'holding the ring' until the country could benefit from the arrival of North Sea oil – then expected in the 1980s – a development that would transform its fortunes.

Wilson regarded Heath's flirtation with bourgeois radicalism – during the 'quiet revolution' – as a grievous, destabilising error. The old actor-manager (by this time more cynical and worldly wise than the stunned, innocent Heath) would appease, not confront, the trade unions. So Wilson inaugurated a novel system of national management. It was called the 'social contract' – an arrangement whereby government and unions cooperated to determine the domestic policy of the nation. Even the composition of his cabinet was to be drawn up in agreement with trade-union leaders, who were given a say over who got what job in some of the domestic and economic ministries.

By bringing the union leaders into the very heart of government Wilson was not (as some of his critics alleged) taking the country to the verge of 'red revolution'. He was rather marching to the beat of the ancient drum of paternalist statecraft, exhibiting the traditional instincts of England's ruling class when it meets a challenge to its vital interests. Domesticate, do not enrage, the insurgent; appease, do not confront, the opponent; maintain power by the appearance of sharing it.

And the union leaders played their part. As day after day they were to be seen on Britain's television screens emerging from 10 Downing Street it was as if the ermine was already wrapped around their shoulders, draping them in the embrace of an ancestral acceptance more worthy than any mere industrial reward. Their members had other ideas; but that particular rude awakening would await the next prime minister, the real architect of the 'social contract', Wilson's successor James Callaghan.

JAMES CALLAGHAN

Britain's eighth post-war prime minister 'kissed hands' (the term still used when the monarch graciously appoints the prime minister) on 5 April 1976. Jim Callaghan was a small-'c' conservative. He did not like change, and he identified with the status quo, the established political and social forces in the land. He was also an old-fashioned patriot – a successor of those working-class Labour patriots who had identified with Britain's imperial role and the elite which ran the empire and the country. Like Harold Wilson before him he was very deferential to the Queen and very pro-monarchist. He resisted the moderniser's attempts to change royal finances and get the Queen to pay income tax, and in 1977, jubilee year, he led the cabinet in a long discussion – as long as some of the discussions about the earlier IMF visit – about what gift to give the Queen for her jubilee. (They settled on a silver coffee pot.) With his premiership any pretence of modernisation was over.

Callaghan came from a southern-English upper-working-class background. He was a merchant seaman, and then an employee of the Inland Revenue, and as a young man made his way in Labour politics through the Inland Revenue Staff Association. Like others from a similar background (such as George Brown, Ray Gunter and Bob Mellish) he relied heavily upon right-wing trade-union votes for political advancement. Callaghan could relax easily with trade-union leaders, a social coterie with which he felt at home. For all his seemingly detached political style, and his apparently cold self-assurance, Callaghan was socially insecure, like so many from his background. Consequently he invested immense emotional capital in the Labour movement.

One of his cabinet colleagues could suggest,

> An endearing feature was his genuine gratitude to the Labour party for all the opportunities it had given him. He was justly proud to be the only politician of the century to have held all four of the senior offices of state: Chancellor of the Exchequer, Home Secretary, Foreign Secretary and, finally, Prime Minister. In turn he thought he owed the Labour party his total loyalty and this meant accepting the trade union link, bloc votes at conference and the arguments between right and left. These were, in his view, an inevitable part of the Labour party and they had to be endured.[2]

Nothing could shake Callaghan's determination to work with the trade-union leaders, and although the 'social contract' became increasingly shop-soiled during his tenure in office he stood by it to the end. The Callaghan-led Labour government was even more collectivist in its underlying assumptions and ethos than that of Wilson. Wilson – university-educated and meritocratic – had, after all, at least flirted with social modernisation as an objective, believing that weakening trade-union power was one way to create a more open and socially mobile society. Callaghan, on the other hand, was by background a trade-union employee and a trade-union-sponsored MP, who assumed that the only possible method of improving the conditions of the poorer, weaker and less wealthy sections of society was by 'collective advancement' under the auspices of the Labour movement, working within a framework of established economic and social relations.

THE IMF VISIT

Callaghan's 'social contract' deal with the trade unions was to fall foul of a serious run on sterling during the early months of his premiership. And in order to staunch the run Britain was forced to turn to the IMF for a massive loan. After the IMF team visited Britain the Labour government was forced during the winter of 1976/77 into seriously limiting the growth in public spending – as Anthony Crosland put it in a speech in Manchester some months earlier, 'the party's over.'

It was a pivotal time for Britain. For these IMF-induced spending cuts placed the 'social contract', with what was still a militant trade-union movement, under further strain. The Callaghan cabinet was divided between those who sought to accept the IMF's terms (led by chancellor Denis Healey), those who wanted a further negotiation for better terms (led by Tony Crosland), and those who wanted to walk away from the loan altogether, and if necessary implement a siege economy (led by Tony Benn). At one stage, in order to burnish his credentials as a national leader who would not be pushed around, Callaghan went on television and raised the issue of the expense to Britain of stationing the British Army of the Rhine in Germany – a non-too-subtle threat that if Britain did not get from its allies in the IMF (the Americans and Germans) decent terms, then the country's commitment to NATO might be brought into question.

Under pressure from the IMF Callaghan slowly but surely began to turn a corner onto a new route – one that would ultimately lead to Thatcherism and to a whole new, 'neo-liberal', approach to the economy and society. Consulting his son-in-law, Peter Jay, ahead of his 1976 Labour conference speech, Callaghan asked him to produce some paragraphs which would 'make the fur fly'. And in front of the serried ranks of staid trade unionists at the conference he stunned those present as he proclaimed,

> For too long, perhaps ever since the war, we postponed facing up to fundamental changes in our society and in our economy. That is what I mean when I say we have been living on borrowed time. For too long this country – all of us, yes this conference too – has been ready to settle for borrowing money abroad to maintain our standards of life, instead of grappling with the fundamental problems of British industry…The cosy world we were told would go on forever, where full employment would be guaranteed…that cosy world is now gone…We used to think we could spend our way out of a recession and increase employment by cutting taxes and boosting government spending. I tell you in all candour that that option no longer exists, and that insofar as it ever did exist, it only worked on each occasion since the war by injecting a bigger dose of inflation into the economy followed by a higher level of unemployment as the next step.[3]

In reviewing the historical importance of this speech the economic columnist William Keegan reported Robert Hormats, a former White

House economist, as saying that 'that speech…demonstrated to us that the UK had changed course. Without that speech it would have been difficult to obtain support in the US.'[4]

But Callaghan did not stop there. Under the shadow and pressure of the IMF he also became the first post-war prime minister to talk the language of the neo-liberal think-tank the IEA (Institute of Economic Affairs) about the 'dominance' of producer over consumer interests in post-war Britain. He was later to suggest that

> I also wanted to support the producer, but felt that the balance had shifted too far, to the extent that welfare services, and especially local government, were increasingly run entirely for the convenience of those who worked in them without concern for the needs of the ordinary citizens (and voters) who paid for them through taxes and who tried to use them…In fact, in all my many dealings with the National Union of Teachers at the time I never once heard mention by it of education or children.[5]

Support for the cluster of ideas around 'neo-liberalism' and monetarism had few friends in the Labour or Liberal Parties in the mid-1970s. Isolated figures like Parliamentary Labour Party chairman Douglas Houghton, trade-union leader Frank Chapple and Liberal MP John Pardoe would turn up at free-market think-tanks like the IEA and CPS (Centre for Political Studies), as would some of the officers of the Social Democratic Alliance, but these were minority pursuits. Whatever support neo-liberal economics secured from within the British left had more to do with the necessities of life following the IMF crisis than with any systematic ideological conversion to market-based economics. Even so, Callaghan's 'conversion' would serve one key function – to open the door to the later more comprehensive attack on the post-war consensus.

A 'WORLD ROLE' AGAIN

Jim Callaghan's administration also opened the door for a much more pro-Atlanticist and pro-American foreign policy. The 'Yes' vote in the 1975 referendum was in no way a prelude to Britain moving closer to Europe strategically. In fact exactly the opposite. Callaghan was ideologically more distant from Europe even than Wilson. His traditionalist attitudes – with a reactionary tinge – and his 'little Englander' instincts resisted too close a relationship with the continent.

At the same time, with the Cold War 'hotting up' around the world as the Soviet Union expanded its influence (following the American defeat in Vietnam), the British government felt it needed the 'special relationship' more than ever. And Callaghan was reinforced in this Atlanticist instinct by his fellow social democrat German chancellor Helmut Schmidt. The West Germans in the mid-1970s, conscious of being on the Cold War front line, were pursuing a 'special relationship' of their own with Washington. Schmidt's administration, although a 'good European' one, was somewhat wary of France on security matters – and sought to persuade Callaghan to continue with the British nuclear system in order that France would not become the only European nuclear power.

Callaghan's instinctive traditionalist Atlanticism had been on display in January 1975 when the British Labour government – in an echo of Ernest Bevin – took a crucial decision to extend the life of the Polaris submarine fleet and British nuclear weapons. Wilson and Callaghan acted in secret to approve the 'Chevaline project' to update the British nuclear deterrent. Chevaline was a new missile system which had been developed largely in the USA and, again, made Britain highly dependent upon US goodwill. Chevaline became operational on the submarine HMS *Renown* in 1982. This project was kept secret by Wilson and Callaghan from government, parliament and people, and was only announced to the public some seven years later – by Margaret Thatcher's defence secretary Francis Pym. In the post-1974 'social contract' between government and trade unions drawn up by Wilson and Callaghan, the union leaders had a say over a wide range of domestic policies, but the government was specifically shielded from trade-union involvement over foreign policy and defence.

Callaghan's detachment from Europe was repeated when in 1978, only three years after the pro-European victory in the national referendum, Britain took the decision to stay out of the newly established forerunner of the euro, the exchange-rate mechanism (ERM).

In many respects Jim Callaghan – both in his approach to Europe and in his flirtation with economic neo-liberalism – was foreshadowing the coming era of Thatcherism. Indeed even before the votes had been counted in the 1979 election he was predicting his defeat and suggesting that the country was embarking upon a major change of course. In one of the most extraordinary lines ever uttered by a senior politician in an election campaign, he said, 'there are times, perhaps once every thirty years, when there is a sea-change in politics. It does not matter what you say or what you do. There is a shift in what the public wants and what it approves of. I suspect there is now such a sea-change – and it is for Mrs Thatcher.'[6]

PART 3
Thatcher's Janus-faced revolution

9 THE ROAD TO THATCHERISM

Margaret Thatcher won the 1979 general election with a majority of 59 seats over the two main opposition parties. Thatcher was not just the first woman to rule in Downing Street – she was also a serious ideologue with decided views and a clear vision for the country. This vision, though, was not on prominent display when on the morning of 5 May the newly elected leader of the country travelled to Buckingham Palace to 'kiss hands' with a very different Briton – the hereditary head of the British state, the Queen, Elizabeth Windsor.

Born within a few months of each other (Margaret Thatcher on 13 October 1925, Elizabeth Windsor on 21 April 1926) these two women had made it to the top – but by sharply distinct routes. Whereas the Queen had been anointed by the Archbishop of Canterbury on behalf of the divine, Thatcher had made it on her own – she was the daughter of a grocer from Lincolnshire, had been a research chemist and a parliamentary candidate, and had risen through the ranks of the male-dominated Conservative Party to the highest elected office in the land.

The Queen at 53 was presiding over a country riven by industrial and social division – the undeclared British 'civil war'. The year 1979 was but a lull, a temporary peace treaty between the state and the miners' union, and almost everyone knew that a titanic struggle was still ahead (although few knew that the new Conservative prime minister had well-worked-out plans for defeating what her party saw as nothing less than a trade-union insurgency). The Queen and the royal family had kept a very low profile during the great industrial disputes and social disruptions of the mid-1970s. The likelihood was that 'the establishment', including the royals, would not survive a victory for the miners in the coming struggle. So although the relationship of the Queen and Mrs Thatcher was formal, even stiff, the Queen had a very personal interest in the success of the new prime minister.

But although Thatcher, when 'kissing hands', might have seemed to the Queen a fairly normal Tory prime minister – who could be counted on simply to defend 'the establishment' against the gathering extremists in the trade unions – she was, in fact, no such thing. The departing prime minister Jim Callaghan had seen her as representing a 'sea-change', and he had read her right. For the 'sea-change' he was alluding to was not simply a change of party but a change of direction – or, more precisely, the emergence of a new, radical, idea or ideology called the 'free market' or 'neo-liberalism'.

This idea had seduced and then captured Margaret Thatcher. She had won the Conservative leadership in 1975 as the candidate of the right, on a platform that rejected Heath's centrist U-turn. And while leader of the opposition during the late 1970s she found herself increasingly influenced by a insurgent group of radical-right market enthusiasts including Sir Keith Joseph, Alfred Sherman, Ralph Harris and Arthur Seldon (of the IEA), Madsen Pirie (of the Adam Smith Institute) and American economists and strategists around the Heritage Foundation in Washington DC and the then governor of California, Ronald Reagan. She proclaimed herself to be a follower of both the philosophical libertarian Friedrich von Hayek and the monetarist economist Milton Friedman.

These people represented what amounted to a transatlantic insurgency – a rejection of the whole post-war social-democratic consensus. In the USA they sought nothing less than to dismantle Franklin Roosevelt's 'new deal' and President Lyndon Johnson's 'great society' programme – and the 'big spending' and 'big government' they represented. In Britain they sought to 'roll back the frontiers of the state', lower taxes and public spending and, crucially, give business its head through deregulation.

It was a radical and ambitious agenda, indeed an historic one – and it was fortified by the certain belief among its leaders that the social-democratic, welfare era started by the post-war Attlee government was dysfunctional and coming to an end. And like all radical insurgencies it was engaged in an uphill task. After all, this new economic philosophy had being promulgated, in weaker form, before, by Edward Heath during the 'quiet revolution' of 1970–72, and the same interest groups – primarily the trade unions – which had forced Heath to back away from the strategy were still entrenched. Thus Thatcher's new radicalism, although exciting growing interest among journalists and in think-tanks, was, nonetheless, ultimately viewed as a fancy – as coherent theoretically but ultimately inapplicable to Britain. It simply went against the grain.

Thatcher – unusually among modern 'leaders' – was both an ideologue (with a strong sense of mission) and a highly practical politician. She knew that her ambitious economic restructuring of the country could not be carried through in the lifetime of one parliament. She needed at least a decade, if not longer, in order to overcome the inevitable initial resistance and to acclimatise people to the benefits she fervently believed the 'free market' and deregulation would ultimately bring.

There was little doubt in her mind that in order to succeed she would, ultimately, have to confront, and overcome, the power of the trade unions, particularly that of the NUM. She saw left-wing influence in local government (particularly in the Greater London Council (GLC)) and among the 'socialist generation' in the civil service, the universities and the media as powerful roadblocks, but was clear in her mind that it was the power of the unions that had effectively ended the government of Edward Heath and could end hers too.

However, her immediate objective was to fully secure her political position as prime minister. And for that she needed to win elections.

THATCHER'S 'LANDSLIDES'

Thatcher's first government became deeply unpopular almost immediately – primarily because of the downward turn in the economy and rapid growth of unemployment (reaching over three million in 1981). Yet surprisingly she was to win both the 1983 and 1987 general elections in what were termed 'landslides'. In the 1979 election the Conservative share of the vote was 43.9 per cent, and this share fell by 0.2 per cent in 1983, and again by a further 1.4 per cent in 1987. The Conservatives were able to translate this series of minority votes into a series of 'landslides' of parliamentary seats because they benefitted from the vagaries of a multi-party electoral system which delivered a disproportionate number of seats to the party which could secure over 40 per cent of the vote.

The fact that Thatcher's Conservatives were able to secure just over 40 per cent of the vote in three successive elections was no mean achievement, given the growing unemployment and social and industrial conflict which the new economic strategy brought in its wake. The intriguing question is why the Conservatives did so well.

Part of the explanation obviously lies with the deep unpopularity of the Labour Party as, after 1980, it moved to the left under the leadership of Michael Foot. This was particularly so in much of the south and the midlands where, outside London, Labour's vote almost disappeared.

Yet from the Conservatives' point of view there was also a positive side to the story. A careful reading of the detailed electoral statistics reveals that the new neo-liberal economic strategy of the 1980s was able, over time, to create genuine support for itself among a growing 'middle-class' electorate. And 'middle class' here is not meant to depict solely the traditional Conservative enclaves in the home counties and among the suburban salariat. One of the most intriguing aspects of the politics of the 1980s has been the changing voting habits of one of Britain's most pivotal voting blocs, the skilled manual workers. Between the elections of 1983 and 1987, the percentage of these workers (and their families) who voted Conservative rose by 4 per cent.[1] This helps to explain the historically (and remarkably) high level of Conservative votes recorded in predominantly urban safe Labour constituencies throughout the southern half of England. Such erstwhile Labour strongholds as Thurrock, Walthamstow and Wolverhampton North-East were gained by the Conservatives in 1987; and in seats like Barking, Dagenham, Coventry South-West and Corby (as well as in a range of other predominantly urban and highly unionised constituencies) the Conservative vote reached levels that it had never seen before.

Previous decades had witnessed fluctuating 'working-class' support for the Conservative Party, but what was new about the 1980s was the sheer size of the conversion in particular blue-collar areas in the southern half of England. The electoral map of southern England began to lose its class flavour as the traditionally 'working-class' seats could no longer be so easily distinguished from the rest. This electoral consensus, however, represented something even more important. A process was obviously underway which was beginning to blur the lines between the old, stubborn, British social stereotypes of hourly-paid workers living in council houses (who voted Labour) and the salaried middle class with mortgages (who voted Conservative). 'These divides,' it was suggested by the *Economist* of 16 May 1987 'are now crossed by millions who would be called upwardly mobile if the yuppies had not got to the term first.'

The class inequalities which the 1980s had somewhat 'ironed out' in the southern half of England had stiffened in the north (including

Scotland). During the years of the Thatcher revolution large tracts of the urban north and of urban Scotland were untouched by the economic changes proceeding in the south (and the rising trend in unemployment north of the Trent had ensured that, far from eroding social barriers, ancient social divisions were, if anything, hardening).

The old image of 'the north' as one vast wasteland was never particularly apt, for such an image hardly took into account either the areas of northern prosperity or indeed southern poverty. This image somehow tended to omit from view the vast number of acres held in private ownership throughout the north and Scotland, the sizeable middle-class suburbs surrounding many northern and Scottish cities, and indeed the quasi-bourgeois character and aspirations of some of the more prosperous families in the mining areas. Thus the reaction of 'the north' to the popular capitalist experiment of the 1980s was more complicated than the traditional image would normally have allowed. In fact, during the 1980s 'the north' was only marginally less well disposed to the Conservatives than was the rest of the country. Between 1983 and 1987 the Conservative vote fell by only 2 per cent in the north-west and by 2.3 per cent in the north (Scotland was the genuine exception, where it fell by 4.3 per cent and the Labour vote rose by 7.3 per cent).

The consistently solid level of public support (with percentages around the low forties) for Thatcher's radical economic strategy of the 1980s contrasts sharply with the notion that Britain had become utterly resistant to change. By the time of the third Conservative election victory, the London correspondent of the *New York Times* could argue that 'None of the opposition strategies seemed to admit the possibility that in an ossified society – where inheriting has long been deemed the only truly proper way to acquire wealth – Mrs Thatcher's strivers' code might exert an almost clandestine appeal.'[2]

Of course a series of election victories for the Conservative Party during the 1980s based upon a popular vote never rising above 43 per cent is hardly the same thing as a popular national mandate for radical change. Nor does it tell the whole story about the underlying instincts and opinions even of those who voted Conservative. For among Conservative voters those who identified themselves with economic change (and wanted more of it) were probably outnumbered by those who sought the defence of the status quo, who voted Conservative as a means of keeping Labour out. If anything, 'old money' probably supported the Conservatives as fervently as did 'new money', landowners as determinedly as the new entrepreneurs, and the older traditional middle class in greater numbers than the upwardly mobile 'workers'. A marked shift in the underlying social attitudes of the Conservative voting constituency should not therefore be pushed too far. Although popular motives can never be properly adduced from polling results, it would seem likely that a large percentage of Thatcher's vote in both 1983 and 1987 was still grudgingly given.

THE FALKLANDS MARCH-PAST: NO ROYALS PLEASE

Of course any account of how the Tory Party was able to convert to its cause so many blue-collar workers during the Thatcher years needs to include some mention of the so-called 'Falklands factor'. On 2 April 1982 the Argentine government launched an invasion of the Falkland Islands, legally a British territory. The response in the House of Commons was a fascinating lesson in how the old instinct of empire and dominance was still alive and well among the British parliamentary and political elite. Michael Foot spoke for the Labour Party in patriotic terms imbued with Churchillian rhetoric, and in essence called for the use of force to expel the invader. It was as if this invasion of some small windswept islands by a Latin American government was the last straw in a series of humiliations for the post-imperial power; its *amour propre* had been offended. And the decided position of the whole House of Commons – with the exception of a few Liberal MPs and the former chancellor Roy Jenkins – was that the empire needed to strike back.

Margaret Thatcher, with her premiership hanging in the balance, needed to lead the strike-back, indeed to oust the junta from the islands, in order to save her premiership. And, following the dispatch of a task force to the area, the Argentines were indeed ejected, and surrendered in June 1982.

This was sold as a patriotic war and as an historic British victory – and it was to form part of the proffered story of the revival of British power from its decline in the 1970s. The fact that the USA's help (in Ascension Island and in military materiel) was crucial in determining the outcome of the conflict was down-played.

Before the conflict in the South Atlantic, polls showed that the Conservative Party was losing significant numbers of votes in southern England to the new SDP – Liberal Alliance, but that after the 'victory' the Conservative vote hardened and Thatcher's popularity rose. Indeed Thatcher rode such a wave of nationalist and patriotic popularity that she was able, in a most unusual development, to take, on her own (with no royal present), the salute of the forces in a march-past, appropriately enough in the City of London.

THE MINERS' STRIKE OF 1984

Having got through to an election victory in 1983 – with the help of the 'Falklands factor' – the next hurdle for Thatcher emerged in the following year, when the NUM found itself in dispute with the National Coal Board (NCB) over projected pit closures. The prospect of a conflict between the NUM and the state aroused considerable anxieties within the Conservative Party and government. Ever since 1971 – when the NUM unexpectedly won what was to become the first of a trilogy of industrial battles with the elected government – British politics had proceeded in what amounted to a twilight world of authority. The question raised in the first general election of 1974, 'Who governs Britain: government or unions?', remained a legitimate subject for speculation well into the 1980s. (Some months before the 1983 general election a European diplomat politely asked an embarrassed Tory MP whether the NUM president, Arthur Scargill, had a 'veto' over the further development of the Thatcherite revolution. 'He surely,' enquired the foreigner, 'will not allow privatisation of energy?')

The initial instinct across the established political spectrum, including the 'old establishment', was to appease the miners' union, for so stark a confrontation was obviously taking risks with the social fabric and thus with their place within it. Indeed, Thatcher herself had earlier appeased the miners when she yielded to the union in a dispute a year after coming to power. However, by 1984 there was a strong consensus in the political class to see off the latest strike. Intriguingly, the royal family remained completely silent during the dispute – there were no private or public displays of sympathy for the striking miners as there were later to be for the rural lobby during the fox-hunting ban dispute. In confronting the miners, the Thatcher government and the 'old establishment' were all in it together. But it was clear that this decision to confront the union was yet another high-stakes gamble by Thatcher.

The strike started in March 1984 and quickly became what amounted to an industrial civil war. At the Orgreave Coking Plant near Rotherham in June 1984 a battle scene, similar to a civil war, saw ten thousand combatants line up on each side. No shots were fired, but the police used horses and truncheons, and there were many serious injuries. Other confrontations occurred throughout the country. The miners were fatally weakened in their struggle when other unions refused to support them, and when it became clear that the Thatcher government had made serious contingency plans – including new controversial policing policies – to keep the electricity grid operating. Unable to bring enough pressure to bear on the economy and society, the NUM voted to return to work on 3 March 1985, a year after the strike had begun. It amounted to a major defeat and humiliation for the union and its leader Arthur Scargill; and it saw the beginning of the end for coalmining communities through the British coalfields, areas of Britain which have subsequently seen high unemployment levels only mitigated by a growth in call-centres.

Yet had the strategy to confront the NUM failed – and the dispute gone Arthur Scargill's way – then not only would the NUM have established 'veto power' over at least some aspects of the liberal economic strategy but also the re-emergence of an undercurrent of fear for the future of the social fabric would have strengthened the hand of the Tory 'wets'. Thatcher's revolution, and possibly Thatcher herself, would have been over. As it turned out, the conflict with the NUM (and indeed Britain's 'trade-union question') was finally settled in the late spring of 1985 when thousands of defeated miners – the 'lions who had been led by donkeys' – returned to work, covering their humiliation at the hands of the Thatcher government by marching in columns under their banners with bands playing. Thatcher had prevailed yet again.

By the spring of 1986, though, the prime minister was confronting yet another threat to her premiership when the 'Westland helicopter affair' came remarkably close to removing her from office, this time through an attempted 'palace coup' within the 1922 Committee of Conservative backbenchers. 'Westland' was essentially a contrivance, and an opportunity for Thatcher's remaining opponents to oust her in time to allow another prime minister to see himself into the job before the coming election. Thus the merits of the issue became of less interest than what the affair revealed about the line-up of 'dry' and 'wet' forces within the Conservative Party seven years into Thatcher's era. It was soon quite clear that the radicals had indeed won the battle for the Tory soul, for the 'wets' simply could not muster the parliamentary numbers needed to overcome a determined resistance from Number 10.

Margaret Thatcher overcame most of the rebellions against her from within her own party because the question of whether to remove her or not only served to concentrate the minds of Conservative MPs on the lack of any credible successor. The connecting theme in Thatcher's successful battle with her own party during her years as prime minister was that ultimately the party stuck by her because she was a winner, above all electorally. And she was to prove the point again in the general election of 1987, when she was returned to Downing Street for a third time – with another large parliamentary majority. Thus the triumph of radicalism within the Conservative Party, and the revolution known as Thatcherism, was only made possible by the string of election victories accumulated by the party under her leadership.

THE DIVIDED LEFT: THE ROAD TO APOSTASY (REG PRENTICE)

Thatcher's election victories, however, need to be set in a broader political context. It had been a truism of British politics during the twentieth century that divisions on the left help the Conservatives. Such was the case when Labour edged out the Liberals as the major opposition party during the 1920s; it was also the outcome of the Labour government break-up in 1931. It is also a truism that divisions on the left are endemic, a part of the furniture of British politics, a product of deep ideological tensions, indeed irreconcilabilities.

These strains, however, were contained for a good three decades following the 1945 political settlement. Yet they began to surface again during the 1970s as the uneasy coalition between the socialist and social-democratic wings of the Labour movement began to fray at the edges. A split between these two wings nearly occurred when a dramatic realignment of British politics almost took place in December 1976. Jim Callaghan's majority in the House of Commons had disappeared and consequently a very small number of Labour MPs could have effectively brought down the government. For some years past the arguments for a realignment had been taken seriously by a section of the Conservative Party which had been close to Macmillan. Since 1973, Reg Prentice had taken a lone path, one which would eventually take him out of the Labour Party and into the Conservative fold. In the meantime, in league with Roy Jenkins, he had sought ways of bringing down the Callaghan government.

His advocacy had struck a chord with some Conservatives, among them Robert Carr, Nicholas Scott and Patrick Cormack. These, and others, were beginning to meet, together with Labour MPs, on an increasingly regular, though informal, basis. A meeting finally took place in Julian Amery's house – with Amery himself, Patrick Cormack, Maurice Macmillan, Reg Prentice, John Mackintosh and Brian Walden – to argue through the case for bringing down the Callaghan government. The consensus emerged that an attempt was worthwhile, and Prentice, who had come straight to the meeting from a Labour cabinet meeting chaired by Callaghan, made arrangements to meet secretly with Margaret Thatcher.

Prentice has reported that

> The key people would be Margaret Thatcher, Roy Jenkins and David Steel, in that order. Margaret would have to lead such a government, as the Conservatives would be the biggest party in it, although they lacked a majority in the House. Would she be interested? If she were, then Roy Jenkins would be the one person in the Labour Party with a wide enough personal following to bring in a substantial Labour contingent. Only if this happened would the Liberals be likely to join. Arrangements were made for me to see Margaret Thatcher. Nobody else was present and no notes were taken. I do not recall all the details of the discussion, but I remember her strong views on the economic crisis, so much more incisive that anything I had heard at the Cabinet table. She was angry and worried at the drift of events and was afraid that the government would 'fudge' the issue again. As to a political realignment, she did not commit herself, but I was left with the impression that she would feel bound to participate if there were evidence of wider support. The clear implication was that I should take further soundings.[3]

Everything therefore hinged on the attitude of Roy Jenkins. He was technically a backbencher, but he had an office in the cabinet secretariat building – as he would be taking up the presidency of the European Commission on 1 January the following year. As an MP still, he was politically and constitutionally available to take part in the contemplated political moves. Jenkins, however, was to reject the overture, and the opportunity. He told Prentice that 'the proposed realignment would lead to a government nominally "national" but in fact "Conservative".' He also argued that 'Although I would be a senior figure in the new government, supported by other right-wing Labour members, we should be supporting an essentially Conservative administration, rather like Ramsay MacDonald and his friends in 1931.'[4] Jenkins was at that time haunted by the 'MacDonald analogy', with its image of 'betrayal'. At the same time, he obviously believed his refusal to 'break out' during the 1970s was another kind of betrayal. The formation of the SDP, in which he was the incomparable guiding hand, was, in a sense, an act of redemption on his part for these past missed opportunities.

And it was Margaret Thatcher's inordinately good fortune that the electoral fissure between Labour and the SDP which was produced by this political earthquake was to give her revolution a fair wind for another ten years.

THE SDP AND THE DEFEAT OF THE LEFT

The SDP was launched with great fanfare on 26 March 1981. It was founded by four senior Labour politicians, Roy Jenkins, David Owen, Shirley Williams and Bill Rodgers, the 'gang of four'. For some time before they broke with Labour there had been rumblings of discontent within the Labour Party about its increasingly left-wing direction. For some years the Social Democratic Alliance (of which I was joint secretary) had agitated within the Labour Party against this ascendant left and, after 1979, in favour of a new breakaway party. Roy Jenkins, then European Commission president, agreed, and in 1980 he also started campaigning for a breakaway party (a 'centre party' as he dubbed it) and a realignment. He talked of 'breaking the two-party mould' of British politics.

After considerable hesitation the three other senior Labour politicians finally joined him. The time for a new party was highly propitious. As unemployment rose the Thatcher government was deeply unpopular, but at the same time so was Labour – as it moved to the left under the leadership of the nuclear disarmer Michael Foot. Polls showed that the new party was ahead in large numbers of seats – mainly in the Tory south of England – and it seemed as though it was indeed on course to hold the balance of power after the election and 'break the mould'.

But the new party had some real weaknesses. It was an avowedly social-democratic party launched just as the social-democratic era was dissolving. So there was something rather defensive about it – defending the old order against the extreme left. David Marquand's major pamphlet, written specifically for the newly formed party, was appetisingly radical – he called it 'Russet-Coated Captains', referring to the radical officers in Cromwell's new model army – but the social democracy for which Marquand (and the SDP) stood, though innovative (especially on constitutional reform and Europe) was simply not an insurgent force. It was defending the established order, but offering a better way (than Thatcher's) to defeat the left.

Also, its four leaders were far too narrowly drawn socially. None of the original four were from extravagantly privileged backgrounds, none born into real wealth or status. Roy Jenkins – although his demeanour and accent belied it – came from a middling Welsh family. His father, though by no means a typical workers' representative, had gone to prison for trade-union activities, a fact which caused his mother some embarrassment. David Owen's ancestry was Celtic, a fact about which he could sometimes become emotional. Bill Rodgers was a Mancunian, a grammar-school boy with provincial roots. Shirley Williams hailed from a self-consciously intellectual family which seemingly rejected the conformist upper-middle-class standards of the day.

As the playwright John Mortimer wrote,

> Mrs Williams it seems was born with a silver spoon in her mouth, perhaps one of those her mother, the writer Vera Brittain, who inherited wealth from a family business in the Potteries, used at her elegant tea parties attended by a maid…She had a father, who, as his son candidly admits, gave the appearance of being a frightful snob. The temptation to take such a spoon and stir a chipped mug of strong Typhoo in the nearest and greasiest working man's caff must have been irresistible.[5]

Yet all of them went to Oxbridge, and not one was a trade unionist. I tried to insert former deputy prime minister George Brown (a populist and a former right-wing trade-union leader) and the electricians' trade-union leader Frank Chapple into the leadership to provide a broader-based 'gang of six', but to no avail. And the party soon came to be tagged by its opponents as little more than a group of elitist progressive middle-class 'claret drinkers' (allegedly claret was Roy Jenkins's favourite drink).

Finally, the new party never truly settled upon a strategic objective, for its leaders were divided on which party it sought to replace (Jenkins was in favour of replacing the Tories, Owen Labour).

The 1983 election was to be the great test for the new party. If it could not make a breakthrough then it would make no breakthrough at all. It came very close. The SDP received only 2 per cent less than Labour in the national popular vote and came a close second in a shoal of southern English constituencies. The unrepresentative electoral system, though, meant that the new party received only a handful of seats compared to its large national vote and the Conservative Party gained a disproportionately large parliamentary majority. The dream of 'breaking the mould' was over. The SDP passed into the history books.

However, although the SDP had not broken the mould of the two-party system, it did succeed, with the help of Labour's extremist left, in fatally weakening the Labour Party, putting it out of office for a long time. At a reception at the SDP conference late in 1983 one of the trustees of the new party offered the following conclusion as to what it had all meant: 'Well, we may not have broken the mould, but we have dished Labour, and for a generation.' He was not far off the mark. Furthermore, with three parties instead of two contesting the 1983 election the vagaries of the electoral system produced a large enough Tory majority to allow Thatcher to ditch her left-wing 'wets' and go for the full 'revolutionary' agenda.

When the dust had settled, the much-trumpeted 'realignment of the left' had ended up with an ironic twist: those Keynesian social democrats who had set up the new party had helped forward, by the very act of dividing Labour and thus helping Thatcher, the end of their own social-democratic era. Had Jenkins, Williams, Rodgers and Owen, in those early, heady days surrounding the launch of the new party, known how they were playing into Thatcher's hands they might not have embarked on the endeavour at all.

Yet the SDP affair cannot be seen only in this grimly ironic context. The declaration of the new party in 1981 was not a random event produced by careerist politicians; rather it had its roots in the contradictions of Labour's, and Britain's, history. Labour had nearly split apart several times during the 1960s and 1970s. But somehow its explosively combustible contradictions always seemed to be contained, yet another testimony to the sluggish hold of tradition on the mid-twentieth-century British. The great battles of principle and ideology were always seemingly subsumed under the inertia of traditionalist habit.

These contradictions in Labour were, of course, part ideological – between the social democracy of the moderates and the marxism of the left. But they also echoed another, deeper, British inner-conflict – between modernisation (and the necessary national adjustment to a reduced role in the world) on the one hand, and the traditionalism of both left and right (continuing the 'grand delusion' of British power).

It is worth reflecting upon what indeed could have happened had the SDP succeeded in 'breaking the mould' of the party duopoly as early as 1983. Had the SDP–Liberal Alliance held the balance in parliament for a generation, Britain would have taken a different road to that taken by Margaret Thatcher. It is likely that the trade unions would have been cut down to size but not destroyed; that the state would have been somewhat reduced, but not systematically handed over to business; and that, most importantly of all, while the market and deregulation might well have been introduced into more areas of the economy, there would have been no unbalanced, spectacular growth of the off-shore Wall-Street-led 'casino capitalism' of the 1990s and beyond. Britain would likely have retained its mixed, and balanced, economy. Also, the pro-European SDP–Liberal Alliance would likely have ensured that the British played a fuller role in the moves towards European integration in the 1980s and 1990s and become a leading player, alongside Germany and France, in deciding Europe's future – one more to Britain's liking than the one that resulted.

But none of this was to be. By failing to secure a few thousand votes in the all-important 1983 general election the mould remained intact. Thatcher won outright, and Britain set off down the road towards a new, and revolutionary free-market and globalised future.

10 THATCHER AND THE QUEEN: TWO VISIONS OF BRITAIN

I always feel ten years younger – despite the jet-lag –when I set foot on American soil.

Margaret Thatcher, 2002

In July 1986 the *Sunday Times* reported claims from the Queen's advisors that there had been 'a rift' between the monarch and Margaret Thatcher over a range of policies – including differences of opinion over the Commonwealth and rising unemployment. So serious were the rumours that Buckingham Palace took the unusual step of issuing a formal denial.

Such a 'rift' was not unexpected. By 1986 the prime minister was flush from her victory over Arthur Scargill and the miners, and the road was open to the completion of her revolution. She was beginning to bestride the smallish British scene like a colossus, and was becoming an international political star – promoted, among others, by President Ronald Reagan. Indeed she was becoming almost presidential. But, presidential or not, Britain was a monarchy, and it had a Queen.

The 'rift' was dampened down, and there was to be no open political confrontation between monarch and prime minister. Yet even so it was becoming clear that there was indeed a confrontation, even a clash, of visions. Of course the Queen's vision had not changed much from the time of the coronation. She saw Britain as still very much a top-table power with a worldwide global role based around the Commonwealth of Nations (of which she was head) and the Anglican Church (of which she was also the head). Margaret Thatcher certainly saw Britain as a global power, but completely rejected the Commonwealth as a vehicle for this role. For her British power was based upon the American 'special relationship'.

But it was in their vision of 'England' and 'Englishness' – both the Queen and Thatcher were decidedly 'English', at least culturally – that they differed most sharply. For the Queen the vision was essentially paternalistic: a country in which everyone was cared for (after a fashion) but a land of 'ranks and orders' where everyone knew their place. And in her private life she lived this vision. It was, is, an essentially arcadian existence – a land full of villages and thatched cottages, rural and equestrian – indeed rather feudal, a world which is ill at ease with the modernising influences of both industrial capitalism and democracy. Jonathan Raban, an English writer who went to live in America in the 1990s, used to argue that it was a world, something of a fantasy-world, which had many proponents among middle-class people in England.

> On a clear windy top of Highgate Hill there is a community of ardent villagers. They wear country clothes – riding macs and headscarves, tweeds and Wellington boots – and talk in gentry voices, braying bravely over the tops of taxis. They have their church [of England], their tea-shop, their family grocer, their village green, three village pubs, and the Highgate Society with its coffee mornings, its knighted President and its evening lectures.[1]

The prime minister's vision of her country was much, much different. Thatcher did not see herself, not then and certainly not later, as a protector and defender of old England and of the values and way of life represented by the Queen. Her heroes were industrialists and entrepreneurs and the great English fighters for freedom and commerce. Thatcher was a genuine radical. So radical, in fact, that she wanted to change Britain out of all recognition. So radical, in fact, that her political and social vision amounted to a programme for transforming Britain – into a copy of America.

In her early years she gave little appearance of being such a revolutionary. Brought up as a provincial middle-class Englishwoman she seemed a typical southern English small-town rural-cum-suburban lady. Yet, like so many bright and ambitious young grammar-school children of the time, she had to adapt to the class-bound and 'county' world of the late 1940s and 1950s in order to succeed. She took the subtle personality-changing first step – elocution lessons – and would thereafter sound and appear the almost perfect 'twin set and pearls'

English county tweedy Tory. She was in fact, though, very different. And her deeper identity was to come out later.

By the standards of the time the young, aspiring, Margaret Thatcher was a fish out of water in the Tory Party. A meritocrat in a party that valued inheritance, a suburbanite in a party still highly influenced by big landed interests, a developing ideologue in a party suspicious of systematic thought, and a woman of strong opinions and principles, who loved a good fiery argument – in a man's club. In fact there was very little of the Tory traditionalist in her at all. Yet during the 1950s she was to make her way in the party – in the 1951 and 1955 elections she fought the safe Labour seat of Dartford in Kent.

Soon after she entered Downing Street, however, it was becoming clear that she was attracted neither to the governing ethos of her own party nor certainly to the socialist alternative (no matter how meritocratic). She had more in common with the values and attitudes of a different country altogether – the USA. She was to say, some years after she left office, that 'I always feel ten years younger – despite the jet-lag – when I set foot on American soil.'[2]

Many East Anglians of Thatcher's generation have always had a soft spot for Americans – dating from formative years in wartime Britain when American soldiers and airmen came into contact with the locals. They liked their directness, their enthusiasm and their optimism about the possibilities of life. Margaret Thatcher herself once wrote that there is 'something positive, generous and open about the people'. In any event this American way was, for her, a deal better than what she often saw as the elliptical over-sophistication, hypocrisy and, above all, appeasing instincts of the Tory governing class.

She had a sense of, as she put it, 'belonging to America'.[3] And as prime minister in the 1980s she saw herself as struggling, often against the odds, to bring American-style capitalism to Britain. And in the process, in all but name and manners, and of course formal nationality, she became an American.

A great part of her attraction to the USA arose from the great ideological struggle of the Cold War. Thatcher believed deeply in the reality of the struggle, and of the threat from Soviet power. In the 1970s détente was at its height and there was a sense the West was losing the East–West struggle as Soviet influence was seen to grow around the world, particularly in Latin America and Africa. Thatcher saw America, the leader of the West, as the only bastion against communism. She saw the republic as 'the last best hope'.

In Britain decline was in the air. The Heath government had, in effect, been defeated by the miners' union when it failed to get a majority following its 'Who governs Britain?' appeal in the February 1974 general election. And the subsequent Wilson government's 'social contract' was widely seen as a further surrender – both to the miners and to the wider trade-union movement. It was a period rife with talk of 'ungovernability' and 'extremism'.

It was during this period, in late 1975, that I first met Margaret Thatcher. I was a Labour member elected to the GLC and joint-secretary of the Social Democratic Alliance, she was leader of the opposition. She had heard of my outspokenness about the Labour extreme left. Through a mutual acquaintance, her assistant Richard Ryder, later to become Tory chief whip, I was invited to her home in Flood Street for a chat. Two things now stand out from that get-together. Something had obviously happened in, of all parties, the Tory Party, for I was met by a cultural role reversal. Margaret's husband Denis greeted me, but the husband then remained in the kitchen as the wife, her assistant and I went upstairs to her living room for a chat. Also, and very unusually for top Tories of that era, this Tory leader was an enthusiast, almost a crusader – a bubbly woman who was also highly intellectual – in the sense that she was interested in ideas and abstractions. She was dogmatic in her beliefs but also loved argument. What shone through, though, was an Englishwoman who, the moment she talked politics, transmogrified into a replica of an American suburban conservative – without the religion. She exhibited the kind of political fierceness and commitment – and a disdain for liberals, socialists and communists, which she saw as melding into each other – that I was later also to witness in Reagan's Washington among right-wing Republican activists.

She saw 'free markets' as bringing freedom and democracy in their wake, and capitalism as unleashing merit and enterprise around the world. In an echo of American right-wing rhetoric of the time, she fervently believed that America had saved the world before (on D-Day) and would do so again; and that the Europeans, particularly the French, were 'weak sisters', riddled with socialist thinking and bureaucracy. Some time after she left the premiership Thatcher revealed just how much she actually believed in this right-wing American view of the world. 'In my lifetime,' she reflected, 'all our problems have come from mainland Europe and all the solutions have come from the English-speaking nations of the world.'[4]

Not surprisingly, Thatcher was to go on to become the most thoroughly pro-American prime minister of the post-war era. Her relationship with Ronald Reagan simply solidified her love affair with America. His straight, no-nonsense, folksy approach appealed to her. However, even she was to have a 'Greece to Rome' moment when she reportedly remarked privately about the president, 'Poor dear, there's nothing between the ears.'[5] Even so, she came to see that Reagan's simple, straightforward approach was basically hers too, and she soon realised that the clear, uncomplicated political messages of 'the great communicator' were necessary for the prosecution of their joint cause.

Above all, though, it was their convergence on Western strategy and policy that made the match. Abandoning détente with the Soviet Union was the key unifying point. As leader of the opposition Thatcher had developed an anti-détente approach that set her aside from governing opinion in the West. She sought a stronger attitude towards the Kremlin, an increase in defence expenditure, and achieved considerable global publicity for her anti-Soviet views when, while still opposition leader, the Kremlin dubbed her 'the iron lady'. When she became prime minister in 1979 there was a sense that the Western guard might be changing; and the American conservatives, mainly gathered around the governor of California, Ronald Reagan, began to court her. The Soviet invasion of Afghanistan in December 1979, some few months after Thatcher had become prime minister, brought détente to an end and her approach to the fore.

Reagan became president in January 1980, and his national-security team – including Richard Allen and Bill Casey – visited Britain just before his inauguration. As part of their trip Ed Feulner, president of Reagan's favourite Washington think-tank, asked me to arrange a private lunch for them at Brown's Hotel in London to introduce them to a variety of British opinion-formers – and these included financier Jimmy Goldsmith, television journalists Alistair Burnett and Michael Charlton, and some Tory MPs. It soon became clear that even before they had taken over in Washington Reagan's officials were treating Margaret Thatcher very seriously. They were highly conscious that a new phase of the Cold War was dawning, and that the two new leaders could make a real difference.

And, as it turned out, the Reagan–Thatcher Cold War duo did change the global scene – and in the process it gave, for the first and only time, some real meaning to the term 'special relationship'. For a short time during Reagan's presidency the Anglo–American relationship became something of a two-way street; and Britain surpassed Germany as 'first among equals' in the gallery of US allies. Thatcher herself in 1985 could say with confidence that 'I feel no inhibitions about describing the relationship as very, very, special.'[6]

For Margaret Thatcher, her total support for American policy around the globe was not a submission to America and its interests. Rather it was part of the natural order of things during the Cold War. For her, as for many British politicians across the spectrum, Britain during the Cold War was only one part of a bigger ideological cause – the 'free world' and the idea of democracy for which it stood. She once said that 'America's cause is, and always will be, our cause.'[7] In Thatcher's world view the American president, in this case Ronald Reagan, would be the automatic, unchallenged leader of this cause, and the British prime minister his chief of staff. And they would be serving a single – ideological – vision.

When Reagan came to Britain in June 1982, following Thatcher's success in the Falklands, he gave a major address to parliament. The speech was vintage Reagan, a highly ideological and optimistic speech about the great cause of 'freedom and democracy' and the need to pursue it worldwide. The reception showed the divisions in the Tory Party at the time between the ideologues with their sweeping universalist ideas and the more cautious, more interest-based, realists. While Thatcher, obviously moved, nodded vigorously in agreement, Reagan's approach obviously jarred on some of the 'wetter' Tories – Francis Pym and William Whitelaw in particular. They were less than enthused by the 'free world' rhetoric but, like good, loyal, subordinate allies, they sat straining to be similarly moved.

For Thatcher, as for many Americans (both Republicans and Democrats) the 'free world' meant 'free markets'. For her, the two ideas were indissoluble. The West stood for clear economic principles, such as free enterprise and limited government, and those who did not agree – social democrats and socialists of various hues – were weakening the West in the Cold War struggle. Thatcher shared with most American political leaders a fundamentalist approach to the market. It was an approach that both sought to marketise as much as possible, remove as many restrictions to the market as possible, and, crucially, saw the market as having a political function – as extending human freedom and individual sovereignty. Thatcher was an extreme individualist in the mould of the American writer Ayn Rand, a view of the world that led Thatcher, in her most famous of all pronouncements, to argue that 'there is no such thing as society. There are individual men and women, and there are families.'[8]

Thatcher had honed her belief in individualism and the 'free-enterprise system' at the feet of the classical liberalism of Enoch Powell, Keith Joseph and the IEA during the 1960s and early 1970s. They had introduced her to the Austrian thinkers Ludwig von Mises and Friedrich von Hayek and, in the contemporary debate, to the Chicago School monetarist Milton Friedman. The IEA had been set up by the millionaire entrepreneur Anthony Fisher and from its inception was led by Ralph Harris and Arthur Seldon. In the 1970s Harris and Seldon hosted hundreds of IEA lunches, held in their small, cramped offices off Smith Square in Westminster – events which, literally, changed the thinking of a generation. And Seldon's house parties in his rambling home in Sevenoaks – always drawing a mixture of bright politicians, journalists and academics – were vibrant affairs, and had about them the atmosphere of a coming new orthodoxy. Seldon was able to write about the great adventure in his well-received book *Capitalism*, published in 1990.[9]

Harris and Seldon were ideology in action. They were utterly committed, clear and compelling arguers and thinkers; and, as with all good iconoclasts and successful campaigners, they had a credible target in their sights – the failures of the British economy in the 1970s and the consensus that supported it. Harris and Seldon put these failures squarely at the door of the social-democratic policies and structures of Keynesian and welfare economics (whereas unbalanced trade-union power and geostrategic questions such as oil-price rises were not particularly highlighted). They played this theme for all it was worth. And as the very high levels of inflation and unemployment of the 1970s eroded confidence in the established consensus, opinion-formers were prepared to listen to a radical alternative.

These market-fundamentalist gurus had a big influence not just on Margaret Thatcher's economic philosophy, but also on Thatcherism's US geopolitical orientation. For Harris and Seldon, the USA was their intellectual home, for the other great capitalist economies on the continent were seen as too 'statist' and 'quasi-socialist', stubbornly stuck in the social-democratic consensus that they were trying to break in Britain. For the IEA thinkers, US society, and not just its economy, was worth copying: and social reform in Britain should centre around overhauling and privatising the British welfare state, including health and education, to give more freedom and choice to the individual.

There was something of the appearance of an old-fashioned English nationalist in Ralph Harris. A working-class lad from Tottenham in North London, he affected a 'Colonel Blimp' persona with his RAF bearing, his pipe and warm beer, and his affable, ironic, complaining about 'Johnny Foreigner'. It was therefore something of a natural progression when Harris became a leading light in the anti-EEC and anti-EU campaign groups, particularly the Bruges Group. A bitter opponent of European federalism, he saw it as associated with socialism. Arthur Seldon, on the other hand, was less hostile to the EEC. He was no Tory, always describing himself as 'whiggish', and was suspicious of the nationalist impulses lurking within anti-European breasts. Seldon possessed none of the traditionalist English prejudices about Europe. He saw Europe through free-market eyes – as a huge internal market which Britain needed to be a part of; and he would constantly remind Eurosceptics that Britain could, should it want to, retain its 'precious sovereignty', but only at the expense of increasing poverty at home.

Yet, all in all, no matter these home-grown ideological influences on her, Margaret Thatcher came to power in Britain on a prospectus essentially made in Chicago. Her philosophy and her governments were not a one-off or a uniquely British affair. For they represented only a part of a much wider transatlantic movement that in the 1970s campaigned and in the 1980s and 1990s ultimately succeeded in altering the economies and societies of much of the Western world.

In essence Thatcherism was the British version of an American-led neo-conservative insurgency developing throughout the West. The intellectual origins of this insurgency can arguably be traced way back to the early revolt in the USA against the 'big government' programmes of Lyndon Johnson's 1960s 'great society' (that themselves had built upon Franklin Roosevelt's 'new deal' in the 1930s). This revolt surfaced first of all at the Republican convention in 1964 when the radical conservative candidate Barry Goldwater defeated the Republican liberal establishment, and set the Republican Party on a course which took it to the right both economically and socially – and ultimately led to a 'southern strategy' in which the old Democratic Party hold on the American south was defeated. At a party for conservative Republicans in 1985, just after Reagan's second victory, a member of his administration in the Department of Defense, Bruce Weinrod, pointed out to me all of those who had come into politics during the 1964 campaign in order to support Goldwater's run for the White House. He pointed to more than half.

In the late 1960s in Chicago, Milton Friedman was giving this Goldwater revolt of the free-market fundamentalists some very heavy intellectual firepower. But the ideas offensive only got seriously underway as 'great-society social democracy' – which in essence was continued by Nixon into the early 1970s – faltered in the mid-1970s under the impact of oil-price rises. Under Reagan after 1981 these programmes (excepting the defence budget) were contained and a new orthodoxy of market economics and market fundamentalism took its place. In power and interest-group terms what had happened was a serious accretion in the power of corporations and a weakening in the countervailing power of both the state and trade unions. When communism fell in the 1990s, with consequently huge increases in global markets and the global labour market, the power of the private corporate sector was further enhanced. And market-based solutions came to be renamed 'neo-liberalism' – a doctrine which spread out around the world, establishing its ascendancy through growing globalisation.

This contemporary 'neo-liberal consensus' is a worldwide phenomenon, but remains in essence American-led. The growth of markets around the world quite naturally – without design – promotes the 'American model' of economics, and in its wake even the American model of society – the American way of doing things. And Britain's Thatcherite revolution of the 1980s and 1990s was part of this wider change, and should be seen in this global context.

As this revolution took hold, doing things the American way became the gold standard for Britain's political class, but crucially also for the country's most powerful opinion-forming interest group – the owners of the changing British media. The Murdoch press – the *Times* and the *Sunday Times*, the *Sun*, the *News of the World* and the Sky TV network – and the Conrad Black empire were emerging as major ideological powerhouses behind neo-liberal and geopolitically pro-American ideas and values. The BBC and other media were by comparison to the Murdoch and Black media much less committed, less sure of themselves and less possessed of a sense of ultimate triumph. In consequence, they provided no serious counterbalance. And thus progressively during the late 1980s and 1990s the neo-liberals helped inform and condition thinking in the country, and established what amounted to a new British consensus. It was a view of politics and life that saw the world in much the same way as would Americans in America. This Thatcherite American revolution – as much as Tony Blair's own political will – became the political basis for Britain's later support for post-9/11 American global policy and the invasion of Iraq.

THATCHERITES, THE CITY AND 'THE ANGLO-SPHERE'

Britain's elites in the City and in the political class were, almost by definition, attracted to the American economic model. They also, for the same reasons, tended to deride the European economies and through them the European project itself. Perhaps the most well-connected anti-European Thatcherite of his generation was the journalist John O'Sullivan. I first met O'Sullivan at the London University debating society in the early 1960s and he has remained a friend ever since. A journalist on the *Daily Telegraph* during the 1970s, he was a bitter critic of Edward Heath's government, so much so that, though a Conservative, he voted against his party in the February 1974 general election. He became an early supporter of the rising Margaret Thatcher and later served in the Number 10 policy unit, becoming her speechwriter and close advisor. Later still he helped her with her autobiography. O'Sullivan always was, and remains, a free-market true believer, and in the 1970s and 1980s he perfectly embodied the core neo-liberal support for America and opposition to the EEC and EU. For O'Sullivan, as for many Thatcherites, the EEC was Keynesian, corporatist and socialist – a depiction reinforced when Thatcher and the Commission fell out in the 1980s and then highlighted when Commission president, French socialist Jacques Delors, visited the TUC and began his none-too-disguised campaign against Margaret Thatcher.

O'Sullivan's market fundamentalism, though winning in his native land, ultimately unhooked him from a life in England, and in the late 1980s, launched him, quite naturally, into the home of neo-liberalism, the USA, and into the Washington conservative think-tank the Heritage Foundation. He later became the editor of the American conservative journal the *National Review* (following the editorship of conservative journalistic icon William F. Buckley) and then the editor of the Washington quarterly the *National Interest* (founded by the neo-conservative Irving Kristol). He has subsequently settled in the USA, and married an American.

I once asked O'Sullivan, when we were both in New York in the early 1990s, about Thatcher's deep-seated and visceral opposition to

European integration. Were there any other reasons, apart from the obvious ideological ones? The answer was surprising, and fascinating. It could be found in the photographs – in the contrast between the team pictures of the European leaders at EEC summits and the one-on-one Thatcher–Reagan White House photos. 'You see,' said O'Sullivan, 'she's simply not at home in Europe – too many leaders. Gets lost among them. When she's in the States, though, she's one-to-one with the US president, and she shines.' As with Margaret Thatcher, so with media-conscious Tony Blair.

Another market fundamentalist who saw America as the 'model', if not quite the 'saviour', was the Tory MP John Redwood. Redwood, an ardent Thatcherite, was, like O'Sullivan, an ideologue. And, again like O'Sullivan, his free-market ideology translated into a love affair with the US market economy and into a systematic opposition to the 'corporatism' of the EU. In his 2001 book, appropriately titled *Stars and Strife: The coming conflicts between the USA and the European Union*, he broke what had amounted to a taboo and openly talked of a future in which Britain became the fifty-first state of the union. Without actually advocating such a course, he argued that 'we could try to become the 51st state of the American Union' and suggested that 'there would be no language barrier, and less of a legal, cultural and political barrier than submerging ourselves in Europe.' And he asserted that this option was one which Harold Wilson had toyed with in the 1960s.[10]

John O'Sullivan and John Redwood were the advance guard of a broader grouping – mainly of neo-liberal financial journalists and Eurosceptic Tories – who wanted closer formal and institutional relations between Britain and the USA. Worried about European influence, but aware that the 'fifty-first-state option' was an impossible dream, they sought other ways to bind Britain irrevocably to the USA. In the late 1990s ideas started emerging about Britain joining the North Atlantic Free Trade Area (NAFTA, a group comprising Canada, the USA and Mexico), and British Eurosceptics arranged a trip to London for some US congressmen (including Senator Phil Gramm of Texas) to investigate the possibility. British membership of NAFTA was, though, a shortlived idea, for it soon emerged that Britain would have to leave the EU in order to take part in NAFTA – and many Eurosceptics, although they might welcome the idea, saw leaving the EU as both unpopular and a truly Herculean task.

Yet some conservatives refused to let the idea completely die out, and from time to time it was refined and re-floated in the guise of a broader free-trade agreement involving the whole EU and NAFTA – a kind of grand transatlantic trading bloc. (The idea – in very general terms – was even given a welcome by European Commission president José Manuel Barroso in 2006). At the same time some Thatcherites, seeking to break Britain off from Europe, started toying with a new concept, the 'Anglo-sphere'.

This 'Anglo-sphere' had no formal organisational basis, but was an attempt to describe, and to build on, what was seen as the common heritage and interests of the English-speaking world – the USA, Britain and Australia primarily – and, crucially, to distinguish it from the rest of the EU-dominated West. For a time, Thatcherite British opinion-formers, like historians Niall Ferguson and Andrew Roberts, joined O'Sullivan in using the term and attempting to get the idea off the ground. But it was this very 'Anglo-sphere' that in 2003 went to war in Iraq; and, following the failure of this mission, the term fell into virtual disuse. (For some time the terms 'Anglo-Saxon countries' or 'Anglo-Saxon economies' had been used to describe the USA and Britain; but it was something of a misnomer, as the USA was certainly no longer ethnically Anglo-Saxon.)

Not all ardent Thatcherites were devotees of the 'free market' and visceral pro-Americans. The journalist, Frank Johnson, a friend and colleague of O'Sullivan's in the leader-page editorial team at the *Daily Telegraph* in the 1970s, was more laid-back about both the market and America. He supported Margaret Thatcher (or 'the lady', as he often called her) not through the prism of economic ideology but because he saw her as attempting to reverse the decline of the country – primarily through tackling Britain's 'trade-union problem'. Because he was more interested in European history, and less ideological and analytical, than O'Sullivan and Redwood, he was less attracted to the USA and less opposed to Brussels. Indeed, like many traditional Tories, he saw – even if he did not like – the case that joining fully the EEC/EU could place Britain at the heart of a new big power bloc in the world. Disdainful of the routine politicians at the top of British politics, he was a great admirer of big historic figures, not least General De Gaulle.

LABOUR'S ANGLO-SPHERICS

The Thatcherite Anglo-sphere garnered support way beyond the market fundamentalists in the Tory Party. Some Labour social democrats were among her most vociferous supporters – both publicly and privately. They saw aspects of the Thatcher revolution as providing an opening for their own brand of politics. In her early years as opposition leader and prime minister she often proclaimed that she favoured a more meritocratic Britain; she certainly believed in upward social mobility; and she was opposed by the two groups that many social democrats of the time hated the most, and blamed for Britain's problems – aristocratic Tories and left-wing socialists. Also, many of Thatcher's secret (and not so secret) supporters within Labour's ranks were schooled in the conflicts within the Labour movement of the 1970s, and they saw Britain's politicised trade unions as a serious threat – and saw Margaret Thatcher as the only politician in Britain willing to confront them.

Brian Walden, Labour MP for Birmingham Ladywood and later television interviewer, was one such. In the 1970s he had became progressively isolated within his party. He had started off in politics in the 1960s as a Gaitskellite, indeed as one of Gaitskell's parliamentary inner circle. And during the 1970s, as he watched his party move dramatically to the left, he made few compromises with the advancing forces. He was very pro-American (he supported the USA in the war in Vietnam) and pro-NATO. At the height of the Cold War and the left–right struggle in the Labour Party, when the left was riding high, Brian Walden, John Gilbert (later a Labour defence minister) and I were together at a party and we raised a glass to the map of the USA on the wall. Walden's toast said it all: 'Where would we be without them?'

He detested Harold Wilson's political appeasing of the Labour left, and would regularly unleash, from the back benches, his considerable invective against the prime minister – and against what he saw as the 'phoney middle-class moralism' of many on the left. Walden was his own man, and not much of a team player. And in a move that increased his political isolation he stayed out of what he considered to be the incestuous and somewhat prissy middle-class grouping that in the late 1960s was gathering around Labour's right-wing leader-apparent Roy Jenkins.

Walden was, arguably, the most effective old-style parliamentary orator of his generation, the kind of speaker the chamber of the House would fill up to hear. He was not in any sense a Tory. He was, rather, a Birmingham radical – and a populist radical at that – and he admired, and shared a pronounced Midlands accent with, Enoch Powell. He did not possess the discipline to be a party leader; but he had the flair, eloquence and sense of history that made a great parliamentarian of the old type. He was not a party man; and this independence (and daring) of spirit gave him the space and freedom to support Margaret Thatcher's revolution, which he did with gusto. His contribution to Thatcher's domination of the 1980s was no small thing: for in 1980, in a final act of ingenious sabotage against the Labour left, he voted, together with Neville Sandelson and three other right-wing Labour MPs, for left-winger Michael Foot as Labour leader – specifically in order to ensure that Labour had a leader who would make the party unelectable. He succeeded. And he later went off into a highly successful career as a television presenter and interviewer.

David Owen was another Labour supporter of the Thatcherite revolution. Like Walden he was in no way a socialist, and he saw the trade unions as 'over-mighty' and needing to be cut down to size. Also like Walden he was a natural Atlanticist, and was never, like the Jenkinsites, a fervent European (he was later to head up a Eurosceptic grouping and, should a referendum on Europe have taken place in 2005, he was positioning himself to become a leader of the 'no' campaign). Married to an American, Owen was always outside the traditional class system – neither an aristocrat or aristocrat-*manqué*, nor a trade unionist. He brought a refreshing American style of professionalism and telegenic charm to British politics. He was a modern, media politician in a way that the more staid Roy Jenkins could never aspire to be. Of all the four SDP leaders who set up the party he was the most pro-Thatcherite. Unlike Jenkins, who opposed the Falklands War, he supported it, indeed proclaimed his support regularly in television appearances. He also supported the Thatcherite trade-union reforms of the late 1980s. He was also the most instinctively pro-American of the SDP top leadership, and this American leaning, together with his global economic interests, probably accounted for his developing anti-Europeanism in the 1990s.

As the 1980s developed, this pro-American sentiment among right-wing Labour people played surprisingly well with more traditionalist Tories – not because of any love for America and Thatcher's open and raucous democracy – far from it – but because 'junior partner' status, much more than European involvement, would allow them to play the world role to which they still aspired. Also, a 'junior partnership' to Wall Street was beginning to appeal just as much as the 'junior partnership' to Washington.

THE BIRTH OF 'ANGLO–AMERICAN GLOBAL FINANCE'

The 'free world–free market' ideology – and the allure of America and its power – that gripped the minds of the Thatcherites contained the seeds of an even bigger revolutionary idea that, as the 1980s developed, began to seize the minds of Britain's elites: that of 'globalisation', or rather economic and capital 'globalisation'.

Globalisation chimed well with free markets because capital globalisation was a sure way to free business from national governments and their regulatory instincts. It also played well with the endemic ideology of Britain's political class – British 'greatness' and Britain's 'global role'. During the Thatcher years the idea took hold that Britain would be 'great again' through immersion in the 'global' as opposed to the European economy. And to make us fit for 'globalisation' the country's sluggish and high (labour) cost manufacturing industries needed to be let go in favour of the country's service and financial sector. Britain would, as in imperial times, become a dominant world finance centre, a global financial powerhouse based in the City of London. And the 'big bang' (of 1986) would make this happen. It was all part of the process – it was argued – of making tired old socialist Britain more efficient and more competitive, able to survive in an increasingly competitive world. But it also sowed the seeds of what was later to become the 'City of London problem': the dire over-extension of British global banks and the British financial system.

This rush to finance also played into the anti-industrial ethos of Britain's traditional ruling groups. In the 1970s and 1980s being 'something in the City' was almost as socially acceptable as being a landowner, certainly a grade or two above a career in 'industry' or 'trade'. Indeed in the 1970s and 1980s, as we have seen, critiques began to emerge about the overly tight nexus between the public schools, Oxbridge and the City of London – as a generation of the educated and privileged young, normally men, succumbed to the attraction of the world of short-term finance rather than the longer-term, more strategic perspectives of industry. It was still the case, well into the industrial age, that 'in the world's first industrial nation, industrialism did not seem quite at home.'[11]

THE CITY, HOLLOWING OUT AND PRIVATISATION

This emphasis upon finance and the City of London went hand-in-hand with a disastrous hollowing out of the industrial base of the British economy as manufacturing jobs were, by comparison, declared 'uncompetitive' and lost. In 1979 the manufacturing sector provided about 28 per cent of total employment. Between the end of 1978 and the end of 1982, there was a 1.4 million rise in the number of unemployed.

Over the same period, the number employed in manufacturing industries fell by 1.5 million. This job loss can be traced to a substantial and sustained collapse of manufacturing production between 1979 and the end of 1980.[12] It is more than likely though that this collapse – a collapse that was to continue through the next decades – was not caused just by monetary or fiscal policy, but also by 'Dutch disease' – the effect of North Sea oil production as it caused sterling to appreciate and led to a rise in the relative price of British manufactured goods. As a result, British manufactured goods became uncompetitive and production contracted sharply.

Of course this restructuring of Britain during the Thatcher administration could not be carried through without a serious erosion of the power of the trade unions and the publicly owned sector of the economy. Once the miners were defeated in 1984 the Conservative government was able, in a phased legislative programme, seriously to weaken trade-union power. And the still rather large public sector was dismantled by a series of 'privatisations' – a radical process originated politically by Nicholas Ridley's Nationalised Industries Policy Group in 1976, set up to examine the desirability and practicalities of ridding the state of such responsibilities. This concept, described initially by Ridley as 're-privatisation', was referred to in the group's report as 'denationalisation', probably in deference to Margaret Thatcher, who disliked the term 'privatisation'.

The list of privatisations secured by the Thatcher administrations was lengthy. It included Cable & Wireless (1981), Amersham International (1982), Associated British Ports (1982), Britoil (1982), British Telecom (1984), Enterprise Oil (1984), British Gas (1986), British Airways (1987), British Airports Authority (1987), Jaguar plc (1987), Leyland Trucks (1987), Royal Ordnance (1987), British Steel (1988), water (1989) and electricity generation (1990).

Intriguingly, in an early example of City dominance over government, the Thatcher government broke its own rules about state intervention and at the height of the privatisation boom in 1984 came to the rescue – a state rescue – of the Johnson Matthey Bank. A longstanding city company specialising in gold and other precious-metal refining, Johnson Matthey had branched into banking in the 1960s, but hit problems when some of its high-risk loans went bad, forcing it to the point of bankruptcy.

OILING THE REVOLUTION, WASTING THE RESOURCE

Thatcher's revolution was to be oiled from the North Sea. Ahead of the 1979 general election there was a growing awareness that whoever won the coming contest would inherit the bonanza of North Sea oil. The mid-Thatcher years saw North Sea oil tax revenues peak at a healthy £12 billion (1984–85), then fall slightly to £11.3 billion in 1985–86. They were then to fall to around £2.5 billion per year over the period of the new millennium, rising again to average over £6 billion from 2001 to 2007.

Yet in many respects this oil bonanza was to become a wasted asset – from, that is, the perspective of both sides in the British political debate. The left increasingly saw the wastage in terms of a refusal to use oil revenues to modernise the country's infrastructure, whereas the right saw a loss of an opportunity to use the proceeds to reform the burgeoning welfare state. And in another early sign of how an economy dominated by private global capital would re-order the economy (and society!) the profits from oil were accrued by the private oil companies and thence found their way into the growing global economy. The Norwegians were to establish a state oil company and a 'sovereign wealth fund' using North Sea oil revenues. The economist John Hawksworth of Price Waterhouse Coopers has written that had the UK done likewise – a plan initiated in 1978 by Tony Benn but subsequently axed by Nigel Lawson – the country would have accumulated by 2008 a fund on some readings of around £450 billion, making it one of the world's largest.[13]

THE LEGACY OF IMBALANCE

The Thatcher administration, and the Thatcher-consensus that followed it, so restructured the British economy in favour of finance (and other services) that it became seriously unbalanced. This imbalance was both tolerated and encouraged by Britain's political class for three decades – and public acquiescence in this 'new economy' was secured by rising living standards (increasingly sustained by higher levels of debt) and a welfare state saved by North Sea oil: under Thatcher's government welfare spending remained broadly the same.

11 THATCHER: 'CLOSER IN SPIRIT TO OLD IRONSIDES'

Thatcherism was all about economics. But as time went by her neo-liberal economic programme was to have huge social consequences – many of them expected, but many unintended. Intriguingly, these changes came to change the face of Britain. And they posed a bigger threat to old England and the authority of its institutions and elites, including the monarchy, parliament and the Anglican church, than did even the reforms of 1945–51 (when, although the welfare state expanded, the old ruling establishment remained in control).

The age of Thatcherism saw a marked loss of deference. People simply no longer 'knew their place'. Certainly the militant trade unionists of the 1970s had played a role in challenging authority, but so too did the growth of Thatcherite consumerism and individualism. In sum, the commercial and market revolution unleashed by Margaret Thatcher ended for all time the dominance and authority of the old traditional aristocratic elites, as it served to unfreeze Britain's frozen class structures. In the social and cultural sense – though certainly not in the income and wealth sense – the 1980s revolution ushered in a more 'classless society'.

This 'classless' potential of capitalism had been a recurring theme of the guru of Thatcherism, Sir Keith Joseph. A member of a leading Anglo-Jewish family who represented a northern constituency in the House of Commons, Joseph was, by background and temperament, a social egalitarian. The distinguished American political scientist, Samuel Beer, an acute reader of the English, described his approach, linking it back to the Victorian liberals:

He shared the Victorian liberals' vision of a classless society which could be achieved by a 'common value system'…He regretted that 'Britain never really internalised capitalist values'. On the contrary, the rich man sought to get away from his background in trade and industry, giving his son an education 'not in capitalist values but against them, in favour of the older values of army, church, upper civil service, professions, and land-owning'. With his praise for liberal individualism and his rejection of Tory paternalism went an equally bold rejection of the patrician mode of rule.[1]

Joseph was entering territory into which many a contemporary 'radical' analyst would not dare to tread. Like some of the old radicals, this modern free-market radical was going to the root of the matter. By arguing that his country's uniquely contorted class system was based upon something far more profound than the mere arrangement of formal economic power, Joseph was raising the infinitely more tricky and fundamental question of the cultural power of English paternalism. Britain's real 'class problem', he was suggesting, could be dealt with only at the highest levels, by operating on the exclusive, restrictive and hierarchical values emanating downwards from such bastions of privilege as the professions, the upper civil service, the army and the established church.

'Internalising' capitalist values in these areas of British life was a revolutionary nostrum, threatening the whole structure and security of what was still a paternalist nation and the ancient establishment which brought it into being. 'Truth to tell,' noted a Sunday newspaper as though it was a revelation, 'Thatcherism is profoundly egalitarian, in the sense that its moral message is the same for everybody, for all walks of life, for rulers as much as ruled…old aristocratic values have been consigned quite expressly to the dustbin of history.'[2]

The levelling social effect of radical capitalism has also been a theme of another leading member of the neo-liberal nucleus around Margaret Thatcher, Geoffrey Howe. Howe (like Joseph and Thatcher herself) is essentially a Tory outsider, a Welshman and a self-improver. He came to prominence during the abortive modernising phase of Heath's 'quiet revolution', when he introduced the 1971 Industrial Relations Act. He has described himself, in very un-traditional Tory terms, as a 'quiet revolutionary', and prefers to think of his economic liberal philosophy as descending from a somewhat egalitarian non-patrician nineteenth-century lineage.[3]

Margaret Thatcher later built upon Howe's political theme that by embracing the free market the Conservatives had become a socially egalitarian party. In March 1988 she asserted, 'It's not just the socialists who want a classless society. So do I – and, unlike them, I really mean it.'[4] Tory MP Norman Tebbit went further: 'One by one,' he argued in April 1988, 'the bastions of class privilege...have fallen to that most remarkable of animals: a Radical, Populist Conservative Party.'[5] Howe, Joseph, Thatcher and Tebbit all saw Britain's archaic class system as an obstacle to the creation of a modern 'enterprise culture'. Tory leaders were still somewhat reluctant, however, to take the 'classless' issue beyond the small print of isolated public speeches, and into full-blown campaign rhetoric. Such an abrupt change of rhetoric would have sounded somewhat contrived, and anyway would not be appreciated by the more traditional Tory base.

THATCHER THE BOURGEOIS RADICAL

Traditionalist reservations about Thatcher grew with every passing month, as Conservatives began to realise that she was no Tory of the old school. Above all, they were fearful that her new radicalism might, by confronting the unions, also destabilise their own world. Labour's shadow foreign secretary, Denis Healey, had attempted to exploit these fears during the 1987 campaign by exposing Thatcher's known anti-establishment instincts. 'Thatcher,' he asserted, 'has declared war on the BBC and the Church of England.'[6] A leader in the *Sunday Telegraph* of 7 June 1987, published on the eve of polling day, also struck a high-Tory traditionalist note, one which spoke for many who in the end also voted Conservative. Entitled 'Bourgeois triumphalist threat to Mrs Thatcher', it issued a warning:

> Wealth-creating is a good thing...in their case [that of the new financial elite] the possession of wealth seems to carry with it absolutely no sense of obligation or service whatsoever...To some extent the resentment they provoke is due to envy, since they flaunt their wealth with a degree of brazen insensitivity the like of which has not been seen since the days of the Edwardian nouveaux riches. But the resentment is also due to genuine concern that the values yuppies espouse, or rather the lack of values, threaten this country's long record of civilised governance.

This concern to ensure 'civilised governance' echoed more widespread fears among many Conservative supporters about whether or not a more entrepreneurial society would endanger the kind of 'stability' with which traditionalist Tory voters had historically felt comfortable. A healthy economy fired by entrepreneurial spirit and values was not – so the argument went – *ipso facto* a stable society. Yet these same Conservative supporters were aware that the 1970s had not been a stable decade either. Economic decline had produced serious social instability and, what is more, an instability which led to collective defences (through trade-union action) rather than individual action. In an age in which deference was waning and aspirations were rising, a rich society was likely to be more stable than a poor one. Hence traditionalist Conservatives, in the absence of any 'acceptable alternative' (or 'soft option' as it was dubbed by the Tory 'dries'), continued to support, albeit reluctantly, Thatcher's radical proposals.

THATCHER'S 'NEW BOURGEOIS' CONSERVATIVES

This 'disestablishment' of the Conservative Party – perhaps the most remarkable political development of the 1980s – was the end-product of a reordering of social power within the party which had been underway over the whole post-war period. It was a Pareto-style 'circulation of elites' – in which the upwardly mobile, commercial, and populist faction of the party (the 'dries') edged ever nearer to an ascendancy over the landed and 'liberal' wing (the 'wets') – and evident with the political demise of a generation of 'one nation' Tory paternalists. During the 1980s such leading 'wets' as Norman St John Stevas, Jim Prior, Ian Gilmour and Lord Carrington were progressively replaced at the cabinet table by more radical and meritocratic figures like Geoffrey Howe, Keith Joseph, Nigel Lawson and Norman Tebbit.

Later still, this vanguard was supplemented by a whole new generation of younger Conservative politicians – like John Major, John Moore, Cecil Parkinson, Kenneth Clarke and Norman Fowler, who represented the more classless grass-roots base emerging through the Conservative Party itself. The party leadership was no longer dominated by the landed classes or the very wealthy. People with very different formative experiences and values had taken over the helm.

The ageing Harold Macmillan, ever acute, once declared that he was shocked to hear on 'the wireless' a senior Tory cabinet minister (Norman Tebbit) speaking with an 'East End' accent. However, this kind of traditionalist opposition to social change within the party tended to be expressed either privately or in terms of impotent resentment – as when 'Knight of the Shires' MP John Stokes (following a speech by Tebbit to the Radical Society praising the modernisation of the Tory Party) wondered, somewhat facetiously, whether there was any room left in it for the landed interests.[7]

In many respects it was the career of Tebbit (more so even than those of Howe, Joseph or Thatcher) which typified the changing social composition of the historic party of crown and land. An airline pilot from Edmonton, holding a seat in suburban north London, Tebbit's demeanour and style were more akin to those of the lower-middle and working-class politicians of Labour. His regional accent, untainted by received pronunciation, was somewhat jarring to shire Tories, but was a sign of things to come.

These 'new Conservatives' were part of a mutually reinforcing internal party dynamic which ran through the politics of the party during the 1980s. The new breed of Conservatives helped Thatcher to establish her ascendancy over the party, and she in turn used her influence to widen further the social base of the leadership. And in turn (again) as the party became more classless Thatcherism's writ within the party ran ever more powerfully.

Margaret Thatcher's ascendancy over her own party was a remarkable achievement, by any recent historical standards. It is a story made all the more intriguing by being against the grain and the odds. It involves doses of political courage, no little guile, great luck and considerable tenacity on the part of Britain's first woman prime minister. There are many twists and turns along the way in this tale of the in-house revolution within the party. Thatcher's winning of the leadership in the first place was something of a fluke. And ever after, her Tory opponents waited for a suitable excuse to weaken, and even oust, her.

These changes in the Tory Party were, of course, not being wrought in isolation. They represented a changing Britain. Britain's old 'social pyramid' – brilliantly portrayed in the *Monty Python* sketch of upper-class, middle-class and working-class people all knowing their place – was being chipped away at its foundations by a more individualistic society and being replaced by a 'diamond-shaped' social structure. At the centre of the 'diamond' was a huge 'middle class' – at once the most numerous and the most dynamic grouping, which would set new manners, tone and style for the nation.

Such a 'flattening out' of the traditional 'social pyramid' would, on the face of it, be welcome news to those generations of radical critics who had seemingly so despaired of the country's antique class system. During the high tide of post-war social democracy a whole bevy of social critics had discussed little else than the malign nature and character of 'class' in Britain. George Orwell, John Strachey, Richard Hoggart, Michael Young, Anthony Crosland (and others) had set a critical tone which was taken up by a generation of post-war consensus politicians – one-nation Tories and the Labour social democrats alike. The speeches and articles of people like Hugh Gaitskell, Ian Macleod, Harold Wilson, Edward Heath and Roy Jenkins were replete with calls for such egalitarian social goals as the creation of an 'open society', the 'opening of society to the talents', a 'classless society', and the need for 'social mobility'.

Their 'classless' words, however, were never really matched by deeds. Class solidarities and 'tribal' sentiments hardened, rather than weakened, during the years of the post-war consensus, finally leading to the bitter class confrontations of the 1970s. One (less than charitable) explanation may be that these essentially meritocratic politicians of the post-war consensus had already – before they had even uttered a socially egalitarian word – been co-opted by Britain's smoothly efficient patrician polity. Whatever residual egalitarian sentiments remained to be expressed were, therefore, in reality weakly held.

Another explanation lies with the realities they faced. They simply couldn't make a silk purse out of a sow's ear. No matter how committed to egalitarian social change they may have remained, these reformers of the 1960s could not implement their ideas within the framework of the society in which they operated. How could a 'classless' society be encouraged in an age dominated by assertive and self-conscious trade unionism? Or through the mechanisms of a public sector and professional class still dominated at their apexes by the still-strong older type of Oxbridge elite.

Yet another explanation may lie in the fact that the post-war critics of 'class' were heavily influenced by the elitist Fabian way of looking at the world. The post-war Fabians were certainly social reformers, but of a peculiar type. Sons and daughters of empire, they were schooled in notions of hierarchy and order. The very last thing they wanted for Britain was to open it up by extending property rights and widening choice for ordinary people. When they were in the mood to challenge the total economic system, they went overboard, and (like Sidney and Beatrice Webb) embraced Soviet communism. Otherwise, they were content to see reform in a paternalistic concern for 'the poor'. A bourgeois, individualistic society driven by 'popular capitalism' was not for them.

In this sense Thatcherism succeeded in outflanking the British left in the battle for ideas. She and her adherents could with some measure of credibility argue that they were the true radicals. They were committed to the 'free society' and the 'open society' in an era in which the left were flirting with varieties of command socialism and trade-union syndicalism. But more importantly they could argue that only a real radical market-driven change could shake up Britain's antiquated class system for them.

America was the model. By contrast the British left remained both worried by and disdainful of the US model. Their leading social thinkers saw Britain in paternalistic terms: George Orwell, in a famous aphorism, which said much about his native conservatism, saw Britain as a family. It was 'A family with the wrong members in control', but 'still, it is a family'.[8] Hoggart seemed to find the regional and hierarchical distinctions of British life, which he analysed so incisively, a pleasing, rather than a disconcerting, patchwork. And Crosland once suggested that America's open and mobile society would create in Britain 'psychosomatic illnesses on a large scale'.[9] In other words, a more open and socially mobile population was good rhetoric, but not a heartfelt objective. The fact was that little headway could be made among the socialist generation by evoking the model and images of America, Australia or even post-war Germany. Bourgeois capitalism, with its images of the nation as a series of families and individuals (as opposed to 'one happy family' or indeed 'one unhappy family'), had little appeal. Indeed, it would often meet with a fierce reaction.

In this sense the Thatcherites succeeded, at least temporarily, in wresting the mantle of reform, even radical reform, from the left (to prove the point in 1987 Mrs Thatcher was instrumental in setting up 'The Radical Society').

A NATION OF ENTREPRENEURS?

The ultimate test of the durability of Britain's 'classless revolution' of the 1980s would, however, rest upon the strength of the social base of small capital ownership and accumulation. Put crudely, the more personal power people possess – the greater the number of 'islands of freedom' – the more irreversible the middle-class revolution would become. By the 1990s the growth in small businesses, though, was still minimal. The West's more mature bourgeois competitors were still producing far more 'new' entrepreneurs than was post-1980s Britain. The much vaunted 'wider share ownership' campaign ended up as a rather meagre affair. Twice as many people owned shares in 1987 as in 1980; and employee-share-ownership schemes had been enlarged from around 30 in 1979 to over a thousand in 1987. But this only scratched the surface, incorporating into the enterprise culture only a very small section of the manual working population.

On the other hand, the new radicalism did take one decisive step to widen 'at a stroke' the ownership of private capital. It sold off council houses, allowing, so its advocates argued, members of 'the working class', trapped in the serfdom of council ownership and control, to take over at least one part of their lives: their homes. The addition, between 1980 and 1988, of one million to the number of home owners can hardly be undervalued in terms either of reality or of symbolism. Joel Krieger has ascribed to this process a serious political dimension, coining the term 'the ideological suburbs' to describe the potential effect of council-house sales upon the wider political contest: 'those attracted by the appeal [of home ownership] could feel good about themselves: they were not simply abandoning socialist community for individual interest but participating in a broad inter-class modernising movement.'[10]

THATCHER AND THE RURAL LOBBY

Under Thatcherism Britain became more suburban – and 'middle England' was born. In 1986, over half way through Thatcher's own time in government, more than two million families moved home, more than in any year since the war. The pattern of movement in that one year suggests substantial additions to medium-sized towns and their environs. Towns such as Milton Keynes (which added 60,995 people), Peterborough (37,752), Northampton (36,910), Telford (30,106), Colchester (26,749), Bournemouth, Chelmsford, Aberdeen, Widnes, Wigan and Redditch all gained at the expense of losses in the big cities: London (740,781), Glasgow (166,193), Manchester (145,375) and Liverpool (134,371). In the process the south of England was slowly becoming one large classless suburb. And as the older 'working-class' ghettos in the large cities dissolved the new areas of population were located in what were essentially the suburban environs of the growing towns. These new suburbs brought in their wake a more classless, consumer environment (including American-style shopping malls).

As Britain became more and more suburbanised, it seems, looking back on it, quite remarkable that one of the most densely populated landmasses in the world could have sustained, well into the twentieth century, such large tracts of uninhabited land. In the name of protecting the countryside, Britain's planners placed ring-fences round both the medieval 'village' and the industrial nineteenth-century 'city'. This frozen 'village and city' pattern was ultimately dependent upon a freezing of social and geographic mobility, and was further secured by piling 'the propertyless masses' of the old inner cities into tower-block developments, rather than allowing a freer and more lateral pattern of development. The suburbanisation of Britain thus posed the most serious threat yet to the old 'cities and villages' model (and mentality) which sustained the class structures (and images) of post-war Britain.

That the image of the 'English village' had (has) its charm, entrancing locals and tourists alike, can hardly be in dispute. And even amid the social changes of the 1980s and 1990s its hold on the English imagination – as a refuge from the rigours of modern life – remained as strong as ever, particularly among those whose lives are essentially urban. And the idea of England as nothing more than a series of 'villages' was also imposed from above, particularly by cultural leaders and by the lifestyles of the royal family, not least Prince Charles (who by the 1980s was becoming a campaigner for the rural lobby). But rural charm had its darker side. In evoking such a positive image for 'the village', Britons also, implicitly at least, accepted pre-capitalist and pre-individualist habits of mind. The 'village', by definition, is small and thus exclusive; too large a village becomes a 'town'. Also, in many of the villages of southern England the old British class system was still played out in miniature form. Modern-day 'lords of the manor' still presided over a social hierarchy derived from medieval times. Below them, there is a local 'gentry', a local vicar and, further down, a modern propertyless 'peasantry', usually hidden from view on small council estates.

During Thatcher's era Conservative rural England was on the defensive. As resistance to suburbanisation grew, defenders of the 'rural interest' were increasingly placed at a moral disadvantage – as the 'not in my back yard' instinct became a famous acronym (NIMBY) depicting both selfishness and hypocrisy. Nicholas Ridley, the Thatcherite secretary of state for the environment, annoyed many of his own traditional Tory supporters by declaring that 'I cannot and will not say that because I have a nice house and a good life I do not care about anyone else', and that 'the city dweller's life should be made a misery in order to save others a picturesque view.'[11] This social and cultural battle – between the southern 'ideological suburbs' and static village England – became a major feature of the Thatcherite age.

'LITTLE ENGLAND' UNDER PRESSURE

Perhaps, though, the biggest of all the threats to the traditional, and traditionalist, way of life wrought by the Thatcherite era was the coming of 'globalisation'. The fact was that Thatcherite economics – or neo-liberal economics – knew no national boundaries. The very first act of the new Conservative government in 1979 was to remove exchange controls; and this symbolic departure – perhaps even more than entry into the EEC in the early 1970s – represented a fundamental act of adjustment on Britain's part to the modern world outside its borders. British capital was finally fully free to expand overseas – to the point where, in the late 1980s, it had become the single most important foreign investor in the USA. In return, foreigners bought up more and more of Britain – encouraged not only by a welcoming government but by weakened trade unions and a more 'competitive' domestic environment. This increasing penetration of the domestic economy by foreign capital produced a 'culture shock'. One by one, some of the country's most 'English' of institutions fell into the hands of foreigners. Harrods went to the Arabs, Rowntree to the Swiss, 'quality' Sunday newspapers and 'prestigious' publishing houses to Australians and Canadians. Also, and more crucially, a people only previously allowed to see the world through the lens of their elites, were to have available to them foreign-owned television channels. The British were also beginning to get used to mass foreign travel as millions of 'working class' Britons took their holidays abroad in southern Europe, principally in Spain – where many also bought into the property market. These invasions made it increasingly difficult to see Britain as some kind of isolated 'national' economy whose future could be shaped by the fine-tuning of its mandarin class. In its place appeared a new reality: the country as little more than an offshore territorial 'entity' upon which a complex of financial, industrial and commercial players (some domestic, some foreign) could work their separate and multiple wills. In sum, Britain was becoming 'globalised'.

And what was more, this 'globalisation' was very much an aspect of public policy. The Thatcherite mantra was clear: Britain needed to make its way in the world, and could only do so by becoming 'cost competitive', by selling things people throughout the world wanted. In return Britain needed to open its markets to the world.

Thatcher's own political rhetoric was redolent with global, and globalising, words. Thatcher's ministers would remind anyone who would listen that Britain, from the works of Adam Smith through to, and beyond, the Manchester Liberals of the nineteenth century, had pioneered the modern conception of free trade. The old adages still rung in modern Tory ears: 'Britain is a trading nation or it is nothing'; 'If Britain has to choose between Europe and the Open Sea, it will always choose the Sea'; 'Trade follows the Flag.' These were also aphorisms of empire, and therefore sounded pleasing to Tory ears.

Of course the 'global imperatives' of the Thatcher era differed considerably from the global outlook of imperial times. The 'white man's burden' was certainly outward-looking, but it saw only an ever-widening global horizon filled with English manners, language, religion and rule. Thatcher's 'globalisation imperative' meant that the world increasingly impinged on Britain – not the other way round.

'CLOSER IN SPIRIT TO OLD IRONSIDES'

In a half homily to Thatcher's social revolution, the leading Irish public intellectual of his generation, Conor Cruise O'Brien, drew an interesting parallel with England's first outburst of serious bourgeois sentiment in the seventeenth century: he argued that

> The political division of modern England in regional terms corresponds quite closely to the line of division at the time of the first English revolution. Then, as now, the line ran between the South and East on the one hand, and the North and West on the other. The old domain of the Puritan revolutionaries is now the domain of Mrs Thatcher. The old Royalist areas are now held by Mr Kinnock's socialists...I don't think this is a mere curiosity or fortuitous paradox...Mrs Thatcher likes to be compared with Queen Elizabeth I and Queen Victoria...I think the Iron Lady is closer in spirit to Old Ironsides [Oliver Cromwell].

This analogy with the country's seventeenth-century revolution was obviously overdrawn. But in 1980s Britain there was indeed a sense that real, lasting, change was underway, that an older Britain was being replaced, that old loyalties and authorities were being questioned, that traditional institutions were no longer to be venerated for simply existing, or having existed, but rather would now be judged according to 'value for money'. And this applied not just to traditional industries and to the professions but to the ancient institutions like parliament, the courts and the monarchy too. For in the 1980s, as in the earlier upheaval, a militant 'middling' class was flexing its muscles, and drawing its political strength from the sense of influence – and power – accruing to new centres of money, trade and commerce.

MONARCHY IN TROUBLE: 'HM TAX DODGER'

That the British were becoming more assertive, more individualistic and decidedly less deferential than their predecessors was taking its toll on authority. Consumer power – a key idea of the Thatcher age – was taking off in the High Street as during the 1980s the religious (and trade-union) lobby lost its fight against Sunday trading laws. There was also the beginning of today's assertive opinion culture and the introduction, to cope with it, of 'interactive' culture on TV and radio. And media corporations ceased imposing the high-minded and turned increasingly to entertainment.

It was hardly surprising that in this atmosphere even the most sacred of all British institutions – the monarchy and royal family – were also becoming subject to popular – or consumer – will. Having two women at the very top of British public life provided the Queen with some unwelcome competition, but the upshot of Thatcherite consumerism was to introduce a dose of instrumentalism into the monarchy question: the public was allowed to ask of the monarchy, as of all institutions: did it provide 'value for money'?

One of the legacies of Thatcher's age was that the taboo on royalty was broken. Previously, even under Labour governments, even in the tabloid press, hardly a word against the royals was heard in Britain's public media. Indeed newsreaders on the television would rarely mention a royal story without contrived smiles. And the royals, and particularly the Queen, were defended throughout the political class, even among left-wing politicians who would be natural republicans – as Jeremy Paxman argued 'over the twentieth century, the British monarchy could hardly have had a better defender than the Labour party.'[13]

Yet the late 1980s and early 1990s was to see all that change. A new bitingly critical mood developed, partly to do with the marital problems of the younger royals, but it also underlined a new lack of deference. Serious criticism of the Queen herself broke out in 1992 following the publication of Andrew Morton's 1992 *Diana: Her true story* (written with Diana's obvious cooperation). Diana's role as innocent and aggrieved commoner – and the Queen as a cold-hearted and insensitive traditionalist – began to be propagated by an increasingly sentimentalist mass media, and Diana's continuing role as a underdog fighter threatened the royal family, indeed the institution of monarchy itself. This highly unusual anti-royal sentiment peaked after the hasty decision of the government to pay for the damage caused by a fire at Windsor Castle in 1993 met general opposition from the public, displaying a new critical inclination, particularly on royal finances. On 12 February 1993 the *Daily Mirror* ran a front-page story on the finances of the royal family under the headline 'HM tax dodger' alongside a cartoon of a greedy Queen calculating her taxes. 'The Queen is set to become Britain's biggest tax dodger – paying as little as £2 million on her vast fortune.'

Elizabeth Windsor had, as they say, 'ascended' the throne in 1952. Forty years later, by the beginning of 1993, the house of Windsor had become something approaching a laughing stock. The idealised dream family of the 1950s and 1960s had collapsed. Her sister, her daughter and two of her sons all seemed incapable of sustaining marriages with what commentators still cutely describe as 'commoners', while the troubled life of Princess Diana had kindled the public's sympathy. And, most troublesome of all for royalists, the Queen was beginning to look less than dignified. Her initial refusal to pay any taxes at all, together with her later decision (taken after considerable pressure) to pay *some* taxes, exposed a surprisingly wilful, unedifying stubbornness in the royal personality. It was no wonder that the Queen would refer to 1992–93 as her 'annus horribilus'.

Following the collapse of her marriage to Charles, Diana continued to destabilise the monarchy. She became outspoken and was carving out a role for herself as what amounted to an 'alternative royal'. It was extremely damaging not just to Charles but to Buckingham Palace as well. And when Diana died in a car crash in Paris on 28 August 1997 public sympathy for her came close to sweeping the house of Windsor away.

THATCHER'S JANUS-FACED REVOLUTION

In late 1990, as the dust settled on the momentous 1980s, and the new prime minister John Major took over the reigns of power, the new contours of British life wrought by Thatcher's 'revolution' were becoming visible. The defeat of the miners in 1984 meant that no longer would the threat of trade-union militancy – as in the mid-1970s – act as a veto on business-friendly change. The country was now able to set out upon a radical new economic course, a course increasingly being described as 'neo-liberal', one in which markets, particularly financial markets, would rule, the private sector would be ascendant, and the much traduced old social-democratic ways of doing things would be abandoned. And when, in 1989, the Berlin Wall came down, world communism was defeated and new markets opened up, this 'neo-liberal' project was given another shot in the arm. 'Market forces' became 'global market forces', giving transnational capitalism, both banks and non-financial corporates, much greater bargaining power over nations and labour. And in Britain the newly deregulated City of London ('freed up' by the 'big bang') was leading the way towards great new profits and increased financialisation of the economy.

This 'revolution' was certainly beginning to sweep away cobwebs, and was seen by increasing numbers of commentators as a modernising and galvanising social force. The neo-liberal age was creating a new and vibrant non-deferential middle class.

Yet at the end of 1990, as Margaret Thatcher stood down from the premiership, the old ways were still there. And ironically in some ways her 'revolution' had strengthened, rather than weakened, traditional England. A simple audit of power in 1990s Britain following the Thatcher administration (and in the early years of the Major government) reveals a country whose traditional elites and institutions were still intact, indeed had more than survived the convulsions of the 1970s and early 1980s. These decades had seen a serious trade-union-led attempt to alter the balance of power and redistribute wealth and income in Britain – an 'irreversible shift of power to working people and their families'; but with the defeat of the miners in 1984 this attempt had failed. But 'the winners' were not just the broad 'home counties' middle classes, but also, importantly for the future, Britain's traditional rich – the big-wealth-owning upper and upper-middle classes from landowners to corporate leaders. For the big truth about the 'Thatcher revolution' was that, for all its modernising rhetoric (and reality), 'old money' and old habits had survived – more than survived – and in the coming decades would serve to leaven the dynamism of 'new money' and new ways of doing things.

I was away from Britain during the early years and middle years of Thatcher's administration, and I well remember meeting up in Washington with the journalist Alexander Chancellor, who was visiting. I was still a believer that Thatcher was the incarnation of 'Old Ironsides' rather than yet another defender of the traditional English super- and mega-rich, and was probably over-egging her 'meritocratic revolution'. Chancellor didn't agree with my thesis at all, and with no small relish pointed me towards a news item from home. 'Have you seen the stuff on Willie Whitelaw? She's made him an hereditary.'

Edward Heath had ended the practice of creating hereditary peers, and the assumption was that Thatcher would be even more resolute. But towards the end of her premiership she relented and awarded the hereditary honour to William Whitelaw (who became Ist Viscount Whitelaw, KT, CH, MC, PC, DC) and two others: Earl Tonypandy and the Earl of Stockton. It was a small matter but very revealing.

In this sense Thatcher's 'revolution' had its very decided limits. Its leaders may have set out to create the conditions for a modern, progressive middle-class social revolution – but the continuing limited spread of wealth and the new ascendancy of big business over the countervailing powers (state and trade unions), opened the way for the country to become more and more unequal and ultimately in the late 1990s and beyond, something of a playground for the rich and deeply privileged (both British and foreign).

And the 'revolution' served another unforeseen function: the re-emergence of British complacency. For it became a victim of its own perceived success. Margaret Thatcher's victory in the Falklands and the later turnaround in the economy was to spread the idea that 'Britain is Back'. It was to be a notion with fatal consequences – as it re-asserted the dormant superiority and complacency in elite political culture. For many, with 'Britain back', there was no longer any need to challenge the leadership groups of Britain's way of life; and certainly no need to rethink the nation's position in the world, particularly no reason to take part in further European integration. The imperial nostalgia of Britain's leadership groups, with their fatal inability to adjust to the modern world, was still intact. And it was, like the British monarchy and the Queen herself, to show its continuing power, its seeming enduring hold on the national imagination, during the coming decades.

PART 4
The beginning of isolation?

12 MAJOR AND THE BIRTH OF EUROSCEPTICISM

John Major became prime minister in November 1990. He was born in 1943, the son of a former music-hall performer; he attended a grammar school, but not university; and he rose through the ranks at Standard Chartered Bank. In many respects he was the embodiment of the socially mobile society Margaret Thatcher had stood for, and thus was a fitting successor to the great lady. And he became Tory prime minister in large part because, at a crucial juncture in the race to succeed Thatcher, he raised the class issue against one of his main opponents, Douglas Hurd. Hurd was an identikit Etonian – possessed of an easy, mildly superior, manner and a languid, worldly wise approach to politics. He had the classic air of imperial rulership about him. Michael Heseltine was the other serious candidate, and whoever stood against him on the final ballot would probably secure the still very large number of Thatcherite votes, Heseltine being from the other wing of the party. So Major needed to shunt Hurd out of the race. And he did so with one devastating phrase – when he claimed in his campaign 'manifesto' that 'in the next ten years we will have to continue to make the changes which will make the whole of this country a genuinely classless society.' The obvious inference was that Hurd was the wrong kind of Tory to succeed Thatcher.

It was a commentary on the new values espoused by the Thatcher Tory Party that such an appeal could have had such an effect. Major's success was, in one sense, a fitting ending to Thatcher's administration. Her 'revolution' would go on: but under a new kind of Tory who represented, as she did but more so, the erosion of the traditional social profile – public school, Oxbridge, hint of land – of the Tory leadership class. It seemed, at the time, to be well in tune with the radical social objectives of Thatcher's popular capitalism. It was also a sure sign that the age of deference – deference, that, is to the old style of rulership – was coming to an end.

END OF THE COLD WAR: ANOTHER 'BRITISH VICTORY'

John Major took over in Downing Street during a period of momentous geopolitical change. The fall of the Berlin Wall had preceded Margaret Thatcher's departure by just over a year, so it was clear before she left office that Soviet communism had been defeated. And many in her party and in the country believed that this was 'her victory', as she had played such a crucial role, with President Ronald Reagan, in opposing and rolling back Soviet power. Among many Conservatives it was also seen as a victory for Britain, as the country had played such a pivotal role as US chief ally during the forty-year contest.

There was, though, an alternative analysis: that the end of the Cold War was mixed news for Britain, in the sense that it left the country in something of a limbo. With the Soviet threat gone American leadership through NATO no longer possessed its previous rationale for existence, and thus Britain, the chief cheerleader for the USA in NATO, would no longer possess such an important role. In these circumstances to believe that Britain had won a victory could be seen as yet another example – one of many – of misplaced hubris. As it turned out, though, reports of NATO's death were greatly exaggerated, as both NATO and US leadership of the West survived intact well into the twenty-first century, though in a less united and coherent manner, and thus Britain was able to continue in its junior-partner 'global role' for some years yet.

However, for continental Europe the end of the Cold War was a real watershed in its relationship with Washington – and it was to usher in a new era of European unity. Germany was formally reunited on 3 October 1990, and Europe's leaders, worried by the consequences of this new power of eighty million arising in the heart of the continent, moved quickly, under French leadership, to bind the newly united country into the West. The result was the Maastricht Treaty, agreed in December 1991 and formally signed on 7 February 1992, which set up the 'euro-zone'. The creation of the euro – giving Europe a central bank with control of interest rates and monetary policy – was the boldest piece of supranational economic integration since the creation of the single market in 1957. And it placed Britain – still uneasy in its European policy – in an awkward position.

JOHN MAJOR: AT THE HEART OF EUROPE

In virtually John Major's first foreign-policy move as prime minister he was to issue a memorable statement from Downing Street that signalled his wish for nothing less than an historic change in the country's foreign alignment. He declared – in what looked at the time like a huge snub to Margaret Thatcher and a reversion to the Edward Heath years – his desire to see the country 'at the heart of Europe'. Major was a sympathiser with the aims of European monetary union, and had earlier taken Britain into the precursor of the euro, the exchange-rate mechanism (ERM), much against the better judgement of his own prime minister. Also, while a seemingly loyal supporter of Thatcher, he had never been party to her visceral anti-continental – and pro-American – sympathies, and he had come to the premiership following what amounted to a pro-European palace coup from within the cabinet.

For a time it seemed as though Major might well tilt Britain's foreign alignment away from Washington and towards Europe. Major was not one of nature's Atlanticists – and apart from a minor interlude at the Foreign Office he had not been very involved in defence and security matters, and therefore did not embrace the culture of Washington-led NATO. Also, his relations with the USA became strained when President Bill Clinton took over the White House following the presidential election in November 1992. Clinton, who did not get on with British Tories, believed that Major had improperly interfered in the American election campaign in 1992 in order to aid his Republican opponent, George H.W. Bush.

The test of whether Major was truly in the business of reorienting British foreign policy towards Europe was to come within weeks of his taking over in Downing Street. In December 1990 the European leaders, including Major, moved to set up an inter-governmental conference (IGC) to plan for the euro – and also, so they said, for 'political union'. The conference was scheduled to last for a year; and for Britain, and Major, it was to be a fateful year. Fervent pro-Europeans believed that in the IGC negotiations Britain should 'go for it', help shape the outcome, and become a founding member of the planned euro-zone, introducing the new currency with the others in the late 1990s. Once it was clear that Britain was actually planning to be a founder member of Euroland it would bring to an end the two decades of Britain's awkward and often hostile relationship with its neighbours.

In guiding the furious European debate in the Tory Party Major was, though, dealt a difficult hand. He was by no means a free man. The 'palace coup' that had brought him to Downing Street continued to sour relationships with the still very strong Thatcherite grouping in the party; and following her ouster Thatcher herself was to remain an active 'Eurosceptic', exerting considerable political influence in the background of Tory politics for the next fifteen years. Major was aware that these Thatcher supporters on the backbenches could always effectively veto any attempt by him to join the euro at launch date. Even the Maastricht Treaty – in which Britain stayed outside the euro-zone, only agreeing to 'opt in' at a later date – was bitterly opposed by the Tory 'Eurosceptic' rebels (led by a future Tory Party leader, Iain Duncan-Smith).

And in the middle of these euro negotiations Major was faced with a major geopolitical crisis which would dominate his first weeks in office and affect the rest of his premiership. Out of a clear blue sky Saddam Hussein had invaded Kuwait, and on 17 January 1991 a USA-led coalition started 'Operation Desert Storm' to evict the Iraqis from the small sheikhdom. The conduct and outcome of the Gulf War was a great demonstration of American military prowess, and reminded the European allies of their dependence on US power to protect their oil supplies. President Bush was proclaiming that a 'new world order' was coming into being. And following his success in the Gulf it certainly seemed that American global leadership would be an indispensable aspect of this new world order. This belief that America would remain the 'indispensable power', as secretary of state Madeleine Albright would later describe the USA, reinforced those who gave priority to the American connection over the European.

More damaging still for the European cause in Britain was the collapse of the Yugoslav Federation and the subsequent Balkans conflict. During 1991 the German government was becoming the major power in the area, and Chancellor Kohl took the fateful step of encouraging Croatian independence. And the German chancellor may well have lit the touchpaper which ultimately exploded and broke up the federation. Indeed the Bavarian interior minister could say that 'Helmut Kohl has succeeded where neither Emperor Guillaume nor Hitler could.'[1]

But Washington did not want Germany or the EU to become a pre-eminent power in the region, and the Clinton administration influenced the Izetbegovic government into refusing to sign the peace agreements arranged by the European leaders in 1993. Instead, Washington sought NATO control of the area. And when the federation then fell apart in ethnic conflict, and the EU was unable to deal with this problem 'in its own backyard', the USA later entered the Balkans fray and took the lead role in the Kosovo conflict and the NATO air war over Serbia which ended in June 1999. This Balkans episode was a great defeat for Europe. The major European powers were divided on what to do and whom to support. And the geostrategic lesson was clear: that Europe could not act to deal with a crisis even on its own continent, and still needed to call in 'Uncle Sam' and 'the new world' to 'redress the balance of the old'.

Although out of power, the Balkans crisis provoked quite a debate among Republicans. The 'realist' old guard led by Jim Baker (later to chair the Iraq Study Group which reported in 2007) wanted to keep the USA out of the Balkans. He famously put it that 'we have no dog in this fight.' However, many neo-conservatives saw it differently, seeing the Balkans crisis as an opportunity to weaken Europe, put US power on display and develop a unilateralist approach sidelining the UN. Leading neo-conservative Richard Perle has reportedly argued that the USA-led air war against Serbia was a useful precedent – 'the first precedent' – for the USA to act unilaterally in overriding a UN Security Council resolution, a precedent which was followed in the later Iraq invasion of 2003.[2]

In Britain during the 1990s the lessons of the First Gulf War and the Balkans crises were clear: Europe was not, any time soon, going to supplant the USA as a global power, and Britain, still in search of a 'global role' for itself, had no urgent need to review the 'special relationship' and draw closer to the EU.

Yet, these geopolitical lessons aside, it was to be a more 'domestic' economic event that decisively turned the British against European integration for another decade or so. In September 1992 the Major administration was suddenly rocked by what amounted to a national humiliation – which quickly turned into a source of British hostility towards the continent, and particularly the Germans.

'BLACK WEDNESDAY'

On 16 September 1992, 'Black Wednesday', Britain was forced to leave the ERM. This event, which seemingly surprised the country's political and financial elite, did not, though, come out of a clear blue sky. It had a long gestation period.

The story starts on 8 October 1990, when the British government, at the prompting of Douglas Hurd and John Major, decided that Britain should enter the ERM. It did so with great fanfare, but without the courtesy of consulting its partners either about the entry itself or about the rate of exchange, which was set at a damagingly high (and grandiose) rate of over 3 deutschmarks to the pound. This unilateral decision was accepted by the European partners, but not with enthusiasm. It was widely seen as high-handed. Jacques Delors declared diplomatically that although he was happy with the decision of the British government he remained vigilant.

The chickens were soon to come home to roost. Some 23 months later, serious pressure began building on sterling, and the Treasury was unable to keep the currency above its lower limit. In a last-ditch effort to remain within the ERM the British raised interest rates to the dizzying level of 15 per cent. But it was all to no avail, and on the evening of 16 September the chancellor, Norman Lamont – with a young PR advisor, future prime minister David Cameron, by his side – announced that Britain was withdrawing from the ERM.

In Tory circles, and in the press, this withdrawal was seen as nothing less than a national humiliation – on a level with that of the Suez crisis in 1956. And, just as in the aftermath of Suez, the sense of bitterness in high places was palpable. Sections of the press turned on the Germans, who were blamed for their high-interest-rate policy and for their refusal to help Britain out (interestingly, the German government was later to accommodate Italy by agreeing to widen the ERM bands). And as the crisis sank in among the general public, it was the Conservative Party and John Major who were to be blamed for the humiliation, and Conservative poll ratings collapsed from 43 to 29 per cent in one month. They were never to recover, and would remain at this low level for 14 years.

The humiliation was all the more searing because of the sense – felt widely – that Britain had restored her 'greatness' during Thatcher's reign, and that somehow the exit from the ERM was an expulsion. Thus a regained national pride had somehow been thwarted – and by, of all people, the wartime enemy, the Germans.

Thus the scene was set for the emergence of a xenophobic backlash against Germany, manipulated and orchestrated by sections of the tabloid press, led from the offices of the Murdoch empire. Strong anti-continental feelings were to last right through the years of the Major administration and beyond. British 'Euroscepticism' was born.

The fact was that both the British and the Germans had fallen foul of the exigencies of the new situation in Europe following the end of the Cold War – particularly the initial economic and financial difficulties caused by German reunification. But the British remained sore, and Major's government struck out in a more detached direction – with its 'wait and see' policy towards the euro. British *amour propre* was not soothed when some days after the pound had fallen out of the ERM Kohl made a none-too-veiled threat in the Bundestag: he declared, obviously referring to the British, that 'no one in Europe – and I repeat, no one – should labour under the illusion that it is in a position to go it alone.'[3]

For nationalists and Eurosceptics 'Black Wednesday' may have been a short-term national humiliation, but it soon came to be seen as 'White Wednesday'. For in one fell swoop Britain was out of the ERM, free to continue to determine its own interest rates and to print its own money. Still smarting from the German decision, Britain's political and financial elites could balm their wounded pride with the appealing idea that they were free and independent agents in the global economy.

Major's government never recovered from 'Black Wednesday'. And his attempt to push through parliament the ratification of the Maastricht Treaty – in which Britain joined the glide-path to euro entry but didn't join – led to a bruising fight within the Conservative Party, the bitterness from its fallout leaving deep scars. 'Black Wednesday', Maastricht Treaty ratification and the loss of popular support all conspired to create a serious party crisis in which an anti-euro faction of Conservative MPs formed a 'party within a party' and for a time lost the Tory whip. This grouping, which included MP John Redwood, was to form the heart and soul of the contemporary British Eurosceptic movement.

These Tory Eurosceptics – they were, in reality, much more 'anti' than they were 'sceptical' – carried on a successful parliamentary guerilla warfare against the Major government with the ultimate aim of getting it to abandon its residual commitment to future euro-zone entry. They sought, by rejecting euro entry, to turn the Tory Party against the whole EU integration process – with the ultimate aim of either turning Europe into a free-trade area or, should that not be possible, getting Britain to leave the union altogether. A decade later this small, and somewhat eccentric, grouping had succeeded beyond its wildest expectations. In two elections, 2001 and 2005, Britain's Tory Party had opposed euro entry and in so doing pushed Labour onto the defensive on the issue.

Labour leader Tony Blair was forced to pledge a referendum before any entry into the currency zone. By New Year's Day 2007 – even though the *Financial Times* could report the historic news that the euro was in sight of competing with the dollar as the world's reserve currency – the British *zeitgeist* had turned, seemingly decisively, against Europe.[4]

THE BELEAGURED PRO-EUROPEANS

Ever since Margaret Thatcher turned against the European project in her Bruges speech in 1987, the pro-Europeans were always in the minority in the Conservative Party. And ever since 'Black Wednesday' in 1992 they have been on the defensive, fighting little more than a series of rearguard actions.

Even so, during the 1990s the pro-Europeans were still a force to be reckoned with in the Major cabinet. Tory luminaries such as Michael Heseltine, Kenneth Clarke, Geoffrey Howe, Chris Patten, Douglas Hurd and Leon Brittan all held strongly pro-European views, some even seeing Britain's future within the euro-zone.

Yet as the 1990s progressed this generation of pro-European Tories increasingly seemed somewhat time-warped. Formed in the Heath era, they had all, as young politicians, been active in the successful battle over the EEC in the years leading up to the referendum of 1975, and they had gone on in government to support the Single European Act of 1987. In the early 1970s they had the benefit of a party consensus behind entering the EEC, they had most of the press on their side, they had a failing economy at home and successful economies in Europe, and they could present the leading anti-Europeans as extremists (what Bob Worcester, chairman of polling organisation Polls had called the 'men with staring eyes syndrome').[5]

By the 1990s, however, the pro-European Tories seemed rather nonplussed as they found the political ground shifting from under them: the pro-European consensus had disappeared, the press was mostly hostile, the European economies were believed to be faltering, and Euroscepticism was no longer the preserve of eccentrics. Most importantly of all they were battling against the grain: large sections of the public were increasingly sold on the narrative of British 'independence' and 'greatness,' the conviction, or delusion, that Britain could go it alone.

In the ten years following the end of the Major government they lost battle after battle as a succession of Tory leaders – William Hague, Iain

Duncan-Smith and Michael Howard – all took the party in an overtly anti-EU direction. They waited for Tony Blair to give a lead first on the euro issue and later on the constitution; and when he did not, they refused to take the lead themselves. They simply lost their way, and in the process the European cause in Britain was set back a generation and, as a further consequence, the 'special relationship' with the USA was given a new lease of life and was still flourishing well into the new century.

During the Thatcher and Major governments the two leading pro-European figures, Michael Heseltine and Kenneth Clarke, both held very senior positions. Heseltine became deputy prime minister in the Major government and the leading pro-European in the Tory Party. He had the added aura of being the only man to stand up to Thatcher during her reign, when he resigned from her cabinet over the Westland helicopter crisis. He had secured a surprisingly high vote against her in the first ballot for Tory leader in 1990, and had effectively destroyed her premiership.

Heseltine was, of course, hated by the Thatcherite Eurosceptics, but even so was recognised as a potential prime minister with great popular appeal. His hour came when in July 1995 John Major, frustrated by his anti-European Tory opponents, sought, in a surprise move, a vote of confidence from his MPs in order to settle the leadership issue once and for all. Instead of entering the fray himself Heseltine decided to support Major. Had he stood, Heseltine might well have won the contest, and from Downing Street would have been in a strong position to muster a consensus for placing Britain on the road to joining the euro when it was eventually launched in 1999. It was a huge missed opportunity – both for Heseltine and also for his great cause of Europe.

During the 1990s and beyond, Michael Heseltine shared the leadership of the pro-European Tories with Kenneth Clarke, who became chancellor of the exchequer in May 1993. From the moment he took over in 11 Downing Street, Clarke used his position in Major's cabinet almost single-handedly to block the ascendant Tory Eurosceptics from getting what they wanted – a clear policy commitment against Britain joining the euro. And following the defeat of the Conservatives in 1997, with Tony Blair toying with a quick referendum on the euro, Clarke offered Blair his own support in any referendum campaign the new prime minister might want to call.

In the great European debates of the post-Thatcher era, Michael Heseltine and Kenneth Clarke fought hard for their corner but, unlike the Labour pro-Europeans in the early 1980s, they ultimately balked at going the final yard and splitting their party. Heseltine's timidity was a product of his continuing sensitivity about his assassin's role in ending Thatcher's premiership back in 1990; Clarke prevaricated because he believed right up to the last minute – that minute ending when Cameron defeated him for the Tory leadership – that he could at some future point lead the Conservative Party.

During their tenure at the top these pro-European Tories fought hard against their Eurosceptic opponents, and they succeeded in blocking moves within the Tory Party to take Britain out of the EU altogether. But, ultimately they watched their great cause of Europe lose more and more ground, and saw the British people turn increasingly against Britain joining the euro. Ultimately, unlike the Labour pro-Europeans who formed the SDP in 1981, they put their party before their country.

There was, though, a deeper problem affecting Britain's whole European movement in these years. Thatcher's powerful offensive against European integration had over the years taken its toll on the confidence of the pro-European camp, and a sense of defensiveness prevailed. The pro-Europeans seemed unable to offer a vision to match the one of an earlier generation who had sold the European cause as indispensable for peace in Europe. It amounted to an unwillingness to engage the argument on a fundamental level – to argue the case publicly that many of them were proffering privately, namely that as the USA was retrenching and Asia was rising, Britain was facing being alone in a dangerous world, and needed to be part of the European bloc for its own long-term security.

Ever since Margaret Thatcher made the 'f-word' ('f' for 'federal') and the idea of a superstate unacceptable in the late 1980s, the British pro-European establishment became wary of campaigning for further European integration, let alone for federalist ideas. In pro-European political circles in Westminster, federalists like John Pinder and Ernest Wistrich and their colleagues in the Federal Trust and the Federal Union, were respected but hardly taken seriously. Instead, Britain's pro-European establishment preferred the 'softly-softly' approach to campaigning, hoping to bounce Britain into the euro-zone while no one was looking. Or alternatively trying to sell Europe to the British on technical, tourist grounds, making currency exchange easier – the so-called 'Thomas Cook' argument for Europe. And in the process the key Eurosceptic arguments were not met head on: the successful Eurosceptic campaigning themes of 'British law versus Euro bureaucracy' and 'Democracy versus Brussels unaccountability' were rarely rebutted.

13 MURDOCH AND TABLOID XENOPHOBIA

No one ever lost any money underestimating the intelligence of the public.

H.L. Mencken, September 1926

The Sun Backs Labour.

Sun, March 1997

The growth of Euroscepticism during the Major years was decisively boosted by the increasingly influential tabloid press. From 'Black Wednesday' onwards this new power elite – led by the Murdoch '*Sun*' newspaper – was to create a powerful propaganda cocktail of xenophobia, celebrity and sex. In political terms it was to play directly into the 'grand delusion', and its narrative was simple and powerful: Britain was Great Again – and had been made so by Margaret Thatcher, who had turned the country around – but now her independence and democracy was threatened by shifty and slightly sinister continental Europeans. Britain's role as junior partner to the USA in a series of interventions was not to be treated in the same way: for America, by contrast, 'was a cousin' (ever since D-Day and all that!).

MOGULS AND BUSINESS – EUROPE AND AMERICA

It was hardly surprising that the new media moguls of the tabloid press were so pro-Thatcherite. After all, Thatcher's fight was Murdoch's fight – and vice versa. For Murdoch needed the defeat of the unions – in his case the powerful print unions in Fleet Street – as much as did Thatcher. And by the late 1980s Thatcher's victory was Murdoch's victory – and vice versa. The defeat of the print unions at Murdoch's plant at Wapping ushered in more than a new technology of print production and enhanced power for media owners. It was a building block in Thatcher's wider political success, a success that allowed the later political go-ahead to be given for Murdoch's plans for cross-media ownership.

The political needs of the media moguls – a business-friendly environment sustained by business-friendly parties – was bound to lead to an affinity with America, the home and heartland of business, and support for 'the American model' of low taxes and flexible labour markets. And, conversely, business-friendly politics was bound to lead to a natural suspicion of the EU, and the EEC before it, because of Europe's 'social model' of limitations on business through higher taxes and more regulated markets. During Blair's premiership the most politically influential newspaper owners were the trio of Murdoch, Black and Rothermere (father and son). Murdoch's *Sun* had a circulation of 3.84 million in 1997 when Blair became prime minister, and his *News of the World* had a circulation of 4.37 million. Conrad Black owned the *Daily Telegraph* and *Sunday Telegraph* (the *Daily Telegraph* circulation was 1.13 million) and the Tory opinion-forming magazine the *Spectator*. And the Rothermere family's *Daily Mail*, increasingly influential among women, sold 2.15 million.[1] But it was not just the sheer size of the circulation of these papers that gave their owners great political power. More important was the fear – the fear among politicians of getting on the wrong side of the populist technique of sustained day after day, drip, drip propaganda and news slanting based upon targeting specific issues.

All the moguls had strong connections with the USA. Rupert Murdoch lived there, became a US citizen and had large interests in both US newspapers and television. Conrad Black was born in North America and possessed major interests in Canada as well as the USA. And Jonathan Harmsworth – who took over as chairman of Associated Newspapers from his father, Lord Rothermere, in 1998 – had a classic 'Anglo-American' transatlantic education: Gordonstoun public school and Duke University, North Carolina.

However, 'selling America' too openly to the British people – particularly the need to Americanise the post-1945 welfare state – was always a difficult task. The American socio-economic model – with its private health system – may well have attracted the business class but had a very limited appeal to 'middle England'. Margaret Thatcher well understood this: hence her pledge while prime minister that 'the health service is safe in my hands'. She, and her political and business supporters, also understood that the domestic electoral support for her ambitious neo-liberal 'revolution' did not come out of any desire for a grand ideological pro-American 'free-market' change of economic course. Rather the opposite: it came from a domestic, British, patriotic desire for the restoration of national confidence and success after the debilitating 1970s – and for a strong democratic leader to carry it through.

Thatcher, as well as the businessmen who owned the tabloids, understood that good old-fashioned flag-waving patriotism was the key to winning hearts and minds, and therefore to electoral success. Tabloid nationalism had been born out of this key understanding. And in the late 1980s after, sensing that a renewed pride in nation was a winning line, owners and editors played the patriotic card more and more boldly – and, under the pressure of growing competition for readers, the political posture of this conservative press mutated from a generalised national pride into a rampant, crude xenophobia.

'PAGE-THREE GIRLS' AND XENOPHOBIA

A populist media climate and culture lends itself to the emergence of xenophobia – or extreme, simplistic, aggressive nationalism. And a populist approach has been a feature of the British media ever since the birth of mass newspapers. Yet during the 1980s and 1990s British tabloid populist journalism took populism to a whole new level. Even a cursory review of the tabloids of the 1950s and 1960s will show a level of news reporting and commentary that, although popular, was by today's tabloid standards of simplicity and coarseness both sophisticated and informed.

A milestone in this degeneration was Murdoch's decision to introduce topless photographs on 'page three' when he relaunched the *Sun* in 1969, with the first topless photograph appearing in 1970. It was a sign that tabloids would enter new territory in the circulation wars – and it succeeded. H.L. Mencken famously said, 'No one ever lost any money underestimating the intelligence of the public.'

It was a point that Britain's tabloids took to heart as they systematically engaged in a seemingly unstoppable process of 'dumbing down' both culturally and politically, a process that plumbed new depths. Coarseness and xenophobia seemed a winning formula. In 2000 the *Daily Express* changed ownership and in the process, according to Roy Greenslade 'bowed the knee to pornography, misogyny and vulgarity'.[2] And the valiant attempt in 2002 to take the *Daily Mirror* upmarket failed in 2005.

For a while though, even as tabloids began to change, the degeneration had little influence on wider journalism – what the British still like to call the 'quality' press.

But during the early 1990s, as an even more competitive climate began to bite, tabloid mass populism ceased to be confined, and instead began to set the standards – lower and lower standards – for the wider media.

By the turn of the new century political coverage and content in all the newspapers and on all television channels was being reduced from being policy-led to personality and lifestyle centred. News and commentary was becoming an acknowledged branch of the entertainment industry. Throughout the British media images replaced history, catchphrases replaced thought-out opinion, and journalism replaced genuine expertise.

Indeed the journalists became the experts – and journalists, rather than politicians and academics, became leading opinion-formers. And in the process the commercial interests, which owned the media and employed the journalists, came to possess a larger sway over public opinion than at any time in the recent past. Serious political discourse – particularly geopolitical discourse – in Britain, as in North America, retreated back into universities and think-tanks.

It was this new character of the British media – with its blend of news, entertainment and sensationalism – that allowed patriotic pride to turn into popular nationalism and xenophobia. And it was the 1982 conflict with Argentina over the Falkland Islands that both ushered in, and later legitimised, this new tabloid popular nationalism. 'Gotcha' was the crude and insensitive headline in the *Sun* after a British submarine killed hundreds of Argentinian sailors in May 1982. 'Gotcha' was an early salvo in a new type of raw, tasteless and triumphalist nationalism not even seen during the Second World War. It was clearly designed to appeal to the often inarticulate pent-up feelings of national decline and impotence of millions of people in post-war Britain. And it was a success in that, although bitterly criticised, the *Sun* had correctly identified prevailing majority national sentiment, and found no need to backtrack, let alone apologise.

'Gotcha' was later followed by other 'patriotic' headlines: in November 1990 by 'Up yours Delors', a rebuke to the European Commission president; by 'Up yours Señors' (after England defeated Argentina in the

2002 World Cup); by 'Chirac est un ver' or 'Chirac is a worm' (in a French edition of the *Sun* handed out free in France following that country's decision not to enter the 2003 Iraq War); and by 'One down three to go' (on the death of 27-year-old Brazilian Jean Charles Menezes, shot as a suspected terrorist in a London tube station on 23 July 2003, and later revealed to be an innocent bystander).

'Gotcha' was much more than a sign of coarsening standards. It was a highly political act – as it set the tone for a tabloid nationalism that was later successfully to garner public support for the regular use of force abroad – in the Gulf War, in the Serbian air campaign, and in 2003 in Iraq. The formula for success was clear: tabloid circulation would rise as the humdrum lives of millions of Britons would be enlivened and excited by war and violence in which British dominance was established over foreigners. As long as the bombs and the violence were safely distant, and there was no conscription at home, or indeed much sacrifice, support for war and conflict abroad, and British power, would sell.

Such vicarious valour (sometimes dubbed 'couch-potato courage') is a feature of modern xenophobia that makes it quite different from earlier, twentieth-century, national sentiment – which went hand in hand with mass volunteering (in the First World War) and conscription (in the Second World War and, in the USA, in the Vietnam conflict). And it was this new kind of vicarious nationalism that in the 1990s and into the new century was both reflected in and stimulated by the British populist media. And it travelled well – particularly across the Atlantic. This kind of 'macho' nationalism – in which patriotic sentiment would be whipped up by political and media figures who often had no track record of military service, or indeed who, as in George W. Bush's case, had avoided it – later become a key aspect of Murdoch's media in the USA and a 'product' promoted by Roger Ailes's leadership of the Fox News channel following 9/11.

FOREIGNER-BASHING

British tabloid populist nationalism in the 1990s had two main themes: a positive message and image of British 'greatness' and 'goodness', and the creation of a generally negative image of foreign life and foreignness. A culture of 'enemies' and 'threats' was created, a development made much easier following 9/11. And the tabloids sought to give colour and meaning to the fear and sense of threat by a systematic campaign of demonisation of selected foreign leaders. This demonising was not a part of a principled democratic campaign against authoritarianism and dictatorship in the world. Rather it was a highly selective propaganda tool used to create a mood for war – as it did successfully in 1982 with Argentine General Galtieri, in 1999 with Serbian president Slobodan Milosevic, and in 2002–3 with Iraqi president Saddam Hussein.

The climate of fear in Britain following 9/11 was exacerbated both by the tabloids and Britain's political leadership, who saw benefits in a more compliant public. And public opinion was manipulated – as in the case of the run-up to the Iraq invasion of 2003, when the danger of mass casualties in Britain (through an attack on the country by weapons of mass destruction with 45 minutes' notice) was a claim recycled by many tabloids. This use of fear in order to marshall support for political objectives was a formula that had worked well in the Britain of the late 1980s and 1990s – and after 11 September 2001, it was also used to great effect by George W. Bush's strategist Karl Rove.

Part of this tabloid xenophobia package involved a policy of foreigner-bashing. And within that there was a particular anti-continental angle. A tabloid assault on France was opened by Margaret Thatcher herself when her relations with European leaders deteriorated during the 1980s. François Mitterrand was a particular problem for her. Politically agile, with a sophisticated mind and serious geopolitical ability, he became a good target as the slippery foreigner. For Thatcher, though, a special place in the rogue's gallery was reserved for another Frenchman, president of the European Commission, Jacques Delors, who was everything she both detested and feared. He was an unelected international bureaucrat, a socialist with a taste for intellectuality, and a Frenchman.

Delors threw down the gauntlet to Thatcher when he accepted the British TUC's invitation to speak to their annual conference in Blackpool in 1987, and in her own country, in her own backyard, he taunted the prime minister by talking up the 'social dimension' of EU policy. The result was a sharp response. Thatcher herself proclaimed that she had not presided over the end of socialism in Britain just to see it introduced by 'the back Delors' (and the inevitable *Sun* headline, revelling in its now licensed vulgarity, would reply 'Up yours Delors').[3]

The tabloid attack on Delors brought into sharp relief British post-war attitudes towards France and the French. The British political class has always possessed its fair share of Francophiles – Winston Churchill was one such. The war leader even offered to merge the two nations in the summer of 1940 – although, with the Germans approaching Paris, the exigencies of the time probably explain this extraordinary and extravagant gesture. And since the war literally millions of British people have voted with their feet and set up home in France.

The standard post-war British attitude towards France – good food, stylish, weak government, easily overrun in 1940, overly sophisticated and intellectually pretentious – was not laudatory, but it was hardly hostile. It was only when the troubles between the Thatcher administration and the French hotted up in the 1980s that the tabloids, and Thatcher herself, unleashed an anti-French prejudice that went surprisingly deep within parts of Britain.

France and the French figure prominently in the building of English nationalism, and France has been the chief 'other', the outside force, by which Englishness could be measured, encouraged and honed. It is always difficult to measure the lasting effect of past conflicts on the thinking of present generations, but in raising France as a bogeyman there was certainly something there to mine. In the eighteenth century the country was faced with a series of invasion scares and insurrections orchestrated from France by the ousted Stuart dynasty. They tried an invasion of Scotland in 1708, and in 1715 there was a serious uprising throughout Scotland and parts of northern England in favour of James Edward Stuart, who some thirty years later was still at it, launching an invasion which came close to capturing the capital. Later the events of 1789 and the long wars against both revolutionary and Napoleonic France established France as a revolutionary threat to Britain's established classes – and unleashed a patriotic propaganda offensive against France.

Residual anti-Catholic sentiment was also at work in anti-French attitudes. Ever since Henry VIII the idea of a Protestant England set against a Catholic continent was a subtle, though powerful, image in the forging of national identity. In the contemporary debates about Europe suspicions were sometimes voiced, very privately, about whether the sympathies of pro-European politicians, like Shirley Williams, were fuelled by their Catholicism. Hugo Young describes Margaret Thatcher as having a sense that Roman Catholicism was 'alien', a sense he suggests may have 'begun in childhood when she, the daughter of a fiercely Methodist house, lived opposite a Roman Catholic church and a "Roman Catholic manse", as she once described it'.[4]

Tabloid nationalism also targeted Germany. Stereotyping the German grew easily out of the post-war allied British and American bombardment of war movies which flooded the country – and the media's somewhat gruesome fascination with the Nazi regime and Adolf Hitler. At the political level, though, for much of the post-war era West Germany was seen as a prosperous and stable democracy, a key ally in NATO. But this began to change in Britain following German reunification in 1990 when Margaret Thatcher – and she was joined in this by Mitterrand – worried publicly about the emergence of a powerful new Germany in the heart of Europe.

Both Thatcher and Mitterrand rebuffed the Germans by refusing to attend their unification celebrations in 1990 (President George H.W. Bush, a keen supporter of reunification, did attend). Thatcher went further, and in an unprecedented diplomatic snub held a tasteless seminar at the prime minister's country retreat at Chequers in which academics, diplomats and journalists met to discuss 'the German problem'.

The British prime minister's attitude was fodder for the tabloid nationalists, as it gave official blessing to media caricaturing of Germans and Germany which until then had been relegated to the sports pages during England–German contests on the football pitch.

George Urban, an influential writer and journalist who supported Thatcher, was to reveal the full extent of her anti-German sentiments. In December 1989 he was invited, with other members of the board of the Centre for Policy Studies, to a lunch with the prime minister. He reported the event: '"You know, George," she said, coming quite close to me, "there are things that people of your generation and mine ought never to forget. We've been through the war and we know perfectly well what the Germans are like, and what dictators can do, and how national character doesn't basically change…" and so on.' Urban suggested that 'if the British prime minister feels these things to be true, then we are heading for an unregenerate Europe, and most of our work over the last thirty or forty years, from [Jean] Monnet to the present day, will have been wasted. I only hope my fears are unfounded.' Later Urban confided to me that as far as her attitude to foreigners was concerned he thought she had a 'madness'. It was a 'madness' that I had witnessed in others on the political right – both of her generation and younger.[5]

On top of anti-French and anti-German campaigning, the late 1980s saw the beginning of what was to become a long-running anti-Brussels campaign, one that would last for the next twenty years, and at the time of writing was still in full flood. There were two key aspects of this sustained attack. First there was the supposed EEC/EU threat to 'the British way of life' – a tabloid-constructed cosy 'little Englander' life of warm beer, British sausages and the monarchy. It was a way of life, it was argued, that was threatened by 'soulless bureaucrats' in Brussels driven by a power-crazed need to standardise. And a seductive patriotic/ nationalist message, one made more powerful by the regular insensitivity of the Brussels Commission, was developed.

Indeed, so appealing was the Eurosceptic campaign that a leading pro-European, foreign secretary Douglas Hurd, was forced to agree that the Commission should not involve itself in the 'nooks and crannies' of national life. Hurd had served in Thatcher's government and was too timid to point out that it was Thatcher's own great project – the level playing field of the single market – that could only be properly implemented by an 'intrusive' harmonisation of standards.

The continentals were also portrayed as a threat to British democracy. Thatcher herself had constructed the powerful narrative: 'Britain,' so it went, 'stood uniquely for liberty; and in the war we had stood alone; and then we had liberated Europe, for which all Europeans should be grateful.' It was a mindset derived from a war that could not be let go, that had travelled well beyond the Westminster elite and into the British hinterland. It could be seen in the *braggadocio* slogan 'We won the war!' chanted by English football hooligans in many a continental city in the 1980s and 1990s – themes tailor-made for tabloid nationalists.

The constant tabloid repetition of key words like 'unelected bureaucrats' or 'Eurocrats' increasingly disarmed the pro-Europeans in Britain. The very word 'Brussels' became a term of abuse. Tabloid nationalism had successfully identified a central weakness of the nascent European polity – the fact, that could hardly be contested, that one of the EU's primary institutions, the Commission, was in essence unaccountable and undemocratic. However, the tabloid nationalists of the era had little positive to say about the democratically elected European parliament; nor did they, apart from generalised abuse of politicians as a genre, offer much of a critique of the democratic deficiencies of the Westminster/ Whitehall set-up; nor, in their defence of 'the British way of life', did they place any of the blame on the architect of the single market, Thatcher, or the free-market ideology that had driven it.

'AMERICA IS JUST NOT FOREIGN'

Tabloid nationalism was specifically directed at continental Europe. Few tabloids of the era criticised – in any systematic sense – the 'special relationship' with the USA. Nationalists in the popular media would argue about the need for Britain to be 'self-governing' and to be 'independent,' and saw the threat to such 'independence' coming from Europe though not the USA; also, they would assert British interests as being separate from Europe, but not from those of the USA; and they would suggest that the threat to British democracy and Westminster 'sovereignty' came exclusively from the 'bureaucrats in Brussels' while Wall Street and Washington, certainly in terms of any impact they might have on 'British sovereignty', remained relatively immune to criticism. When challenged about this lack of even-handedness a leading conservative editor said to me, 'I get the point, but to British journalists, America is just not foreign.'[6]

In the tabloids of the time, however, uncritical support for American foreign policy went strangely hand in hand with petty anti-Americanism. The British media generally gave inordinate publicity to almost anything American, particularly the eccentric and the extreme. Critical stories about American life and 'the American way of life' suffused almost every newspaper and many television news programmes – even the conservative tabloid media. During the Iraq War many tabloids, while supporting American policy, would also take critical shots at the American right – the 'guns, gays and God' syndrome in American life. Intriguingly, however, these critical pieces rarely translated into calls for a change in Britain's subservient foreign policy. Rather they represented a turn-of-the-century tabloid version of the 'Greece to Rome' conceits of earlier years.

This mixture of blind support, an underlying superiority and resentment, and a blank refusal to confront and deal with Britain's relationship to American power was the true mark of how far the post-war British had slid into an unhealthy colonial master-and-servant relationship.

By the time of the Iraq War in 2003, however, the 'special relationship' had, for the first time since the Vietnam crisis in the late 1960s, become highly controversial among the wider British public. So much so that Downing Street felt it needed defending. Even Tony Blair argued that the relationship with America should not be a one-way street. Talking of policies favoured by Britain, he argued, on the eve of the Iraq War, that 'we should in return [for Britain's support] expect these issues to be confronted…proportionately, sensibly, and in a way that delivers a better prospect of long-term peace, security and justice.'[7] Even so, the tabloid nationalist press rarely objected when British policy objectives – say in the Middle East or in the Kyoto Treaty controversy – were not taken up by Washington.

NORMAN TEBBIT

The tabloid nationalist campaign of the late 1980s onwards had no more authentic voice than Norman Tebbit. Having come to prominence, as we have seen, in the Thatcher administrations as employment secretary and as Tory Party chairman in the 1987 election, he was an archetypal Thatcherite. A fervent anti-socialist, he saw 'big government' as an enemy of aspiring working-class families. And he saw the 'free market' as opening up the economy and therefore society. He was the quintessential 'Essex man', and in extolling upward mobility he was also talking about his own story, as he later recalled in his autobiography *Upwardly Mobile*.[8]

He was also the leading Tory social conservative of his generation, whose mix of immigration, law and order and nationalism made him something of an inheritor of the mantle of Enoch Powell. Also, his London accent, like Powell's Midlands accent, set him apart from most Westminster Tories and gave him an appeal to the southern white working class. In 1987 I joined him, former Labour MPs Neville Sandelson and Brian Walden, and former Liberal Party leader Jo Grimond, in founding a debating society, the *Radical Society*. Tebbit's reputation at the time, led by the media, was that of a populist 'bully boy', a stoker of prejudices. He was that; but he was also, in reality, a sophisticated politician with a keen, forensic debating talent. Essentially uninterested in foreign policy, he was a 'little Englander', concerned above all to preserve traditional ways. Yet, like many conservatives, he failed to appreciate how it was business interests rather than the state that were eroding these traditional ways. And, again like so many of the conservative Eurosceptics of his time, he saw these 'traditional ways' as threatened only by Europe, not by the forces of the market and the Americanisation of Britain.

Towards the end of his active political career, Norman Tebbit appeared in a weekly 'head to head' Sky TV show with the Labour MP for Grimsby, Austin Mitchell. Mitchell was a social democrat, a Gaitskellite by tradition, and he saw himself as a progressive – and he disagreed with Tebbit about most contemporary political issues. They agreed, however, about the need to resist EU influence on British life, Mitchell seeing it as a threat to British parliamentary democracy.

Mitchell, like many Labour MPs of the time, was willing to criticise Britain's 'special relationship' with the USA – but not as systematically and as fervently as he did the country's membership of the EU. In this respect Mitchell represented a serious strain of sentiment among Labour MPs in the Blair era. Many would be critical, privately often quite severely, of specifics of US foreign policy; but they would never take a public stand against the 'special relationship', or indeed against the centrality of NATO in the post-Cold War era. The 2003 Iraq War placed many Labour MPs in a serious quandary, some even emotionally torn. Many vehemently opposed Britain's siding with America, but in the final analysis, career concerns led many to support Blair. And, for the less career-minded, old habits ran deep. Sticking by America in a crisis was deeply embedded in the mental framework, the very DNA of established Westminster politics.

MANIPULATING THE WOUNDED

The key to the Murdoch/Tebbit tabloid populist nationalist appeal in Britain was similar, indeed almost identical, to the nationalist populism that President George W. Bush, his advisor Karl Rove and the Murdoch-owned Fox News channel employed following 9/11. The writer Anatol Lieven, in his fascinating and insightful work *America Right or Wrong: An anatomy of American nationalism*, identified the well-springs of populist nationalism in America, and particularly among George Bush's base vote: white southerners. He suggests that the key to understanding the xenophobia of white American southern men, is to see them as a defeated people with a wounded sensibility – the kind of sensibility that responds to 'macho' strength and xenophobia.

Lieven argues that this mentality leads to an over-identification with the USA as a powerful country, which places them, for once, on a winning team: and what is more, as the American tabloid lingo would have it, a 'kick-ass team'.[9] In this American case the wounds go back to the continuing effect of the South's defeat in the Civil War, and to more recent mid- to-late twentieth-century wounds inflicted by a sense that 'others' – blacks, new ethnic groups and women – have made advances at their expense.

British tabloid nationalism also played on wounded feelings, in this case those of the British white working-class male's sense of insecurity. By the end of the 1990s fewer and fewer British men over the age of fifty were in the kind of full-time work that previous generations enjoyed and, like their American counterparts, they were feeling increasingly beleaguered. Social changes gave them a sense of declining status compared to 'others', particularly women and new ethnic groups. These British men also felt keenly – because many of them had lived through it – the decline of their country as a world power. It was, and is, an unsettling environment and it creates among these people a sense that 'enough is enough'. And in response xenophobia – with its venting of suppressed racial and national prejudices, and the promise of 'not being kicked around any more' – can easily take hold, becoming the perfect outlet: one willingly provided by the tabloid nationalists.

MURDOCH'S 'ENG·ER·LAND':
THE RED CROSS OF ST GEORGE

Tabloid populism – with its admixture of nostalgia for a lost, great English past and a present-day visceral nationalism – had been a growing feature of British working-class life during the late twentieth century, ever since it became clear that Britain was no longer a world power and was taking a back seat to the USA. But at some point during the 1990s it transformed into a new, and even narrower, form of nation-consciousness: English xenophobia.

English xenophobia was slowly building during the 1980s. But it only began to show itself fully in the 1990s when, suddenly and spontaneously during World and European Cup football events thousands and thousands of English flags – the red cross of St George on a white background – appeared throughout the country. They were flown from vans and from homes, mainly in working-class areas. The 1990 World Cup, 'Italia 90', saw huge television audiences and set the tone for the subsequent contests, and these sporting events provided tabloid nationalism with a rich seam of vicarious valour to mine.

The England team became a nationalist symbol, and support for it was rallied by the tabloids – particularly against old adversaries like Germany and France. Through televised football the Second World War could be replayed, this time as entertainment. And the fact of a sporting context, rather than a political one, could allow tabloid 'creativity' – and bigotry – full reign, with opponents dubbed 'Krauts', 'Frogs' and 'Argies'. And in and around the stadiums during these contests the trademark football chant 'Eng-er-land' had a raw, assertive, xenophobic edge to it.

Tabloid xenophobia in football was sold as innocent, competitive, sporting fun. But at the same time it created a wave of support for more serious ideas – principally the emergence of the idea of England as a separate nation, separate that is from Scotland and Wales. As it happened the organisation of British football played right into the new nationalist 'Eng-er-land' theme. For some quirky historical reason Britain (or the UK) had no football team. Instead, the 'national' game had four 'national' sides – Scotland, Wales, Northern Ireland and England. And thus 'England' rather than 'Britain' became the symbol though which many Englishmen expressed their growing 'patriotism' and xenophobia. And with large amounts of money to be made out of the England team – television coverage, mass marketing of team jerseys and insignia, player sponsorship of products – huge commercial and media interests further promoted the idea of 'Eng-er-land', and a separate England at that. As did 'English' celebrity footballers, like David Beckham, who were joining older 'British' celebrity institutions like the Queen.

But the massive commercialisation of English football was only one reason for the new English xenophobia, and not the primary one. More important was a growing but real sense throughout the country that the UK union was creaking, if not actually breaking up, and that there was a kind of inevitability about Scotland eventually going it alone and Northern Ireland severing its links with the mainland. For many English people it seemed that with the empire gone the Celtic nations in their insistent search for greater devolution were in fact seeking to leave a sinking ship. Following devolution in 1997 there was no majority in either Scotland or Wales for breaking the union, but there was a continuing, indeed growing, sense of Scottish and Welsh consciousness (and nationalism) which resisted, and often resented, English influence.

Scottish national sentiment had been developing during Margaret Thatcher's administrations – when the 'English' Thatcher government in London was bringing in radical economic and social changes north of the border without a mandate from the people of Scotland (where the Conservatives remained in a decided minority). Also, although Thatcher's brand of patriotism sought to give all of the British their pride back, her 'revolution' had been a very English affair, led by a very 'English lady', and it had stirred English emotions, not resonating very much north of the border.

By the time of the 1997 general election the nationalist tide was again running strongly. Many within the London establishment became convinced that the only way in which it could be staunched was by the setting up of a Scottish parliament with some law-making powers. It was a measure of this sense of urgency that Tony Blair's very first parliamentary act was to establish this parliament north of the border.

Yet Westminster's concessions to Scotland produced a backlash in England. The politicians were seen in England as pandering to the Scots. For the tabloid-reading Englishman south of the border 'England', no longer 'Britain', was becoming the repository of patriotic, nationalist, instincts and emotions. And there was a widespread sense that, for all the talk of renewal, England was not what it was, was on the retreat, and was on her own. If an Englishman had at the beginning of the twentieth century been dealt the 'top card in life', now, having risen the furthest, he was falling the hardest. For him, England's finest hour, 1940, was long gone, as was England's last football success – 1966. Globally he had already lost out – to Americans, who had replaced him as the inhabitants of a superpower, to Europeans, who were still the arbiters of style and taste, and even to the Chinese, the new rising power.

From this vantage point, with the empire gone and with Britain fragmenting into separate parts, an ideological version of England was becoming 'the last refuge' of the nationalist 'scoundrel'.

ENGLISH EUROSCEPTICISM

This new English nationalism was not just the preserve of the tabloid classes. Throughout England, in 'the country' and 'the county', a quiet xenophobia had long existed. This refined, more mild nationalism was the key ingredient of the Eurosceptism which increasingly dominated establishment Westminster political life during the Major/Blair years. These Eurosceptics expressed themselves more carefully, and more politically correctly, and they did so without much overt 'flag-waving'. The very term 'sceptic' suggested a measured, less aggressive, approach than the tabloids. But, at root, they possessed the same instincts and values, and took the same positions, and signed on to the same policies, as the xenophobes in the tabloid media. Specifically they opposed any change in Britain's foreign alignment – specifically entry into the euro-zone; and they supported, even with much gnashing of teeth, the 'special relationship' with the USA.

By the turn of the century this Euroscepticism had become the near-dominant political instinct among the 'home counties' southern elites in top positions in the finance service sector in the City of London, in the professions and the 'upmarket' media. And it filtered through to the parties. New Labour, as the Labour Party now called itself, which had started off the Blair era as Europhile, ended the era as a mildly Eurosceptic party. During the same period the Conservatives became more Europhobe than Eurosceptic, so much so that in 2006 their new leader, David Cameron, although determined to project a progressive and green image at home, was forced to de-align his party in the European parliament from Europe's mainstream centre-right parties and instead seek an alliance with some eccentric Europhobe populist parties of the right.

These English Eurosceptics shared one overwhelming characteristic with the tabloid xenophobes: a seriously provincial perspective. They inhabited a vantage-point that saw the Channel as a threat, insisted that Britain, or England, had little or nothing to learn from abroad, and still believed 'sovereignty' was attainable. To these believers in 'Queen and country' the age of globalisation and most of the great changes in the world economy and in geopolitics had seemingly passed them by.

John Major had appeased this kind of thinking, as he had appeased the tabloid press. But in 1997 a new political voice was heard, one that promised at least to inject some new realism into British political discourse.

PART 5
An empire of finance

14 BLAIR: SAVING THE QUEEN, BOTTLING EUROPE

Tony Blair was a very different kind of politician. He became leader of the opposition Labour Party in July 1994, but there was nothing of the party man about him. He was privately educated at a well-known public school and at Oxford, and then became a lawyer. He had very little connection with the Labour Party or the trade-union movement (or with any faction in the party) when he became a parliamentary candidate in a by-election in 1982, and this lack of history stood Blair in good stead in his early years in parliament – for in the mid-1990s Labour was looking to break with its past, and this non-political, seemingly classless, articulate and fresh-faced young man fitted the bill exactly.

He was also capable of being bold and radical. While opposition leader he displayed a rare strength of leadership by succeeding where many Labour politicians had feared to tread: in persuading the Labour Party to draw a line under its past by removing the 'socialist' Clause 4 from its constitution. He projected the image of a modernising radical who would bring a breath of fresh air into the moribund political system, not least through major constitutional change. While opposition leader he developed a significant constitutional-reform programme. And, importantly, he also pledged himself to end the country's 'road to nowhere', resolving the European issue by joining the euro.

Blair represented change. And it was seemingly fundamental. In 1997 during the election campaign against John Major's divided and failing Tories he projected himself as 'Britain's John Kennedy'. His rhetoric was unabashedly progressive. 'I want to create a 21st century nation, based not on privilege, class or background, but on the equal worth of all,' he argued at a Labour party conference. He sought to 'sweep away the forces of conservatism' and attacked 'today's Tory party' as 'the party of fox hunting, Pinochet and hereditary peers: the uneatable, the unspeakable and the unelectable'. It was pure David Lloyd George or Aneurin Bevan. Here was possibly a new British leader who through a classless radicalism and real reform agenda would take on Britain's *ancien régime* and finally lay the imperial ghost, turning Britain into a modern European country at ease with itself. Indeed he stated bluntly that for 'the last half century we have been searching for our identity in the post empire world,' and he did not mince words: 'our destiny lies in Europe.'[1]

The British constitution was a battleground in the 1997 general election. The Conservative manifesto was as traditionalist as any in memory. 'We must protect our constitution and unity as a nation from those who threaten it with unnecessary and dangerous change,' it asserted, and went on in similar mode:

> Alone in Europe, the history of the United Kingdom has been one of stability and security; we owe much of that to the strength and stability of our constitution – the institutions, laws and traditions that bind us together as a nation...Our constitution has been stable, but not static. It has been woven over the centuries – the product of hundreds of years of knowledge, experience and history...Radical changes that alter the whole character of our constitutional balance could unravel what generations of our predecessors have created. To preserve that stability in future – and the freedoms and rights of our citizens – we need to continue a process of evolution, not revolution.

By contrast the Labour manifesto looked positively revolutionary. It outlined plans to exclude hereditary peers from the House of Lords, to hold a referendum on changing the electoral system, to introduce a Freedom of Information Act and, most innovative of all, to set up a Scottish parliament, a Welsh assembly and a directly elected London mayor:

> For Scotland we propose the creation of a parliament with law-making powers, firmly based on the agreement reached in the Scottish Constitutional Convention, including defined and limited financial powers to vary revenue and elected by an additional member system...The Welsh assembly will provide democratic control of the existing Welsh Office functions. It will have secondary legislative powers and will be specifically empowered to

reform and democratise the quango state. It will be elected by an additional member system...

For London, 'following a referendum to confirm popular demand, there will be a new deal...with a strategic authority and a mayor, each directly elected...'

And Tony Blair as prime minister lived up to much of this promise. The Human Rights Act 1998 enabled the European Convention on Human Rights to be enforced by UK courts. The Freedom of Information Act 2000 gave the public the right to apply for official information, and later a UK Supreme Court was established separate from the House of Lords, becoming active in 2009. The programme had its limitations. The Human Rights Act did not amount to a full bill of rights in the sense that it was not constitutionally entrenched and judges could use it to quash secondary but not primary legislation (although a declaration of incompatibility by a court placed immense pressure on ministers to amend primary legislation). The Freedom of Information Act was criticised for containing too many categories of types of information that were exempt from disclosure and for providing for a ministerial override to prevent a release. Perhaps most significantly, devolution took on a pronounced asymmetrical quality. Outside London there was no devolution for England. While most hereditary peers were removed from the House of Lords, the House remained wholly appointed. No referendum was provided on proportional representation. Yet the fact remains that under the Blair premiership Britain became a more 'open society' in some key regards; and by creating a Scottish parliament Britain took a giant leap towards a federal system.

In his first few months in office Tony Blair both acted like, and looked like, a new type of prime minister – one fit for a democratic age, a true moderniser. As opposition leader he had taken an axe to the DNA of one of the great forces of conservatism in Britain – the 'Clause 4 socialism' at the heart of the trade-union and Labour movement. It seemed, with his constitutional-reform agenda, that he might be about to do the same to the broader, national 'forces of conservatism', underpinned as they were by the constitutional *'ancien régime'* of monarchy, Lords and unwritten constitution.

THE DEATH OF DIANA SPENCER

During Blair's time as opposition leader another source of change and modernisation had been at work. When Prince Charles had married Diana Spencer in 1981 she had been viewed by many commentators as a rather empty-headed, 'sloaney' kind of woman. It turned out they were wrong. Diana developed a sure common touch and understanding, and portrayed a warmth that was missing from the Windsor family – who by contrast began to look cold, overly formal and old-fashioned. She was giving Britain a different image – one which did not involve rural pursuits and riding to hounds. Public sympathy for Diana – and antipathy towards the royal family – grew as her marriage to Charles frayed and then broke up. And when it became clear that she was not going to remain silent, but rather return to an enhanced public role as a single woman, she became extremely dangerous to the royal family. She was, in effect, setting up an alternative royal court.

When Diana died in a car crash in Paris in August 1997, Tony Blair, still the new prime minister, caught the public mood by dubbing her 'the people's princess', a depiction that both captured her 'democratic' nature and inevitably compared her unfavourably with the 'undemocratic' royals. And Blair's role in the immediate aftermath of the death was to establish him as the representative figure of modern Britain, of 'cool Britannia', and as the reformer who was having to deal with a stubborn, unreconstructed older Britain in the form of the Queen.

SAVING THE QUEEN

The widespread public belief that in some way the royals had had a hand in the death of Diana, together with the immediate reaction of the royal family – led by the Queen when she kept the family at Balmoral instead of returning to London to meet the crowds gathering there – caused a decided falling off in public support for the royals.

Over the following week the Palace started to adopt a different approach, with the Queen making a live television broadcast on 5 September (including the statement that there were 'lessons to be learnt' from Diana's life), culminating in the vast public funeral which, in the words of the Labour historian-turned-royal chronicler Ben Pimlott, 'fell into none of the recognised official categories of "state funeral", "ceremonial royal funeral", or "private royal funeral"'.[2] There is scope for debate about how far the public mood at this time could be seen as republican, and the extent to which Blair and his Number 10 staff should be credited with the change of tack taken by the Palace. But there can be no doubt that the monarchy had real problems immediately following the death of Diana, and that Blair and his team, particularly his communications chief Alistair Campbell, helped resolve them. In the contemporary historian Anthony Seldon's fascinating account of the events of the time Blair and his aides, who took part in planning the response and funeral with royal officials, argued for a public funeral, against the wishes of the Queen and the Spencer family, and 'argued with increasing force the case for the Queen to leave Balmoral to come down to London, and for the flag to fly at half-mast above Buckingham Palace.' 'Seldon states that

> too much can be made of Number 10's influence during this week [but] 'the imploring of Campbell in particular for the Queen to be seen to be empathising with the national mood of grief was significant...Had the Queen not relented, and remained rigidly away from London, without any sign of recognition of Diana, untold damage would have been done to the monarchy.[3]

One of Campbell's contributions, according to Seldon, was to argue that the Queen's broadcast should be made live; and to insert 'the humanising phrase "speaking as a grandmother" to improve a wooden script' for the broadcast.[4] Campbell's diary provides support for these views. For example, the entry for Thursday 4 September records,

> The mood was really turning against the royals and everyone seemed helpless in the face of it. I called [royal officials] Fellowes and Janvrin and said it was becoming dangerous and unpleasant. The press were now fuelling a general feeling that the royals were not responding or even caring. The ugliness of the mood was growing. Today's media would make it worse and it had got to be addressed...there had to be more big announcements to fill the vacuum and also the royals had to be more visible. In an ideal world, they would come back early to London and mix with people.[5]

Blair found himself, in his own words, with a 'pivotal' role. With St James's Palace apparently fearing that Prince Charles might well be attacked by members of the public on the way to Diana's funeral, the new prime minister became the central figure in arranging a compromise between the Queen at Balmoral and the media mood. He was even probably in a position to force a reform of the monarchy, maybe even engineer its demise (probably after the Queen had left the throne). In his memoirs Blair is clear about the fragility of the monarchy at the time. He described the Diana phenomenon in extraordinary terms: 'She was an icon, possibly the most famous and most photographed person in the world. She captured the essence of an era and held it in the palm of her hand…this was gravely disconcerting for the monarchy as an institution or a business, if you like…'[6] And that was before her death.

Blair has written that 'during those days [after Diana's death] it [the position of the monarchy] certainly felt touch and go.' The new prime minister had no love for the monarchy; he found the Queen stiff and formal, and his weekends at Balmoral 'utterly freaky' – 'I never did country house or stately home weekends.' He thought her view of him was 'a bit nouveaux riches', 'a bit arriviste', and 'therefore suspect'.[7] And as a still very popular young leader of the country Blair was in the position, at the very minimum, to start a national debate on the future of the monarchy.

Instead Blair, when asked directly just after the funeral about the future of the house of Windsor, said on television that 'you are either a republican, or you are a monarchist. I am a monarchist. An ardent monarchist.' And then later, at a banquet, he would become even more fulsome as he toasted the Queen: 'the Queen is the Best of British.' By refusing to open the question 'officially' – there was considerable debate among the people and in the media – he effectively saved the monarchy in Britain at a time when it could have been seriously damaged and indeed placed on death row. He said himself that 'I thought my job was to protect the monarchy, channel the anger before it became rage, and generally have the whole business emerge in a positive and unifying way, rather than be a source of tension, division and bitterness.'[8]

But the question remains: why? Why did he spare the royal family from a national debate and instead come so fully to their rescue? The answer will say a lot about modern Britain. One possibility is that it was just too difficult. It was simply not on his agenda and there had been no manifesto commitment. And anyway it was not worth the fight. And the Queen would have fought, not just about proposals to hold a referendum but also about any slimmed-down royal operation or any modernisation of the institution. And, intriguingly, in any such fight Blair has subsequently revealed that he believed he would lose. He has said, 'we know they [the royal family] still have the power to keep us in our place…' And Campbell made much the same point when he was asked – by Sir Angus Ogilvie

– about whether the royals were over. 'I said I thought while the Queen was there no, but post her and the Queen Mum, things might change fast…They were "extravagant" and "wasteful".'[9]

Another explanation was that Blair, for all his proclaimed meritocratic vision, at bottom rather supported the way Britain organised its politics through its unwritten constitution, its unelected upper house, its monarchy and established church, and the aristocratic and imperial culture of its honours and the like. Blair was, after all, educated privately in a traditional English-style public school and was something of a 'toff' in his manners; and he was, as he declared himself, 'supremely relaxed' about inequalities, even gaping inequalities, in British society. There was minimal passion in him for egalitarian causes. Also there is no evidence that Blair ever possessed republican sympathies. Indeed Blair claims that he was not republican by background, and that his father made sure they watched the Queen's annual broadcast. (His wife Cherie, on the other hand, with her working-class and Catholic background, and her obvious contempt for the world of royalty, was a force in the opposite direction.)

ROYAL TENSIONS CONTINUE

However, there is some evidence that the Queen, or the Palace, or both, harboured resentments against Blair for having shored them up, even saved them – particularly as he made it known to friends and others that he had done so. The leaks from the Palace against Blair's change agenda and the snub to Blair at the time of the Queen Mother's funeral and the 2011 royal wedding (when he was not invited to the ceremony) may well tell the story.

From Blair's vantage point he has revealed the quite sharp personal tensions that existed between him and the Queen. He has accused her of showing 'hauteur' towards him at their audiences, and reported in his memoirs that 'you don't get matey with the Queen…she can be matey with you, but don't try and reciprocate or you get The Look.'[10] He simply could not understand the cold, formal and seemingly uncaring attitude of the Queen in the days following the death of Diana.

On the Queen's part it has been revealed that she objected to Blair's attitude to rural Britain: she reportedly told a farmer who complained about Blair's views on the countryside, 'I know. I tell him [Blair] every week when I see him.' And the Queen was also reportedly 'left exasperated and frustrated by change for change's sake' during Blair's administration.[11] The Queen's traditional, indeed often reactionary, attitude was the kind of approach to life that would tend to grate with the New Labour prime minister.

There were tensions with Prince Charles too – primarily over genetically modified food, the hunting ban and the foot-and-mouth disease outbreak. While prime minister Blair once received a six-page letter about foot-and-mouth in what he described as Charles's 'Daily Telegraph-speak'; and he reportedly remarked pointedly that Charles had not complained when six thousand jobs had been lost at Corus (the steel manufacturer). Blair also offered the view, after a long session with Prince Charles on rural issues, that he thought the heir to the throne was 'well-meaning but misguided', but that 'once they got into an argument, not so well-meaning'. When Blair made his well-reported speech attacking 'the forces of conservatism' in Britain, Blair believed that Charles had thought it directed at him, and had been really 'stung by the... speech'.[12]

NEW LABOUR, THE MONARCHY

(AND THE *ANCIEN RÉGIME*)

However, even though the royals often annoyed Blair and grated on New Labour, the constitutional-modernisation programme was never extended to include reforming the monarchy. Labour's royal critics like the MPs Paul Flynn and Kelvin Hopkins were sidelined. Even the most moderate calls to reform some of the constitutional anomalies arising from the status of the monarchy in the UK were consistently resisted. In particular, the royal prerogative, a device which had largely come under the control of ministers and officials (though some of it was retained by the monarchy) was kept intact by Blair.

While under New Labour no progress was made towards an elected House of Lords, the government did succeed in excluding most of the hereditary peers from the upper chamber – although some remained, as did the bishops. This reform amounted to a denial of the ancient political rights of the aristocracy, and by extension could hardly but call into question the role of the monarchy. The 1997 Labour general-election manifesto had promised that 'the right of hereditary peers to sit and vote in the House of Lords will be ended by statute.' However, recognising the implications for the monarchy, but at the same time attempting to deny them, the manifesto stated, 'We have no plans to replace the monarchy.' It was a great tribute to the enduring social power of the British monarchy that in all the debates over the hereditary principle in the Lords hardly any linkage between the Lords and the monarchy was drawn.

Blair avoided tackling all of the minor, though significant, royal issues that reformers were calling for – including the time-consuming weekly audiences between prime minister and Queen, the honours system, the oaths of allegiance, the bar on discussion of the royal family in the Commons, and the financing of the royals via the Duchies of Lancaster and Cornwall.

One significant development did occur towards the end of the Blair era in 2005. The House of Commons Public Accounts Committee (PAC) carried out an inquiry into the Duchies of Cornwall and Lancaster – land holdings that provided sources of income for the Queen and the heir. It was an historic occasion, as the chairman of the committee, Conservative MP Edward Leigh, outlined:

> This afternoon the Committee of Public Accounts is looking at the accounts of the Duchies of Cornwall and Lancaster. I think this is an historic occasion. The Duchy of Cornwall was created by Charter in 1337 when Edward III created his son the Duke of Cornwall, and the Duchy of Lancaster since 1399 has passed to each reigning monarch to provide a source of income. I think this is probably the first time at which a parliamentary committee has examined the Duchies' accounts in this way. It is an unusual hearing for us, the Committee of Public Accounts, because it is not based on a report by the Comptroller and Auditor General. The Comptroller and Auditor General does not audit the Duchies' accounts and has no right of access to the underlying books and records. I should say that the longstanding policy of this Committee is that we think that he should have such access in order to inform Parliament. However, we make one step at a time. Parliament has been about this business since the 17th Century, so we continue to hope that we will get more and better access as the years pass.[13]

In its report, the PAC was critical of the governance and the lack of transparency of the two duchies – but at no time, like the New Labour government, did it criticise, or even suggest reforms to, the fundamental archaic character of the arrangement.

Blair's successor Gordon Brown took one last New Labour shot at the ancient constitution in mid-2007 when he unveiled plans in a green paper to reform the royal prerogative.[14] These royal prerogative powers, which reformers considered the locus of secretive and un-democratic authority at the heart of the unwritten constitution, allow a whole range of actions to be taken without parliamentary approval – simply by the Queen's signature, on the advice of ministers. They had never been approved by parliament and did not require explicit parliamentary consent to be used (and the courts were traditionally reluctant to become involved). Brown's green paper set them out in all their starkness:

> The Government exercises prerogative powers to:
> • Deploy and use the Armed Forces overseas
> • Make and ratify treaties
> • Issue, refuse, impound and revoke passports
> • Acquire and cede territory
> • Conduct diplomacy
> • Send and receive ambassadors
> • Organise the Civil Service
>
> The Government makes recommendations to the Monarch to exercise her powers to:
> • Grant honours or decorations
> • Grant mercy
> • Grant peerages
> • Appoint Ministers

But the Brown proposal for change was a mouse. His green paper argued that 'in general the prerogative powers should be put onto a statutory basis and brought under stronger parliamentary scrutiny and control.' And it carefully noted that

> No changes are proposed to either the legal prerogatives of the Crown or the Monarch's constitutional or personal prerogatives, although in some areas the Government proposes to change the mechanism by which Ministers arrive at their recommendations on the Monarch's exercise of those powers.[15]

The personal prerogatives of the monarch which were to be left intact included the right to grant (and by implication in theory refuse) a dissolution of parliament; and to appoint the prime minister (which, in circumstances of a House of Commons with no overall control, could imply exercising a degree of discretion as to who was chosen).

The government carried out a general review of the royal prerogative powers over the following two years, as well as eventually implementing some changes, most notably placing the civil service on a statutory basis, and providing a statutory role for parliament in the ratification of treaties (both in the Constitutional Reform and Governance Act 2010). But beyond that it concluded, in language worthy of Sir Humphrey himself,

> it is unnecessary, and would be inappropriate, to propose further major reform at present. Our constitution has developed organically over many centuries and change should not be proposed for change's sake. Without ruling out further changes aimed at increasing Parliamentary oversight of the prerogative powers exercised by Ministers, the Government believes that any further reforms in this area should be considered on a case-by-case basis, in the light of changing circumstances.

New Labour's constitutional-reform agenda, so trumpeted at the beginning of its era, ended in a whimper.

There was, though, one last royal controversy to burst on the scene during New Labour's reign. Shortly before the 2010 general election the role of the monarchy was thrust into the public arena by the possibility that a hung parliament was in prospect. Courtiers and monarchical advisors had always feared that in the event of a hung parliament the Queen could be dragged into political debate – because the prerogative powers gave her, as unelected head of state, the right, in the event that no party had an overall majority, to appoint from among contending political leaders one of them to 'try to form a government'. The successful appointee would then seek to secure a majority in the House of Commons. It was a powerful role and could be portrayed as interfering in the democratic process.

In an attempt to keep the Queen out of politics the rules needed to be discovered – but no one knew what they were, and there was no written constitution to act as a guide. In a comic turn worthy of the constitution's Ruritanian character, the Cabinet Office was deployed to discover – or rather divine – and then tell us all what the constitution of the country amounted to. And it produced a draft 'Manual' which set down the legislation and 'understandings' that amounted to the British constitution in the twenty-first century.

It was only after the establishment of the Cameron–Clegg coalition government in 2010 that political circumstances conspired to produce a reform of the prerogative power to grant dissolutions. A key part of the coalition deal struck between the Conservatives and Liberal Democrats in May 2010 was to introduce fixed-term parliaments of five years. The effect of clause 3 of the Fixed-term Parliaments Act introduced later that year was to abolish the royal prerogative power to dissolve parliament.

It remained an intriguing truth about British public life that during the reign of Elizabeth II none of Britain's supposedly 'meritocratic' prime ministers – Wilson, Heath, Thatcher and Blair – saw fundamental constitutional reform as a meritocratic and 'modernising' issue. Of course any serious attempt to modernise the ancient constitution would need at least to confront the monarchy issue – to reform it if not abolish it – and not one of these politicians were prepared for that. Perhaps it was ultimately a question of power. Perhaps they all believed that the Queen and the royal family, in Tony Blair's intriguing words, 'still have the power to keep us in our place'.[16]

BOTTLING EUROPE

Having saved the Queen and the essentials of the old constitutional order, Blair then faced the daunting question of Europe. It was his chance to be a real moderniser, a true radical, to settle the big question about the country's future. Could he be the prime minister who, as the commentator Hugo Young observed, 'took the opportunity to reposition the national mind'.[17] And finally to lay to rest the lingering imperial legacy? Would he be the prime minister who could look Dean Ascherson in the face and answer clearly that the country had 'found a role'.

Tony Blair had come into office in 1997 pledging a European future for the country. His promise of a referendum on Britain joining the euro-zone was not initially seen as a ploy to push the issue 'into the long grass' but rather as an earnest of genuine intentions. Yet once he had decided he would not hold an immediate referendum, and the polls continued to show a high level of public opposition, euro-zone entry went onto the back-burner, never truly to return. It was soon quite clear that Blair's premiership was not going to usher in any radical change in Britain's foreign-policy alignment. There would be no further British integration in Europe, nor any downgrading of the 'special relationship'.

Only days after Blair had arrived in Downing Street the new, young and eager British prime minister hosted a visit to Britain by none other than the president of the USA, William Jefferson Clinton. Blair had probably already decided that Britain was not going to join the euro-zone any time soon, and that the transatlantic status quo would therefore be preserved. And he announced at the joint press conference with Clinton that he and the president agreed that 'Britain does not need to choose between being strong in Europe or being close to the United States of America.'[18]

Blair had forged a strong relationship with Clinton and the American Democrats soon after becoming leader of the Labour Party in 1994. He had worked on the 'third way' proposals which had originated across the Atlantic in Clinton's Democratic Leadership Council and he authored a Fabian pamphlet 'The third way: new politics for the new century,' published in 1998. The 'third way' formed a bond between the two men, and Clinton became Blair's role model. Blair admired Clinton's 'triangulation' electoral strategy but also Clinton's political persona – the laid-back charm and the engaging lightness of touch with few rough edges or discordant ideas. In Blair's premiership style there was also a clearly discernible attempt to mimic the public-relations approach of the Clinton presidency: from the regular 'presidential' Downing Street press conferences (equipped with 'presidential' podium and red carpet) to – an idea that didn't fly – an aircraft called 'Blair One'.

Blair's close relations with Clinton became even closer when Clinton, after some hesitation, decided to enter the European arena with military force during the Kosovo crisis in 1999. Blair had taken the lead in the political planning of NATO's Kosovo intervention and the air war over Serbia and in getting the USA involved. For Blair, the successful outcome in Kosovo and Serbia proved the value of both American involvement in Europe and the policy of intervention. Indeed the prime minister went to Chicago in late April 1999 to deliver a landmark speech about the merits of 'liberal interventionism'. Kosovo had served to strengthen considerably Blair's Atlanticist and NATO instincts (and somewhat weakened his pro-European ardour).

By the very late 1990s, at the same time as Blair's relationship with Washington was growing ever closer, it was becoming clear that Britain's economy had been reviving during the last years of the Major premiership, and that when Major handed over to Blair in May 1997 he gifted him what amounted to a relatively strong economy. And, slowly but surely, a new narrative began to be constructed by the New Labour public-relations team. It was a theme that built on the earlier ideas of 'national recovery' developed during the Thatcher/ Major era before the humiliating events of September 1992; and it was purpose-built for New Labour's pitch in the next election. The message was simple and typically grandiose: not only was Britain's economy thriving, but so successful was Britain that it could set an example to Europe, even to the world.

In what was to become a central theme of the Blair era, prime minister Blair and his team, in speeches and briefings, began to suggest that the continent needed to learn from us – from the 'Anglo-Saxon' economies – and not the other way round. He and other Labour ministers spoke regularly of Britain 'leading in Europe' and would regularly point the way forward to the laggardly continentals. The assumed superiority of 'Anglo-Saxon' economics over continental 'Rhenish' capitalism was also the constant refrain from Bill Clinton's Washington, most specifically the office of treasury secretary Robert Rubin.

Blair continued to favour Britain's joining the euro-zone when the terms were right, but his new approach – the idea that the British needed to teach the continentals about the merits of 'Anglo-Saxon economics' – was bound to annoy some continental leaders. It would also subtly undermine the pro-European campaign at home. Blair argued to his 'Britain in Europe' supporters that the message of 'Britain leading and guiding Europe' would help gather support among the British for the European project. Yet with Britain doing 'so well' and the continent 'so badly' the question became: why bother joining a failing outfit?

This new hubristic and 'teachy' New Labour nationalism was to meld rather well with the 'ideology' of Britain's new power elite in the tabloid media. For some time, just like New Labour, the tabloids had been able to combine two contradictory messages: on the one hand an overt 'British is best' nationalism, on the other geopolitical subordination to foreigners in Washington and Wall Street. There were no press campaigns by the 'patriotic' press against the 'special relationship'; no systematic questioning of the unequal closeness of the American and British leaderships; and no Washington bogeymen to equal the Brussels Eurocrats. Indeed, this great contradiction was exemplified by the lives of the leading media moguls themselves. For, intriguingly, while their papers pumped out patriotic messages – 'proud to be British', 'sovereignty under threat from foreigners' – these same media moguls were living and working for much of their lives in foreign lands, in New York (Rupert Murdoch), in Toronto (Conrad Black) and in Paris (Lord Rothermere). And the leading voice of British patriotism, Rupert Murdoch, was an American citizen.

Although the main press moguls supported Blair's close relationship with the USA (with particular intensity during the 2003 invasion of Iraq),

Blair would be on the receiving end of tabloid invective whenever it looked as though he might be preparing a pro-European initiative – whether on the euro-zone or the constitutional treaty. In the summer of 1998, following a European summit in Cardiff, the BBC reported that Blair was all set to join the euro-zone immediately following the next general election. The *Sun* immediately responded with a headline describing Blair as 'The most dangerous man in Britain', an intervention that was treated in other media outlets like a major political event. There followed much speculation about whether Blair would secure the support of the *Sun* at the next election. In the event, Blair was to make no pledge about euro-zone entry, and the *Sun* duly supported him in the election of 2001.

In early 2004 Blair began to talk positively about the new European constitution emerging out of the constitutional convention chaired by ex-French president Valéry Giscard D'Estaing. His position was that Britain should ratify the constitution through a parliamentary vote. In almost an exact replay of earlier big European decisions, Blair, threatened by Murdoch, backed down. The *Guardian*'s political correspondent Nicholas Watt reported that 'to the delight of the Tories and Rupert Murdoch, who recently threatened to withdraw support if Downing Street refused to change tack, the prime minister will declare that the "weather has changed".'[19] Having opposed a referendum, Blair now supported holding one. One pro-European Tory insider said that 'agreeing to a referendum was like handing the decision over to Rupert Murdoch.' The *Sun* supported Blair in his third general election quest a year later.

'ONLY TONY BLAIR CAN WIN A REFERENDUM'

Yet, Blair, when on form, was a far better advocate for Europe than the Tory pro-Europeans. When he bothered to campaign for Europe he adopted a more modern, relevant approach than the establishment Tories. He sometimes gave glimpses of what his leadership of a referendum campaign might actually look like should a vote ever be scheduled. It would have been led by Downing Street and Tony Blair personally, and backed by a full New Labour PR operation – with simple, easy arguments put in a straightforward manner to appeal to 'middle England', and with the 'no' campaign opponents being painted as either extremists or stuck in the past.

Indeed, almost all pro-Europeans were keen for Tony Blair's entry into the referendum ring as their champion. Blair had positioned New

Labour as a pro-euro party from the moment he became Labour leader in 1995. And immediately upon becoming prime minister he changed Major's 'wait and see' policy on the euro to one in which the country would 'prepare and decide'. For the whole period of his premiership euro entry remained a publicly proclaimed aim of his government. Even at the height of his geopolitical disputes with President Jacques Chirac and Chancellor Gerhardt Schroeder over European relations with America, he would always argue for it as a goal and would always be prepared to state that 'Europe is our Destiny.' And when the proposed European constitution took precedence over the euro as an issue, he supported joining up, and even proclaimed that he would lead the fight for a 'yes' vote in the coming referendum.

But although the seeming champion of European integration he would never actually appear in the referendum ring – and for a simple reason: because he could not guarantee to himself that a pro-European referendum could ever be won. He believed that the prolonged and one-sided Murdoch press propaganda had made up minds.

A decisive moment in the history of contemporary Britain's foreign policy took place in the late spring of 1997 when Blair placed a pledge in his manifesto to hold a referendum on euro entry should Labour decide to join. This fateful decision to hold a referendum was to frustrate pro-Europeans for the rest of Blair's time in Downing Street – for having once granted a referendum, he could hardly withdraw the idea, but nor could he risk holding a vote, for fear of losing. And at no time between 1997 and 2007, either in the euro or the constitution debate, could Blair guarantee a 'yes' vote. (Ironically, this original decision in 1997 had been a naked political manoeuvre considered essential in order to rob John Major of the chance to wrap himself in the union flag in the coming election; but as it turned out Blair's majority in 1997 was never under threat.)

Tony Blair came very near to calling a referendum just after the 1997 general election, and again just after the 2001 general election. But on both occasions he thought better of it, knowing that a 'yes' vote could not be guaranteed. By insisting on a referendum back in 1997 he had tied his hands. And with every passing year since Blair came into office public opinion inched ever further against entry. In order to win a referendum Blair would not only have to overcome existing Euroscepticism but also a ferocious campaign from the increasingly confident anti-European tabloids, who in any general-election campaign would splash on their xenophobic warpaint.

THE LAST CHANCE

With Tony Blair immobilised over Europe could the pro-European Tories have made a difference? Could they have joined with New Labour to end Britain's isolation from Europe? They did have an opening after 2001. In the general election of 2001 Eurosceptic Tory leader William Hague based his whole campaign on his anti-euro views being an election winner, and went round the country holding up a pound coin and pledging to 'save the pound'. Consequently his defeat was also a big defeat for the Eurosceptics.

The Liberal Democrats had done well in the election, gathering a crop of seats unprecedented in post-war times, and were in a mood to broaden their base in a deal with Kenneth Clarke that he should raise the European issue and set up his own backbench group of pro-euro Tory MPs (in a kind of reverse repeat of the Redwood grouping during Major's government). Two Tory MEPs, John Stevens and Brendan Donnelly, had taken the courageous step of breaking with their party and setting up a pro-euro Tory Party list of candidates for the European elections in the summer of 1999 – and by 2001 they were a ready-made political apparatus for Clarke to join. Yet Clarke refused Stevens's insistent blandishments, arguing that he would continue the fight from within the Tory Party.

After the general election of 2001, with Blair becoming unpopular and Iain Duncan-Smith not catching on with the public as Tory leader, a Clarke tie-up with Liberal Democrats could have had a good chance of holding the balance in the election of 2005. It could have been expected to do somewhat better than did the Liberal Democrats alone, and might well have denied Blair his overall majority, or even reduced the Tories, led by Michael Howard, to third place. In the event, Clarke stayed loyal to his party and served under its new leader, David Cameron.

15 BLAIR AT THE MILLENNIUM DOME: 'SIMPLY THE BEST'

On the stroke of midnight at the turn of the millennium, at the Dome in Greenwich, Tony Blair was with the Queen. They were holding hands and singing 'Auld Lang Syne' – him more fully than her – as they welcomed in the new century. He was only two-and-a-half years into his administration but he had already taken the two fateful decisions which both symbolised and determined the course of the country well into the twenty-first century. He had saved the Queen, and the old constitutional order; and he had put off taking the country into the euro-zone. These two decisions meant that Britain was to stay on its previous course as a country. Under New Labour there would be no radical change of direction. The country would continue the Thatcherite path. At home this would mean tolerating growing inequality – as Britain played host to an emerging mega- and super-rich class while seeing its middle class fragment. It would also mean continuing with the grand delusion of its elites – the search for a 'global role' fit for its former imperial status. New Labour had rejected leading an adjustment to a more modest (and realistic) European role for the country. This continued quest for a 'global role' would, over the next seven years of his premiership, impel Tony Blair towards immersing the country deeper and deeper into global finance (through the banks of the Wall Street-led City of London). And it would also lead the country, incredibly as it would have seemed at the Dome that early January morning, to invading a Middle Eastern nation that did not threaten it.

For the Queen, rather awkwardly singing along that night, she may well have reflected on how Blair's search for a 'global role' rather suited her. She was, after all, the head of a Commonwealth of Nations, a position which she took extremely seriously, which too tight an integration into continental Europe would make completely redundant. And she might well have been pleased with Blair on one other count: New Labour's tolerance for inequality would mean that there would be no serious threat to the super-rich and to inherited privilege.

Indeed the Queen could reflect on what indeed was a great victory. The monarchy was now relatively secure (after the frights of the 1990s). And it was becoming apparent that the Queen had survived the long royal crisis of the 1990s, including the death of Diana, without having made any real concessions. She, and her heirs, still possessed the monopoly on becoming head of state. The prerogative powers of her office were still intact. Her finances were still flowing nicely. The civil list was somewhat restrictive and should be replaced by a percentage of the income from the Crown Estates; but the tax situation of the family had been secured by an agreement with the government facilitated by the former prime minister John Major. Crucially, the monarch remained free from inheritance tax when she passed on her personal wealth to her heir – a tax that would have broken up royal wealth. She was still to be treated differently from all other citizens as she would remain above the law on taxation and continue to be exempt from certain other laws like the Freedom of Information Act or the Equalities Act.

What is more, the new century would still see Britain, alone among Western countries, possessing an established church with the monarch as its head. The Archbishop of Canterbury would still anoint the Queen's successor, meaning that the next monarch would still derive his legitimacy from God, not from parliament or people. The bishops of the Church of England would still sit in the unelected upper chamber. Thus Britain would not be joining the rest of the Western world in formally separating church and state. Nor would Britain be joining the rest of the Western world by creating a written constitution.

After all the talk and agitation for reform, the old order of a constitution was still more than recognisable. The unelected House of Lords was still there. The Privy Council remained untouched. As did the royal prerogative powers. Importantly, oaths of loyalty (to the monarch) were still to be administered to virtually every public official – from judges to members of the armed forces to MPs. And parliament, though it could change things if it wanted, would still bar itself from discussing questions relating to members of the royal family.

The monarchy as the 'fount of all honour' and the honours system would remain – including, in the new millennium, honours derived from the middle ages and imperial times: grand titles such as 'Baron' and 'Baroness', 'Lord this' and 'Lord that', and 'Knights' – though no longer in armour plating and astride horses. And, more importantly for the Queen, the monarch would still possess the right, personally, to appoint a whole raft of funny-sounding 'Garters' – leading figures in the state who would be awarded 'the Order of the Garter' by the Queen herself. It was important to the Queen because she could, by bestowing this award on whoever she wanted, show her pleasure and displeasure. (Intriguingly, at the time of writing neither Tony Blair nor Gordon Brown had been so honoured).

With all these roles and powers intact it would seem that Elizabeth's legacy to her family and country would remain that of a largely unreconstructed monarchy – and unreconstructed constitution. At the height of the crisis the family had been forced under the pressure of events to set up 'the Way Ahead Group', which looked at some radical ideas for slimming down and modernising the institution, but there was now no more need of that.

And there was a social victory here as well. As a countrywoman and landowner the Queen would have been very pleased that Britain had seen off the urban threat – from those people who wanted to break up the great landed estates. The structure of land ownership in the country, after centuries of urbanisation, democracy, Thatcherite suburbanisation and radical reform, was still, from the viewpoint of the landed wealthy, very satisfactory: the UK covers 60 million acres, and two-thirds of it is owned by 0.3 per cent of the population, amounting to 158,000 families, (twenty-four million families live on three million acres). And the social power of this unique class was still strong – exhibited in the strange continuing attraction for traditional social forms and ritual from the constant revivals of the 'upstairs- downstairs' life of England during the empire (of which the soap *Downton Abbey* was, in 2011, the latest) to the still much-sought-after 'social season' at Ascot and Henley and the like. 'Theme-park Britain' (the theme being the imperial past), rather than being an embarrassment, was encouraged.[1]

More generally, rich, very rich, super-rich and mega-rich people were still more than tolerated. Indeed the country, London in particular, hosted the super-rich of the world, with few questions asked about the source of their money. Under every government since Thatcher, and particularly so under New Labour, the super-rich and mega-rich were welcomed. Britain had become their playground. In this sense Britain's head of state and her family were quite representative of the national mood.

It was all a remarkable achievement. However, this victory for the unreconstructed monarchy and constitution was not really the result of clever manoeuvring and manipulation by the Queen and court or deference on the part of New Labour. Rather, it was the result of the essentially unreconstructed nature of British society and social values. As was the case through the ages, the new social and political forces – in this case the Thatcherite/Blairite new middle class – were simply not quite strong enough to overthrow the old order, and thus had done a deal with it – the new had melded into the old.

Also boom times and ample credit had meant that average living standards, broadly speaking, rose. And rising aspirations could always, just, be fulfilled. Of course during Elizabeth's reign, particularly in its recent phase, inequality had certainly grown, but, until post-crash, never enough to matter.

There was, though, a price. The Queen needed Blair to keep the egalitarians at bay and sprinkle some needed progressive confetti on olde England. She allowed herself and the rich and influential people who surrounded and supported her – the English super-rich and old loyalists – to be enlisted in the New Labour project.

And there was one other price. The monarchy and the royal family, like many in the broader super-rich, had, in order to keep public support, to accept the role of celebrity. To keep their position the royals needed to entertain and to perform. No longer were they seen as a natural form of authority.

But apart from these costs the victory of the British monarchy and all it represented – primarily inherited riches, power and influence – over the forces of late-twentieth-century meritocracy was so comprehensive that only something as unlikely as an economic crash, the collapse of finance capitalism, would shake the foundations of this still deeply unequal British society and state. And that, of course, was unthinkable.

'

MORALE RESTORED: 'BRITAIN IS BACK'

Each generation in politics tells itself a story about its country. And for the generation of elite Britons at the turn of the millennium the story was one of renewed success. The ideology of New Labour (represented by Tony Blair) and the institution of monarchy (represented by the Queen) set the tone for the country. And there was nothing modest about it. 'Britain was back.' As an election poster had proclaimed, 'It's great to be great again.'

For many people, as they looked back at the time of the millennium, the narrative was clear: the country had hit rock bottom in the 1970s as industrial strife culminated in the 'winter of discontent'. But, like her or not, Margaret Thatcher and the 'Thatcher revolution' – of which Major and Blair and Brown were all part – had saved the country. She had beaten the Argentinians in the Falklands War, she had handbagged Jacques Delors on the EU budget and put the Europeans in their place, and she had slayed the 'enemy within', the disruptive trade unions, by winning the fight with Arthur Scargill's NUM.

It was a story which the American media could not resist – as *Time* magazine put it, the first woman prime minister fighting for the 'soul of Britain', and winning, had played a transformative role in the country's history. And it was a story retold by Tony Blair himself. He proclaimed himself a supporter of Thatcher's reforms and what he called her 'revolutionary' attack on trade-union privileges, and argued that 'she had the character, leadership and intelligence to make it happen.'[2]

By 2000 Blair was also beginning to argue that the British economy was no longer 'the sick man of Europe' – indeed that it was healthy and vigorous, 'a leader' again in Europe. It was a theme that was helped forward by the problems confronting the erstwhile 'leader', Germany, during its difficult early years of reunification (when West Germany added, overnight, almost 18 million people from the desultory, unproductive eastern states). And as unemployment on the continent rose during the recession, and remained relatively high, the British, whose Thatcherite 'hire and fire' system allowed the creation of large numbers of low-paid jobs, began to look better by comparison. British economic growth rates also began to look healthier than on the continent, where orthodox Bundesbank, and then euro-zone, policies were refusing to go for growth as a priority. And as the rise of China introduced low inflation into the global economy Britain was able to sustain growth levels by low interest rates, which allowed massively increasing private debt levels that kept consumption, and growth, up.

There was an alternative narrative, of course. Critics argued that the Thatcher/Major years had witnessed the inestimable good luck of North Sea oil but had wasted the revenues from this precious resource, and that instead of investing to create a balanced economy the British political class had recklessly gone for broke in deregulating financial services in the City of London. And even during the celebration of the millennium there were voices suggesting that rather than celebrating 'greatness' the British needed to understand their true position. A former Archbishop of

Canterbury put the case. 'We're in a very big world,' he said 'and we're now very lonely…we have lost nearly all our navy and air force and so on…We're a pretty ordinary little nation and yet we don't realise it.'[3]

So whatever Margaret Thatcher and her successors had actually accomplished, they had served one, certain, role: they had vastly improved the morale of the British.

SIMPLY THE BEST: A SUPERIOR, EXCEPTIONAL PEOPLE

For many of Britain's leaders in the mid- to late 1990s – both Conservative and Labour – there was no longer any urgency in the 'Britain in Europe' debate. A consensus was growing that the Thatcher 'revolution' had made the country strong enough and important enough to resume a 'global role' after the traumas of the 1970s.

In December 1994 the then prime minister, no less, could argue in a speech to Conservative women – which one columnist said was difficult to believe unless 'you heard it with your own ears' – that 'The United Kingdom – the greatest cradle of culture and academic and scientific and political achievement in modern times – that's not some trifle to be lightly set at risk…it is the highest cause this party knows – and we will defend it with every fibre of our being.'[4] John Major was echoing Thatcher, who had made restoring British 'greatness' a key theme of her premiership. And even his own foreign secretary, Douglas Hurd, a man from the non-flag-waving wing of the party, was reported as accepting, indeed virtually recommending, the self-important idea of the country as 'punching above its weight' in world affairs. He could argue in 1993 to assembled luminaries at Chatham House in London that 'NATO is one of the principal props which have allowed Britain to punch above its weight.'[5]

This new overblown prideful mentality did not come out of thin air. It drew upon a vein of thinking and belief that had, in fact, never been expunged. For no matter the loss of empire and comparative economic decline, the morale boost of the Falklands War and the modest 1980s and 1990s economic resurgence was all that Britain's leaders needed to justify yet another burst of *braggadocio* nationalism. And they could draw on the long history of a belief in greatness, and upon long-held ideas and images that still resonated.

William Shakespeare could write about this 'sceptr'd isle set in a silver sea' that was 'the envy of less fortunate lands'. And in the late Middle

Ages when England seemed to win almost every battle it entered against a much larger military force (at Crécy they were outnumbered by three to one, at Poitiers by five to one) then 'perhaps for the first time, though certainly not for the last, the English began to suspect that God was an Englishman.' And Bishop Aylmer declared him to be so as early as 1558.[6] Oliver Cromwell believed, with most parliamentarians, that the English were a 'chosen people'. And in the nineteenth century Charles Dickens's Mr Podsnap spoke for many when he opined that 'this island was blest, sir...to the direct exclusion of such other countries as – as there may happen to be.'[7]

Writing as late as the mid-1980s the historian Geoffrey Elton could talk of two English convictions having 'lasting currency': 'that every other realm groaned under despots and that everywhere else the peasantry had to live on mere vegetables, while in England Kings governed with the active consent of their subjects and people ate good red meat'.[8]

The conceit of exceptionalism was never a particularly partisan issue – for not only Tory nationalists but the country's late-twentieth-century radical, liberal and socialist thinkers also mined its rich seams. The idea of England as the special home of liberty and freedom, and English history as the unique struggle against arbitrary rule, attracted many on the liberal left. As Elton suggested, many of them believed that even the 'universal' rights of man were really English rights – 'the rights not of Man but of English men and women'.[9] The leading British socialist of the post-Second World War era, Michael Foot, whose heroes were Lord Byron and William Wordsworth (as well as Tom Paine and William Hazlitt), tended to buy into this idea of England as special. Foot, who made his political name as a firebrand socialist journalist working for the arch-imperialist press baron Lord Beaverbrook, possessed more than a touch of 'little Englander' nationalism. And towards the end of his long political career he formed a kind of bipartisan 'little Englander' intellectual alliance with Enoch Powell in defence of parliamentary power. But in manfully trying to rescue English history from its Tory concentration on the 'kings and queens approach' he would often over-romanticise the parliamentary tradition. In 2006 Foot, on the home page of his website, 'Michael Foot at 90', displayed a quote from Byron that started, 'England. With all thy faults I love thee still.'

This idea of a superior, exceptional, country served to foster the continuing thread of belief – held widely throughout the country, by left, right and centre – that the English were, are and always will be a separate people – forever an island. The physical separation of an island people from the continent was always a powerful factor separating the Germanic tribes in England from those in the rest of northern Europe. And the physical island, and the English Channel, have played a large role in forging identity ever since. In the latter half of the twentieth century the revolution in travel, particularly the jet aircraft, and then more powerfully still the Channel Tunnel, eroded this sense of separation. But for the post-war and post-Cold War generations that now travel to the continent, or live there, the experience of war, and memories of the images of the Dunkirk evacuation, still resonate, and for the moment still balance off the newer sense of Europe.

But more than the idea of an 'island race', it is the English language that has remained the greatest cause of separation – particularly from the near neighbours on the continent. Indeed the story of the development of the English language – and its battle with French and Latin after the Norman conquest – is a key which may well even begin to unlock the mystery of English identity. In the late fourteenth century English was adopted as the official language of government by Henry V and then the great storyteller-poet of the English language Geoffrey Chaucer made his own contribution to the growing sense of Englishness.

The communications revolution in printing and publishing (led by William Caxton) which took hold in the fifteenth century established the hegemony of English among the English and within England; and Caxton chose English (in fact London-English – the brand of English prevalent in London – there being several versions of English) as his publishing language. When his chronicles appeared English was transformed from a primitive form of communication into the language of a new learning, a process helped forward too by the publication and wide dissemination in 1604 of the King James Bible – published in English! And some hundred and fifty years later, by the time of the publication of Dr Johnson's seminal English Dictionary (1755), the English language was fast becoming not only a major language but the primary cultural agency for the spread of English manners and ideas – of Englishness itself. (Of course this emergence of an increasingly popular and standardised English was crucial to popular consciousness of being English. Yet even while this standardised English was destroying French and Latin in Britain it remained seriously fragmented by dialect, a diversity which, intriguingly, has lasted well into the television age of the late twentieth-century.)

All nationalism is about separateness, and this particular history of separateness – of an 'island people' separated from others by geography, by the sea and by language – remains very strong in contemporary English writing, analysis and polemics right up to the present day. Churchill himself talked of 'the island race' and evocatively of 'the island story', and issued the famed declaration that 'if Britain must choose between Europe and the open sea she must always choose the open sea.' In the 1970s the country's most prolific author and one of its leading nationalists and Eurosceptics, Paul Johnson, wrote about 'the offshore islanders' in a book of the same title.[10]

ENDURING HUBRIS

Yet a fascinating question remains: why has such a strong strain of British nationalism, immodest nationalism, and what amounted to a comparatively ripe form of the sentiment, endured well into the late twentieth century, and into the twenty-first? One explanation lies in the formative years of the Thatcher generation of political leaders. After all, Thatcher herself, born in October 1925, was a teenager during the Second World War and an ambitious young politician in the 1950s. This was a time still dominated by empire. The English ruling classes only gave up on their empire after the war, and continued to be beguiled by the enterprise long after the sun had set upon it. And in consequence, the national culture of Englishness was to exhibit a decidedly imperial character well into the late twentieth century. Margaret Thatcher might well have been among the schoolchildren of the late 1930s who were being told 'We're all subjects and partakers in the great design, the British empire...[a] job assigned to it by God.'[11] And in the mid-1950s secondary schoolchildren throughout the country were still assembling for something called 'Empire Day' to be told that they were the inheritors of a world power.

And long after the formal demise of empire, the imperial sensibility still lingered – and fed the idea of a 'world role'. Aphorisms of empire – Churchill's comment about the open sea, 'Britain is a trading nation or it is nothing', 'Trade follows the flag' – continued to dominate political debate. Churchill, an avowed supporter of empire, even during his post-war premiership, put a stop to Labour's process of decolonisation, and further colonial independence had to wait until Harold Macmillan became prime minister. Although Churchill was the last imperialist prime minister, Anthony Eden acted like one, and his invasion of Egypt in 1956 possessed all the hallmarks of the imperial mentality. And as late as 1962 the Labour opposition leader Hugh Gaitskell was evoking not only 'a thousand years of history' but memories of the military support from the dominions at 'Vimy Ridge' and 'Gallipoli' in the First World War as part of his anti-EEC campaign.[12]

With the afterglow of empire still a source of warmth, the new Queen and her court – both inside and outside parliament – continued to play a role that fostered the imperial illusion. And the immediate post-imperial generation of British political leaders – Edward Heath, Harold Wilson and James Callaghan – all still took an oath of allegiance to the Queen. Later post-imperial prime ministers all grew up under the influence of the post-war global ethos and agenda set at the Queen's coronation, and by the 'new Elizabethan age'. At the time of the coronation Margaret Thatcher was 28 and John Major was an impressionable ten years of age.

This image of Britain as a global power was so ingrained that even the humiliation of the Suez affair in 1956 had only a marginal effect on thinking. Lord Franks reflected a general view of the Westminster official class when, following Suez, he asserted grandly that 'Britain is going to continue to be what she has always been, a Great Power.'[13] And there was something in this prediction: for politically Britain still counted in the world as one of 'magic circle' of Western nations – she had a permanent seat on the UN Security Council, a privilege denied to Germany, Japan and China, and for a while was one of 'the big three'. Even as late as the late 1950s Harold Macmillan could, just about, get away with being considered a world leader, and through the Commonwealth of Nations the UK political elite (and particularly the Queen) could still present themselves as leaders of a meaningful multinational alliance of states.

Even the emergence of the USA as a world power that was replacing Britain had a paradoxical rub-off effect upon this continuing imperial mentality, particularly among the somewhat defensive English upper classes. The English elite could legitimately claim pride of authorship of the institutions of the powerful new superpower. And English, not French or German or Spanish, was its language. In the immediate post-war period, during American world supremacy, the levers of power and culture in the USA were still largely controlled by Anglophile white Anglo-Saxon Protestants. Britain could piggy-back and pretend she was a partner in the growing American empire. Even as the country took the decision to withdraw from 'east of Suez' Harold Wilson could still say, in one of the most deluded and grandiose statements of the whole post-war era, 'Britain's frontiers are on the Himalayas.' Coming from such a personally modest man, this extraordinary and bombastic perspective shows the depth of belief within the broader political class.

One explanation for this hold of the imperial mindset on the late-twentieth-century British leadership class was, of course, the sustaining effects of the two world wars. Defeat in war could have expunged the imperial memory. But Britain went through no such catharsis. In the twentieth century Britain's grievous losses in the two wars – both in human and material resources – was in fact a defeat. But no sense of defeat took hold. Ernest Bevin, the first foreign secretary to take office in the utterly crucial period following the devastating war, exemplified this mindset. His sympathetic biographer Alan Bullock put it clearly: 'he continued to identify Britain's national interests with the maintenance of the world role which the UK no longer had the resources to sustain.'[14]

Sixty years later the exact same assessment of Britain's role in the world – to the word – could have been made by Tony Blair. He, like Bevin, saw only one way to secure this 'world role' – and that was as a junior partner to the USA. And in the latter half of his premiership America, and all that it stood for, was to become his 'fatal attraction'.

16 BLAIR'S 'FATAL ATTRACTION'

Tony Blair won the 2001 general election with almost as big a majority as he secured in 1997. Britain, like the West generally, had experienced boom times and New Labour was riding a wave of national good feeling. It seemed as though New Labour had found the magic formula for successful politics in the modern era. Blair had modelled himself on Bill Clinton both as a policy-maker – Clinton was the inspiration behind Blair's 'third way' thinking – and as a politician-celebrity. And Clinton had charmed Blair. The American seemingly knew the way to Blair's heart: he saw the Englishman's need to 'punch above his weight' and his traditional post-imperial need for power and global reach. (He had invited Blair onto Air Force One and Blair had reportedly been much taken with its atmosphere of power.)

BLAIR, 9/11 AND IRAQ

As time went on Blair simply fell in love with American power, and with the trappings of its imperial presidency. And, like Thatcher before him, he came to see the world through American eyes. America was the future: and the future was of a globalised world dominated not just by American economic leadership and military power but also by American liberal values. Blair's view of the world was classic Fukuyama – a future predicted a decade earlier just after the fall of communism by Francis Fukuyama in his famous book *The End of History*.[1] Fukuyama has subsequently changed his mind, virtually denouncing his own earlier analysis, but the British prime minister remained a true believer.

Blair's strengthening worldview was to be reinforced after 9/11 when the USA decided to develop a forward military posture and invade both Afghanistan and Iraq. Not only was American-led economic globalisation going to change the world, but also America was going to police this world through military power and the huge Pentagon budget. Wall Street and Washington (finance, congress and people) were finally as one.

Blair was determined to get in on this act, as were large sections of British elite opinion – in politics, journalism and business. New Labour reflected as well a deep British need to be at the centre of events. So much so that a majority of MPs in this major left-of-centre party would end up shocking, indeed startling, many of their supporters by not just supporting, but allowing Britain to take part in, the invasion of an Arab country that did not threaten it.

THE BRITISH ELITES AND IRAQ

On the morning of 11 September 2001, just as the planes were about to explode into the twin towers of the World Trade Center, Britain's prime minister, Tony Blair, was in the southern English seaside town of Brighton preparing to address the TUC. He was about to deliver a watershed speech which would open the campaign for Britain's joining the euro-zone. It was to be a campaign that would finally resolve the country's long, awkward relationship with Europe and help Britain to fulfill what Blair had called her 'destiny' in Europe.

But just before Blair set off from his hotel to the conference centre, the chairman, Bill Morris, announced the news from New York and that Blair might be delayed. In the event, Blair cancelled his speech, returned to London, appeared on television to announce that Britain would stand 'shoulder to shoulder' with the Americans; and, fatefully, also put Britain's European campaign on hold.

It was a campaign that was not to be revived – for the atrocity in New York profoundly altered New Labour's whole approach to Britain's future role in the world. In Washington the reaction to 9/11 allowed a stalled Bush administration to develop a new, and aggressive, foreign policy. The influential but previously contained neo-conservatives clustered around the American Enterprise Institute and the Pentagon were ready to seize their moment. The 'Statement of Principles' of the Project for a New American Century (signed by Dick Cheney, Donald

Rumsfeld, Paul Wolfowitz, Elliot Abrams, Norman Podhoretz and others in 1997) was dusted off, and for a time became the handbook of President Bush himself. It was highly critical of Clinton's foreign policy, sought a new defence build-up, and called for a new global vision based upon 'military strength and moral clarity'. This political takeover of the US government led to an aggressive unilateralism – including an extraordinary bid for global supremacy which included the invasion of Iraq, despite the absence of a threat to the USA.

This raw assertion of US power had real implications for Britain, for it gave the prime minister a subordinate but special role in which Downing Street as junior partner would be a global advocate of US policy. It was a role perfectly suited to Tony Blair and to many in the British intelligence services and military. After a half century of global decline – with America now off-balance and seeking a sidekick – here was a rare and real chance to place Britain at something near the centre of world events. And Blair took it.

For some time before 9/11 the prime minister had seen himself as a global, rather than European, player – a posture made more credible when Britain stood alongside the Americans rather than as one of many among the Europeans. The Kosovo crisis had been a turning point for Blair. Here were America and NATO, without a UN mandate, laying down the rules for the post-Cold War world. And he went even further, seeing himself as a remaker of the world in tandem with Washington. In a strange, somewhat discordant, speech in Chicago in April 1999, during the air war over Kosovo, he went so far as to outline a new international doctrine. He declared that 'Bismark had been wrong' to say that 'the Balkans was not worth the bones of a single Pomeranian Grenadier'; he singled out Slobodan Milosovic and Saddam Hussein as 'dangerous men'; and, more importantly, he attempted to overthrow the basic UN doctrine of 'non-interference' in other countries' affairs in favour of a new idea of 'regime change'. It amounted to a call for a new world order in which Western intervention and 'regime change', on Western terms and for Western reasons, was now acceptable.[2] For Blair, America (with Britain at her side) would lead the charge in what was nothing less than a rationale for a new updated liberal – or neo-liberal – imperialism. And for Britain's political and financial elite this was a perfect new opportunity to play on the world stage, and fulfill the long-term goal of maintaining a 'global role' for the UK. With 9/11 as its galvanising force, this new Western assertiveness ended in the invasion of Iraq.

Only days after 9/11, with the wind in his sails, Blair returned to this theme at the 2001 Labour Party conference, when he displayed a relish for the coming business of, in his own words, 're-ordering the world'.[3] The formula – which was being worked up in Washington as Blair spoke – was clear: the mission would be couched in liberal tones – 'bringing democracy' – but Washington (with London in tow) was going to 're-order' the world on Western terms. And it was going to do so by a combination of Western military power (to be put on show in the invasion of Iraq) and the ongoing westernising process of globalisation.

On the ground in Britain, though, the public remained hostile to the prospect of an Iraqi invasion. At the time, and for years afterwards, the British public could simply not understand why Blair had sided with Bush and joined in the fateful 2003 invasion. It was, after all, a bizarre, slightly unreal, decision for a Labour prime minister to take. All the opinion polls showed decisive majorities against the invasion, an opposition made manifest by a massive march and rally in central London; the main European partners were against it, the intelligence was not clear-cut; the UN could not be squared. Yet in the face of all this Britain's left-of-centre progressive-minded premier went ahead and committed British troops to the American-led war.

Blair thus nailed his colours, and with them his legacy, to the mast of a conservative Christian evangelical Republican president. Former cabinet minister Chris Patten could write that 'history will judge Blair as a defender of Bush's agenda above Britain's.'[4] It was a coruscating verdict. Blair had taken the 'special relationship' to a new level.

INVASION: THE 'SPECIAL RELATIONSHIP' IN ACTION

By March of 2003 the whole British political class – Tony Blair and his cabinet, the majority of New Labour MPs, and the vast majority of Conservative MPs – took the fateful decision to sign up with George W. Bush and invade Iraq. And the British did more than just support the Americans in the UN, they also sent troops – the largest contingent after the USA. And following the invasion the British, for the first time since imperial days, took over the military occupation of Arab lands (in the south of the country around Basra). Indeed to the late-twentieth-century British mind the very idea of British troops occupying a heartland Arab nation after having toppled its government would have seemed an act of blatant imperialism, a return to inter-war mentalities, and wildly far-fetched.

The Iraq War was a 'defining moment' for Britain's relationship with the Arab world, but also for Britain's 'special relationship' with the USA. It was a rare and decisive either/or moment in the Anglo–American relationship. The Americans badly wanted British support, but were mainly interested in full-hearted diplomatic support in the run–up to war. At no time did they insist upon Britain's sending large numbers of troops. The American defence secretary Donald Rumsfeld had always had misgivings about the need for British – or any other – troops to support 'Operation Iraqi Freedom', and on the eve of war went as far as publicly stating that they were not needed.[5] Again on the eve of war, with Blair's continued premiership in some doubt, the president himself made a last-minute friendly offer to let him off the hook. Bush suggested that Britain need not send troops should it lead to the Blair government falling. Yet even given this opportunity, Blair, in an act of breath-taking eagerness to please, sent the troops anyway.

Britain had some clear choices before it in the run-up to war. It could have sided with France and Germany and stood aside – a course which would have put at risk the country's relations with Washington. But Washington would have tolerated – some in the Pentagon would have preferred – Britain simply supporting the USA politically and diplomatically without sending troops (as Harold Wilson did during the Vietnam War despite pressure by President Johnson to go further). The Americans would also have accepted a British decision to send only a very small, token, non-fighting force. That Blair decided to go the 'full Monty' of an invasion and occupying force showed his utter determination both to please Washington and to play a global role. From Downing Street's perspective, once the decision to support the USA politically had been taken, the damage to public opinion had been done. There was nothing to lose from sending significant numbers of troops, and much to gain in the scramble for reconstruction contracts in the occupation phase.

The spring invasion of Iraq in 2003 was the culmination of an extraordinary phase of Downing Street-directed British foreign policy in which the British prime minister and some of the higher echelons of the intelligence and military establishment not only took momentous decisions but also real risks with Britain's geopolitical position in Europe. By siding with invasion and occupation Blair took Britain into the potentially momentous 'clash of civilizations' as he alienated Britain from Arab and broader Islamic opinion, perhaps for generations. He also divided Europe by breaking with its two senior members, France and Germany. While these countries led the opposition to the war, Blair was joined by Spain's conservative prime minister José Maria Aznar and Italy's ultraconservative prime minister Silvio Berlusconi and the leaders of a host of eastern European candidate countries in supporting the Bush White House.

WHY?

In the months following Blair's fateful decision, large numbers of British people – both within and without the Westminster village – were asking themselves one question about their prime minister. Why did he do it? Why did Tony Blair take his country to war in Iraq when no apparent immediate British national interest was involved? Why did he put at risk his relationships with his fellow EU leaders? And why – a question asked after the revelations that Saddam had no usable weapons of mass destruction – was he prepared to deploy exaggerations and half-truths in order to do it?

Yet as the dust settled following the invasion the answers to these questions, although never stated, became progressively clear. It became obvious that from Blair's Downing Street's perspective, once Bush had made up his mind to go to war, the British prime minister – any British prime minister – had no alternative but to support him. In sum, Britain's 'special relationship' demanded it; when an American president goes to war, and asks for Britain's support, such support must automatically be given.

This time too it was automatically given, although this time there were new factors. There was a split in the Western camp. In all previous great global crises – during the Korean War, the Cuban missile crisis, the Vietnam War (when Western differences were kept low-profile), the first Gulf War and air war over Serbia – the West had been politically united. But over Iraq the major continental powers not only opposed Washington, they campaigned against her in the UN. Blair was forced to choose between America and Europe. But for Blair it was not a difficult or agonising choice. From Downing Street the Western geopolitical power correlation looked clear. Washington was still the stronger of the two Western contestants. Bush was adamant and committed, would go to war anyway. And although an intriguing (particularly so with Russia as an 'ally') new security core was developing between Germany and France, it was in its infancy.

Martin Kettle, a commentator with good connections to Downing Street, suggested that Blair supported the invasion, and post-war US policy in Iraq, for quite straightforward reasons – he argued bluntly that Blair believes that 'what happens in the US defines the limits of the possible for Britain.'[6] According to this Blairite thesis, it was simply 'impossible' not to support the USA.

It was difficult though to sell such a raw idea of subordination to the British public – so a more palatable posture was struck. It had been outlined decades before by Sir Pierson Dixon, Britain's UN ambassador at the time of the Suez affair. He had argued ruefully that 'if we cannot entirely change American policy, then we must, it seems to me, resign ourselves to a role as counselor and moderator.' And he added that 'It is difficult for us, after centuries of leading others, to resign ourselves to the position of allowing another and greater power to lead us.'[7] Half a century later, Blair might not have put it exactly that way; but Britain as America's 'counselor' and 'moderator' was a role he openly advocated as prime minister.

So as the tension rose in the run-up to invasion, the official British line became what the well-informed columnist and author Peter Riddell came to describe as a 'hug them close' strategy – the idea being that by 'hugging them close' Britain would secure greater influence with the Americans than by breaking with them.[8] Blair put out the word that his closeness to Washington was calculated: that in return for his support Bush was agreeing to support a revival of the stalled Middle East 'peace plan' which would secure a long-term Israeli–Palestinian agreement. Four years later, as Blair, again, lent his support to the USA in the Israeli–Lebanon–Hezbollah war he was still allowing it to be known that he was imminently set to get Washington's 'green light' for a new 'peace initiative'.

TONY BLAIR: AMERICAN NEO-CONSERVATIVE

Tony Blair's support for the USA in the Iraq War was simply the tip of an iceberg, a symptom of a much deeper commitment. For by the time of his second term as premier he had basically adopted the whole Bush-American worldview. So much so that, like Margaret Thatcher before him, he came to identify with the USA more than he did with Britain. On

18 September 2005 the British media was abuzz with details of an intriguing and revealing comment by Blair about the New Orleans hurricane tragedy – seen at the time as a turning point in the standing of President George W. Bush. The BBC reported that Blair had told Rupert Murdoch that BBC reporting of the New Orleans hurricane tragedy had been 'full of hate at America and gloating about our [sic] troubles'.[9] The use of 'our' was highly revealing. It revealed not just where the British prime minister's true affection, if not loyalty, may have lain, but also that he saw the Bush presidency and his premiership as conjoined, as one political unit with common friends and common enemies.

Blair's identification with the USA had, though, a considerable prime ministerial pedigree. Winston Churchill identified with America – after all he had an American mother. That identification was also in Margaret Thatcher, who had a close personal and ideological relationship with President Ronald Reagan. Yet the Americanisation of Tony Blair was less easy to understand. Blair had no similar blood or ideological ties. His ties were with the presidency: he was very close to both liberal-moderate Bill Clinton and conservative-cum-neo-conservative George W. Bush. It was his relationship with the Texan that was somewhat odd, and may reveal that Blair's love affair was, at root, all about power – the power and celebrity of the American presidency.

Yet over time the love affair with the presidency turned ideological. Having begun his premiership in 1997 ostensibly as a European social democrat – with an 'ideology' roughly similar to Gerhard Schroeder's SPD and slightly to the left of Clinton's 'third way' Democrats – he later morphed into a full, red-blooded American radical conservative. Blair, breathtakingly, signed on to each of the three components of Bush's brand of conservatism: global neo-liberal 'free-market' economics, global political rule from Washington, and Christian-based 'family values'. It was an ideological package that took him into an unlikely political stable – one populated by Wall Street, the Pentagon and the Christian right and in Europe by ultra-conservative Silvio Berlusconi and José Maria Aznar of Spain. Blair was the lone supposed European social democrat in such company.

Blair became the chief European advocate of the need to accept 'globalisation'. When used by politicians, 'accepting globalisation' was code for the need to accept a business-driven, cost-cutting agenda. To survive in the global economy – so ran the argument – nation states need to ensure that their costs, that is wages and taxes, are competitive. Labour markets should also be competitive – that is flexible enough to make it easy to 'hire and fire'. In the age of globalisation, if governments don't so oblige, then global capital will go elsewhere – principally to lower-cost China and India. In an article in *Newsweek* in 2006 Tony Blair pulled no punches: 'complaining about globalisation,' he said, 'is as pointless as trying to turn back the tide. Asian competition can't be shut out; it can only be beaten.'[10]

Since the end of the Cold War there had been a quantum leap in the power of mobile capital over state and labour, and neo-liberals argued that governments needed to yield to these 'realities'. Blair was in the forefront of such yielding – constantly arguing that the British people should welcome 'globalisation', not resist it, nor even attempt to shape it. All any government could do was to help the population adapt to the inevitable by helping them to compete – primarily by providing suitable skills and education – the origin of Blair's catch-phrase policy priority: 'Education, Education, Education'. Of course in this future low-tax regime governments would not be able to fund the future welfare state and thus the welfare systems needed 'reform' (with a bigger private sector).

Blair – just like the Wall Street economists who propounded this doctrine – was sustained in it by a sense of almost righteous inevitability. There was, they, and he, argued, 'no alternative' to this global capitalist dynamic. Those who went with the flow, like neo-liberal New Labour Britain – would be 'winners' – whereas the 'sclerotic' euro-zone economies would be 'losers'. It was an American message, but increasingly during the first few years of the twenty-first century an American conservative message (as some US liberals in the Democratic Party, worrying about out-sourcing jobs, began to flirt, and more, with protectionism). The message was clear: the West would need to 'accept' losing jobs in its manufacturing sector but would see its service sector grow to make up for the loss, and it was assumed that China and India would continue to demand Western services. And the message had a warning – that any attempt at trying to use trade or other policies to staunch the loss of jobs in the West was 'protectionist' and self-defeating. It was a message that New Labour, no matter its moral and intellectual roots, could sign up to.

The fact was that Tony Blair's government came to believe that Britain and the City of London were one and the same thing. Hywell Williams, one of Britain's most perceptive writers, put it starkly. 'The power of capital over New Labour, with its superstitious veneration of money, created Britain's most consistently business-friendly party,' he argued; and this business-friendly party, as it promoted 'globalisation', found that, for Britain 'all that is left is the power of the City – the true governor of Britain, with a world view of global markets that has ended British independence.'[11]

Blair's New Labour also adopted a key underpinning idea of American conservative economics – the notion that Western societies needed to live with growing gross inequality as a price worth paying for private capital formation. A tolerance for inequality – and for a growing class of super-rich and mega-rich people – had been a feature of several eras of American history, and particularly of what economist Paul Krugman has called the 'new gilded era' of the post-1980s world.[12] Such tolerance of gross inequality had not been present in Britain, certainly since 1945, and not really even during the premiership of Margaret Thatcher – when the stress was on creating a vibrant middle class.[13] But Blair broke with the British post-war consensus, and adopted a much more American approach. In a remark, unthinkable for any social democrat, Blair declared to interviewer Jeremy Paxman just before the 2001 general election that he simply did not worry about growing inequality, or about the growing class of the super- and mega-rich. 'It is not a burning ambition for me that David Beckham earns less money,' he revealed.

This key American conservative idea – that inequality does not matter, that social problems are not caused by social divides or even poverty, but rather by issues arising from 'family breakdown' – helped further the idea that the tax bill for welfare could thus safely be reduced. In the 1980s the American sociologist Charles Murray was hugely influential in this attempted divorce of economic inequalities from social problems, locating them instead in lack of family stability and personal inadequacies. And reportedly Rupert Murdoch's aide Irwin Stelzer played a role in introducing Charles Murray to Rupert Murdoch and thus to British opinion-formers and public through the *Sunday Times*.[14]

American conservatism won yet another battle in its takeover of New Labour when ideas about Christian 'faith-based solutions' began to appear in New Labour thinking. Throughout his premiership Blair was not bashful in proclaiming his Christian views, although he balked at responding fully to journalists who suggested that his relationship with Bush was based upon a shared Christian faith (he deflected questions about joining hands in White House prayer meetings). But he was less open about his growing Roman Catholicism (or his Catholic wife's influence on him); and the word from Downing Street was that he would make public any conversion to Catholicism only when he left office. In any event, although Blair's 'faith schools' schools programme chimed well with Bush's 'faith-based initiatives', they stood out awkwardly in secular Britain – particularly in secular New Labour (or for that matter in old or middle-aged Labour as well). Yet the New Labour prime minister continued to introduce them, and even appointed a member of Opus Dei to the sensitive post of education secretary.[15] Again, more intriguing perhaps than Blair's own American conservative belief system was the fact that it was tolerated by the bulk of Britain's Labour MPs.

BLAIR, MURDOCH AND BUSINESS

This embracing of American-style radical conservatism by Tony Blair was more than an act of true belief. It was also about hard-nosed domestic politics. For, as it happens, Blair's conservative agenda squared nicely with the worldview and global interests of the Australian-American media mogul Rupert Murdoch, owner of News International and the *Sun* newspaper. Blair decided very early on in his career as opposition leader that he needed, at the very least, to neutralise the *Sun*, which he believed had hurt Labour decisively in previous elections.

The power of the *Sun* was based upon its mass circulation. It outsold every other daily. It developed a clear and concise political message that, particularly following the Falklands conflict in 1982, associated Thatcherism with patriotism and national success and the left with the failed politics of national weakness, trade-union militancy and liberal 'softness' on crime. And its political journalism had a knack of articulating basic populist views and appealing to the often-hidden resentments of its relatively low-income and undereducated mass readership against the 'liberal elite' and its 'politically correct' attitudes.

News International became a major player in British politics (in foreign as well as domestic policy) during the crises of the 1980s as Margaret Thatcher won her battle with Britain's powerful trade unions. Initially Murdoch's empire was part of the broad anti-trade-union coalition; and it also developed a radical, and seemingly progressive, meritocratic edge which, under the influence of *Sunday Times* editor Andrew Neil, took as its targets traditionalist Britain – old-money aristocracy, the monarchy and royal family as well as the trade unions.

By the late 1980s it turned into a support system for the Conservative Party's campaign for a business-led economic and political culture under the banner of the 'free market'. It also began its systematic, high-volume opposition to the EEC and EU, and Britain's place in it. Murdoch's opposition to a European destiny for Britain had little in common with the chauvinism and nationalism exhibited in his papers, particularly the *Sun* (Murdoch, in fact, was an egalitarian Australian, and a cosmopolitan globe-trotter who was to marry as his third wife a young Chinese woman). Rather Murdoch's key concern was what he perceived as the anti-business culture of the EU and its highly regulated, high-tax welfare societies – a culture that he saw as hostile to his own media interests as well. His pro-business, anti-Europe values were bound sooner or later to draw Murdoch to the USA. Murdoch and conservative America were a love affair waiting to be consummated. During the 1990s Murdoch built up considerable media interests in North America and, centring his business there, he became an American citizen on 24 August 2003. The successful political journalism of the *Sun* (and Thatcherism) translated well to Bush's America. As Murdoch invested in newspapers and television (particularly the Fox News channel) the key tunes of Thatcherite pro-business patriotism laced with strong law and order played very well indeed. Fox News channel added to this 'Thatcherite' 'core' appeal the values and concerns of the American Christian right – the so-called three 'G's, 'God, Guns and Gays' – that had been missing from Murdoch's British operation.

Blair first met Murdoch in 1994 – privately, over dinner in the Belgravia restaurant Mosimann's. During this get-together Blair suggested that media ownership rules under Labour would not place Murdoch in a worse position than he was under Thatcher and Major. For his part Murdoch indicated that his newspapers were not 'wedded to the Tories'.[16] In July 1995 Blair, then the new leader of Her Majesty's opposition, boarded an aircraft and travelled 24 hours to a remote island off Australia, where he would attend a News Corporation management conference.[17] From this time on, Blair would continue to seek, and to get, Murdoch's support for his premiership. On 18 March 1997 the *Sun*, which had supported the Conservatives ever since Murdoch took over, announced, 'The *Sun* backs Labour' – incidentally on the very day that the Murdoch-funded neo-conservative magazine the *Weekly Standard* declared that US radical rightist Newt Gingrich was not right wing enough![18] Blair went on to win not only in 1997, but, with Murdoch's support, in 2001 and 2005 as well.

Murdoch's backing for Blair may help explain the latter's own transformation from European social democrat into American radical conservative. Irwin Stelzer was a key aide to Murdoch, an intellectual guru and advisor, and a major player in transatlantic Murdoch politics. He epitomised American radical conservatism and, like many Bush neo-conservatives, possesses an articulate and knowledgeable universalist bravura that gives him the gift of proclaiming – with great confidence – the right course for countries other than his own.[19] Stelzer met Blair on many occasions both before and after he became prime minister, and became Blair's advocate in the USA. He saw early on that the Labour leader shared many ideas in common with the American conservative right. 'I know Tony Blair...,' he once said, 'Blair is one of Thatcher's children. I think he knows it.' And he saw Blair's Christian beliefs as potentially linking him – beyond Clinton and the American secular liberals – to the conservative right. Stelzer could assert perceptively that

> one thing is clear...the leader of Britain's left-wing party finds it acceptable, politically, to profess his Christianity and to look to the new and old testaments for a central core around which to develop his political program. Of necessity, that requires a cultural stance not very different from that of America's Christian Coalition.[20]

Whereas Murdoch may have only facilitated Blair's growing American conservatism, he and his newspapers and television stations were decisive when it came to Blair's European policy. Blair had come into office in 1997 with very positive views about Britain's joining the euro-zone, but was never, throughout the whole period of his premiership, able to act on them. Before the 1997 general election he was forced into pledging a referendum on the issue for fear of Murdoch support for Major in the campaign. After entering Downing Street euro entry remained an objective of his government, but fearful of Murdoch's media influence in any referendum campaign he was never confident of winning a vote. Thus a vote was never held, and Britain stayed outside. The *Mail on Sunday* even claimed that in the original, uncensored *Diary of a Spin Doctor*, Downing Street official Lance Price had written that 'apparently we [Downing Street] promised News International that we won't make any changes to our European policy without talking to them.'[21]

Another clear, and stark, example of Murdoch's power over New Labour – particularly on the European issue – came in July 2006. Blair's premiership was clearly reaching its final phase, and Gordon Brown's team was preparing for the future transfer of power. Speculation was rife about Brown's political options. Into this vacuum Murdoch issued what amounted to a public 'ultimatum' or 'warning' to Brown. Brown was told flatly not to try for a quick general election but rather to stay around for eighteen months, during which Murdoch could judge his merits alongside those of the new Tory leader David Cameron. It became clear that Murdoch, ever the vigilant Eurosceptic, was worried that

Brown might hold a quick election, get a new mandate, and then be free to develop his own European policy. At the time it was becoming clear that a new joint German–Italian–French constitutional initiative was possible and might well be launched after the French presidential election in the summer of 2007, just after Brown had taken over. Murdoch feared that the new prime minister might well sign up to it. Murdoch let it be known that the *Sun* – the only paper New Labour's leaders cared about – would not support Brown in any quickly called election campaign. Should he try such a manoeuvre it would support Cameron.[22]

An intriguing aspect of this intervention in British politics by a media organisation run from the USA was, rather than its blatant nature, the nonchalant way it was received by New Labour, the British political class, press and commentariat. There was hardly a peep of protest or a riposte of any note. After a decade of New Labour, and three decades of Thatcherism, Rupert Murdoch, an American citizen, domiciled outside the UK, had become accepted as an arbiter of Britain's future. He had become as powerful as the whole British cabinet combined.

Murdoch's press empire was, though, by no means the sole pressure behind New Labour's growing extreme pro-Americanism. There was also a general pro-American bias among other powerful moguls of the media world – not least the *Daily Telegraph* and *Spectator* owner Conrad Black. The nexus of media and politics which Murdoch and Black bestrode was, in fact, the world inhabited by New Labour – and later by David Cameron's Tories too. Blair's team, and Cameron's, were not strictly 'political' in the classic sense. Mixing the political with modern communications techniques they took the world of the media very seriously indeed, and they treated media barons as legitimate policy-makers. British politics had come a long way since the early 1970s when it was the trade-union leaders who were the 'over-mighty subjects' and held similar power over an earlier Labour administration.

In this process New Labour had ceased to act like a traditional left-of-centre British political party. Rather, with cabinet and party weakened, Blair's team resembled a highly sophisticated public-relations company that – media-friendly, and brand- and image-sensitive – cut out the party (its factions, its MPs, its trade unions and its activists) and made direct contact with the voter. As New Labour embraced this party-less, American-style politics it automatically became more and more dependent upon media support and approval, and upon business and private money for its campaigning. And the media-cum-business community demanded of New Labour business-friendly policies in return.

It was an embrace that as one commentator put it, 'created Britain's most consistently business-friendly party'.[23] And a 'business-friendly party' was an American-friendly party. For New Labour increasingly acted as an amen chorus for the US economic model and as a pressure against British integration in 'social' Europe. And a key part of the business-friendly US economic model was the opening to a global marketised world with its pressures for 'competitive', low-cost, low-wage, low-tax economies with flexible labour markets. As New Labour entered this world it began – often with relish – to join in the Wall Street barrage of criticism against the European social model with its 'inflexible', regulated – indeed 'sclerotic' – economies and hugely 'debilitating' welfare states. So powerful was the hold of this business-led consensus in Britain that even the downturn of Wall Street and the puncturing of the hi-tech bubble in 2000 and 2001, the huge and dangerous financial imbalances of the US economy, and the corruption scandals of Enron and others did not shake New Labour's conviction that neo-liberal economics was the way forward for Britain.

MANDARINS, SPIES AND SUBMARINERS

New Labour's love affair with America, though, was not simply about business-friendly and media-mogul-friendly politics. For as well as the Americanised business and media class Whitehall's traditionalist 'establishment' was also very much on board for the US connection. 'Atlanticism' ran deep in the corridors of Whitehall. When this Atlanticist faction joined up with the Eurosceptic business class in promoting the 'special relationship' it became an unbeatable combination.

An archetypal Foreign Office Atlanticist was Jonathan Powell, an Oxford contemporary of Blair who became the prime minister's chief of staff in 1997 and saw him every day, sometimes more than a dozen times. Picked out by Blair while at the British embassy in Washington, Powell (an affectation has it pronounced 'Po-ell') is a 'devout Atlanticist who is not much bothered about Europe'.[24] Indeed, pro-American Atlanticism runs in the family, for Powell is the brother of an even stauncher pro-American Atlanticist, Lord Charles Powell, who was Margaret Thatcher's chief foreign-policy advisor.

The Powells are in one sense very representative figures – representative, that is, of the governing official mindset of top political Britain. Like Blair himself they are the product of old-fashioned public schools and, again like Blair, have just a touch of the old imperial manner, and of its attraction to power – in this case to the power of superpower America. Like the foreign-policy establishment they represent, their 'Atlanticism' is ingrained, made so by the historic success of NATO during the Cold War years.

Below this top political level – where the Atlanticist 'special relationship' was held as an act of faith – there were the more pragmatic pro-American Whitehall interest groups: the spies and submariners. Britain's intelligence community had a real 'special relationship' with Washington – based on intelligence sharing, not offered to other European nations, which had continued beyond the Cold War years; Whitehall continued to please Washington for fear it would be cut off. This may help explain the seemingly determined behaviour of John Scarlett, the chair of the Joint Intelligence Committee, who throughout the great post-invasion controversy about Britain's intelligence and the Hutton Inquiry into the strange death of a weapons inspector, stood one hundred per cent by Blair and his policy even though at least one other intelligence chief was reported as having severe misgivings about the war.[25]

The role of the intelligence services is shrouded in mystery, but they have two clear and obvious advantages in Whitehall's power struggles: they are the sole possessor of 'knowledge' and 'information'; and they have total and regular access to the prime minister's office, more so than top cabinet ministers.

The other Whitehall pressure group highly supportive of Washington is the British navy, which ever since the late 1960s has played host to Britain's nuclear weapons, which, together with the missiles, are carried in the navy's submarines. To many in Whitehall this 'British bomb' remains the central nervous system of British power and thus the key to the British establishment's 'world role'. Yet, as befits this British nuclear 'world role', Washington is indispensable. For the USA – first through the Polaris and then through the Poseidon agreements – provided and provides indispensable servicing requirements for the submarine force and crucial satellite targeting systems. The British bomb is independent, but only if the British government wants to launch a 'spasm' response. A proper, targeted response needs American input and allows for an American veto over its use, whereas by contrast the French nuclear-weapons system is genuinely independent. These umbilical intelligence and nuclear ties to Washington may explain, perhaps much more clearly than any of the more geopolitical and theoretical attachments to

'Atlanticism' (and 'NATO-think'), why exactly it is that Britain's top leadership needs the Americans and needs to 'hug them close'.

In 2008 Britain's elites were still 'hugging them close' when Wall Street lending crashed. It was a crash that was to take down with it American global economic and political supremacy and American-style 'economic globalisation' – and thus destroy the validity of the three-decade-long pro-American national strategy of Britain's political and financial class. The 2008 crash was a terrible blow for Britain.

17 BLAIR AND THE CITY: AN EMPIRE OF FINANCE

The great crash of 2008 was not just an American event in which Britain was an innocent bystander – for the City of London was deeply implicated as a co-conspirator. Britain's powerful financial institutions, egged on by New Labour (and the Conservative opposition), had engaged in as big a deregulatory credit bonanza as their American cousins. Indeed Tony Blair had become the European cheerleader for the Clinton/Bush/Alan Greenspan (chairman of the US Federal Reserve) global deregulated free-market economy that formed the framework for the huge credit boom.

When Blair became prime minister, Bill Clinton was some months into his second term of office as president of the USA. These two new leaders – both of them left-of-centre politicians – had originally sought to draw a line under the Reagan/Thatcher revolution and had set out on a new course – which they called the 'third way'. And they had the wind at their backs. In 'Anglo-America' the 'free market' years were becoming controversial, increasingly seen as the 'decade of greed'; and pollsters were finding that publics were more willing to contemplate paying higher taxes for better services.

Yet both Blair and Clinton were to turn out to be very good news for the big players in the City of London and on Wall Street – and for the 'globalisation game' that was the financiers' ticket to unheard-of riches. The youthful public-school radical from Islington and the dirt-poor boy from Arkansas had come to power at a time when some of the structural economic changes – which would open the way to the full flow of 'global capital' – had already been secured. Yet they both had a clear opportunity to limit, and even reverse, the process. But, neither Blair nor Clinton showed even the remotest inclination to do so. Instead, with the super-rich riding off into the 'globalisation' gold rush, Blair and Clinton, and the Western political class to which they gave leadership, decided to ride shotgun.

Clinton's opportunity came first. He was elected in 1992 during a sharp recession when a major milestone in globalisation, the North Atlantic Free Trade Association (NAFTA), was top of the American agenda. It was an election in which Ross Perot had achieved a record-breaking 20 per cent of the presidential vote as a third-party candidate dedicated to ending the free-trade agreement. Perot built his whole campaign around the 'hollowing out' argument, famously, and presciently, declaring that once NAFTA was in being 'you will hear a giant sucking sound' as jobs are 'sucked out' of the USA. The anti-NAFTA campaign had many supporters in the Democratic Party, and with presidential leadership NAFTA could easily have been emasculated, if not completely abandoned.

But Clinton had made his bargain with corporate America and, as president, both introduced and became a stalwart defender of NAFTA and the next great burst of 'globalisation'. Also Clinton's abandonment of any serious attempt to bring in a comprehensive health service to America – which would inevitably have created pressure for corporations to pay taxes at home instead of investing abroad – meant that Clinton was even abandoning the attempt to 'shape globalisation' to American needs. Rather Americans would, in effect, be told to accept it, shape up and compete in the world.

The truth was that Clinton had, long before becoming president, embraced US big business and its linked agendas of market reform (deregulated markets and low taxes) and economic globalisation. His first term assured corporate America that its 'globalisation revolution' was safe in his hands. And he made clear there would be no going back when in 1995, as president, he reappointed the intellectual godfather of the revolution, the extreme pro-market, Randian economist Alan Greenspan, to yet another term at the Federal Reserve.

NEW LABOUR JOINS WALL STREET

Tony Blair, who came into office some five years after Clinton, also had a window of opportunity through which to bring a halt to the rampant globalisation then already underway. Blair had taken over from John

Major, and the big question was: would his New Labour administration weaken the Thatcherite imperative of ever-greater marketisation and privatisation, ever greater financialisation, ever-greater integration into the minimal-governance global economy, ever-greater trade with low-cost Asia – in other words, ever-greater globalisation. Would the New Labour government, true to much of its left-of-centre general election rhetoric, usher in a true change of direction?

As it happens there was a new strategic direction, a new, more left-of-centre route open to the new government had it decided to take it during that post-election summer and autumn of 1997. It would have involved some serious adjustments, but it was open to New Labour to embark upon a full-hearted commitment to Europe and to the Europeanisation of Britain – with all that would have entailed for British economic policy, for household debt levels, for the state's relationship with the market and, importantly, for a future more modest and sustainable role for both the City of London and British foreign policy. Such a course would have ended up with a country less dependent upon the global economy, less leveraged, less imbalanced than the Wall Street model which it was later destined to follow.

When Blair took over in Downing Street, the City of London was already the major player in British politics and was seeing its future in Thatcherite terms as inexorably global. Yet at the same time a majority of City opinion was in favour of the country joining the euro-zone. It saw the City as being able to combine global influence with a future as the financial centre of the European hinterland (like Wall Street to the USA). And Blair's New Labour, ever sensitive to City opinion, had fought the election on a pro-euro platform. He had pledged a referendum, and would have won one – particularly if it had been held fairly early in the new regime.

Yet Blair lost his nerve. Had he gone for it, and won the referendum, then Britain, melded into the European economic scene, would inevitably have been set on a course in which British economic policy would become Europeanised. Blair himself was later, while still prime minister, to lament this grave error of judgement. Speaking in Ghent, only a few miles from Bruges (where Margaret Thatcher had famously opened her campaign against further British integration in the EU), he bluntly stated that 'Britain's hesitation over Europe was one of my country's greatest miscalculations of the postwar years...Britain's destiny is to be a leading partner in Europe.'[1]

BRITAIN'S 'GLOBAL DESTINY'

From his earliest days as leader of the Labour Party Blair had, like Clinton, made his pact with Britain's corporate business community. Blair had proved his market credentials when, before becoming prime minister, he formally scuppered socialism (and social democracy) by rewriting the Labour Party constitution. He later went on to become a true disciple of 'free market' themes and big corporate business, and his attraction to the American economic model, the Wall Street model, weakened his desire to commit Britain to a European future. As British prime minister he would regularly lecture the 'sclerotic' social capitalists in Europe about the virtues of the American model.

Blair gave his considerable rhetorical gifts and public-relations expertise to the cause of 'globalisation'. He argued to anyone who would listen that economic globalisation was 'inevitable' and could not, Canute-like, be turned back; rather, it needed to be 'accepted', and adapted to. Both Blair and Clinton tended to avoid making the case for globalisation solely by reference to economics, profits and cheap consumer goods. They sought instead to create domestic support for globalisation by stressing its positive moral content. Clinton saw it as a great progressive force unleashed to save humanity. For him it was a 'world without walls' – 'the only sustainable world'; and globalisation was 'an explosion of democracy and diversity within democracy'.[2] Blair regularly made the same kind of case – and even some months after leaving office he was setting globalisation in a slightly mystical, moralistic and religious context during a speech entitled 'Faith and globalisation'.[3]

By the mid-1990s 'globalisation' was the rage among Western opinion-formers – an army of academics, economists, journalists and pundits also saw 'globalisation' as a positive force in the world. A strong moral case was consistently proffered, with many believing that 'one world', fuelled by the communications revolution, mass tourism and growing trade, was finally in the making. The leading British academic of globalisation, the sociologist Anthony Giddens (who influenced much of Blair's thinking) saw globalisation in these terms – as a truly transformative agency. 'We have a chance,' he said in 2001, 'to take over where the twentieth century failed, and a key project for us is to drag the history of the 21st century away from that of the 20th.'[4] Among Western journalists *New York Times* columnist Thomas Friedman also took a lead in seeing globalisation as progress – with its 'inexorable integration of markets and nation-states'.

Economists and economic commentators tended to take a narrower, more precise perspective – seeing globalisation through economic, rather than political and moral, eyes. Indeed, as John Ralston Saul argued, they saw 'civilisation as a whole through an economic prism'.[5] And, for a time, there was near unanimity of opinion among economists on the subject – in globalisation's favour.

There was also a very strong correlation between 'free market' supporters and advocates of 'the global market' and globalisation. Leading 'free market' economists Martin Wolf of the *Financial Times* and academic Jagdish Bhagwati saw globalisation as both inevitable and good for aggregate global living standards and for Western prosperity (after suitable 'reforms' and adjustments, particularly in Europe). The overwhelming consensus was that Britain and the West needed to adjust to the new global reality and that the forces that opposed such adjustment, protectionists and pro-welfare politicians, would, by interfering in the workings of the global market, end up causing even lower living standards. Even Joseph Stiglitz, a trenchant and bitter critic of prevailing orthodoxies, only went as far as criticising how globalisation was managed – in part under his tenure as chairman of President Clinton's Council of Economic Advisors. His primary criticism appeared to be that the USA used globalisation to advance her own interests. Looking back in 2003 he suggested that 'we had no vision of the kind of globalised world we wanted, and we weren't sensitive enough about how what we wanted would be viewed by the rest of the world.'[6] Stiglitz developed a powerful critique of a world of economic globalisation without global economic governance – but with global governance still an impossible dream, his readers were left not quite knowing whether he believed that the whole post-Cold War project of economic globalisation, and its free-trade component, had been wrong in principle.

THE WASHINGTON CONSENSUS

In the real world of money-making, globalisation was much more than a nice theory – for it was the practical method of opening markets, deregulating commerce and finance, and raising profits worldwide. For the City of London and Wall Street it was heady stuff. The West's finance capitalists were setting rules and norms for the whole world – their own rules and norms.

These rules were to be set out in what became known, appropriately enough, as 'the Washington consensus'. This 'consensus', unveiled in 1989, was a ten-point programme setting out what Western bankers wanted from indebted Latin American countries. It amounted to a regime that would be imposed on countries which fell into debt, a regime that took advantage of distress in order to impose ideological market solutions.

A precursor to this 'Washington consensus' was the structural adjustment programs (SAPs) of the World Bank instituted following the oil crisis of 1973. These programmes ended the passive (and short-term) loan role of the international financial authorities, substituting a more direct and controlling approach which restructured the market of debtor countries to open them to foreign investment and to promote exports in order to repay the debt. In 2006 W. Easterly, a World Bank official and supporter of these SAPs, reflected that 'the over-ambitious reforms of shock therapy and structural adjustment were the flight of Icarus for the World Bank and the IMF. Aiming for the sun, they instead descended into a sea of failure.'[7]

Icarus regularly fell to earth in Africa, where there is considerable evidence that these SAPs were major failures, for the fact was that those countries that implemented the most SAPs had either neutral or negative growth. The same was true for the countries of the former Soviet Union who agreed to SAPs. The World Bank also funded a number of SAP projects that caused considerable environmental damage in Brazil and Indonesia.[8]

The bottom line was clear: the West, through international organisations, sought to draw the less-developed countries, including importantly China, into an integrated market-based global economic system which it would lead and control and which would be run according to its economic precepts. These 'emerging' economies were forced to rise and fall with the West, and were not allowed to develop indigenous markets, the key to long-term economic growth and success. The idea was 'one world, one market' – but 'one world, one market' run from Wall Street.

John Williamson, who drew up the blueprint for the 'Washington consensus', later argued that he never intended his plans to work out the way they did, but they implied and then led to 'policies like capital account liberalization, monetarism, supply-side economics, or a minimal state...getting the state out of welfare provision and income distribution.' (And he added that, for his part, he now hoped, in 2002, that 'we can all enjoy its wake.')[9]

The 'Washington consensus' regime was to be tried out in a major way in the Asian crisis in the late 1990s. Malaysians, Thais and Indonesians were all to get the treatment – what one critic called 'redemption' through 'economic and social self-flagellation'. In other words, in return for being bailed out countries would need to introduce a full 'neo-liberal' 'reform programme' based upon 'opening' markets and 'liberalising' economies. And in the process the way would be cleared for Western economic and financial elites to do business and to make money. And to continue to make money – as through this global 'reform programme' the whole world would turn into one giant Main Street serviced by Wall Street.

As the Asian countries dutifully 'reformed', Western hedge-fund money swept in, and Western hedge-fund money swept out; and left in its wake a devastated and debilitated terrain.

However, not all was plain sailing for Western mobile capital. Malaysia rebelled. Its maverick and articulate leader Mahathir bin Mohamad broke ranks and re-established capital controls and trade protection. It was a rare act of defiance, and was treated in the West as an act bordering on sacrilege. His heresy unleashed 'a tidal wave of contemptuous condemnations' from around the world, 'writing off Malaysia as a basket case and Mahathir as mentally unstable'.[10] Mahathir returned the fire with sarcasm. He declared ironically the Malaysians to be 'stupid' but asked the market liberals to 'leave us to do the wrong things we want to do.'[11] Of course the Malaysian leader did not believe that the rebellious course he had set was wrong, and soon Malaysia was doing well even by the economic indicators used by the Western-dominated international organisations. George Soros could predict that 'if Malaysia looks good in comparison to its neighbours, the policy may easily find imitators.'[12]

Intriguingly, during the Asian crisis China was not one of the countries that Western market 'neo-liberals' could dictate to – in part because the Asian giant's currency remained pegged. In the world of 'free trade' China was the proverbial 'elephant in the room'. For the country has been growing by doing all the things 'free traders' were telling them not to. It has a pegged currency, it has capital controls, and it has refused to 'liberalise' many key sectors of its economy. China, as it emerged, was going to work to its own, not the West's, rules and agenda.

SURVIVING THE CHALLENGES

Yet the finance-led globalised order ultimately survived the Asian crisis. And it also survived three other serious challenges: the 1998 bailout of the mammoth hedge fund LTCM, the Russian default crisis of 1998 and, most importantly, the 2000–1 bursting of the 'dot-com' bubble.

On 10 March 2000 the dot-com industry's main index NASDAQ peaked at 5132, more than double its value of a year before. Its rise had been accompanied by extravagant claims about how the California-based technological 'new economy' was a wholly new phenomenon – a 'new paradigm' – that was going to rewrite the rules of economics and change the world. Yet on 10 March the prick was administered and for the rest of the year and into 2001 the dot-com bubble steadily burst. The IT revolution had run its course – an important new technology but not one that was going to sustain the global economy.

Yet Wall Street did recover. As did the City of London. The Dow Jones bottomed out at 7286.27 on 9 October 2002 and it was then onwards and upwards again. By the end of 2003 it had reached 10,000 (and by January 2006 it broke through the 11,000 barrier). And in the UK the FTSE, which had bottomed at 3721 at the end of September 2002 had risen to 4476 by December 2003.

'ANGLO–AMERICAN' CAPITALISM RULES

In this climate the 'masters of the universe' in the City of London and Wall Street, and their supporters and enablers among the politicians in London and Washington, could be forgiven for believing that American financial genius when married to globalisation was an unstoppable combination. And they could be forgiven, too, for believing that the global economic order that had been fashioned in their image, had been tested and had survived, was now unstoppable.

Thus economic globalisation and Americanisation (of the Wall Street business variety) became one. And supporters of this Global-Americana were not bashful – it was good for the world as America stood for capitalism and democracy. It was a compelling vision. Robert Samuelson has described its outlines when he argued that

after the Cold War, global capitalism offered a powerful vision of the world – prosperity and, ultimately, democracy. Multinational companies and investors would pour technology and capital into poorer regions, creating a transnational mass market of middle class consumers who would drive Toyotas, watch CNN, eat Big Macs – and, incidentally, demand more freedom.[13]

This was the economic neo-liberal counterpart to Francis Fukuyama's famous political and cultural vision of one world in which 'western liberal-democracy' reigned as 'the end-state of the historical process'. For both Fukuyama and the Wall Street visionaries, although they would not say so openly, something like America (or more like America than anywhere else) was what the 'end of history' would look like (although Fukuyama was, much later, to say that he had in mind the EU rather than the USA).

No wonder that in that spring of 2003 the British-born neo-conservative Harvard historian Niall Ferguson – who, in a long line of British writers, was making a name for himself on the American right – could be moved to declare that the USA had the world at its feet, and that the republic was not only an imperial power but was 'good' as well. For many elite Britons US power was a vicarious experience, lending to the sons and grandsons of empire a glow of that imperial nostalgia. 'The reality,' Ferguson argued, 'is that the United States has – whether it admits it or not – taken up some kind of global burden…And just like the British empire before it, the American empire unfailingly acts in the name of liberty, even when its own self-interest is manifestly uppermost.'[14]

GLOBAL MARKET CAPITALISM AND THE MINIMAL STATE

'Liberty' was to be advanced by the market. Indeed the market was American global capitalism's great universalist idea. And this belief in the market developed a visceral quality, a militant conviction that a brave new world was being born. It amounted to a certainty of religious dimensions. Indeed it became a secular religion. William Greider argued that 'the utopian vision of the marketplace offers…an enthralling religion. Many intelligent people have come to worship these market principles, like a spiritual code that will resolve all the larger questions for us, social and moral and otherwise.' And Edward Luttwak described the orthodox monetarism at the heart of the new capitalism as having 'like all religions a supreme god – hard money – and a devil, inflation'.[15]

This new religion was 'Gekko's world view'. It was the vision too of Ayn Rand and her student Alan Greenspan, of Keith Joseph and his student Margaret Thatcher, and of a host of academic economists who followed in their footsteps and were beginning to populate the think-tanks, calling themselves 'neo-liberals'. And it was this 'neo-liberal' world which in the mid-1990s Tony Blair, then opposition leader, had signed on to renew.

This religion of the market made few conversions among the West's masses, but it did enthral and entrance many of the West's elites – and not just the opinion-formers in the big corporate media outlets and at the annual World Economic Forum in Davos. For it even lit fires in the minds of the men in the staid world of officialdom and policy-making. True believers could be found not just in Downing Street and the White House, but also in the great international institutions like the IMF, the World Bank, the WTO, and even in key parts of the European Commission.

These true believers saw the market – the global market – as being nothing less than an expression of freedom itself. 'Freedom' was what America stood for, and this 'freedom' could only be guaranteed by the 'free market' because, so the argument ran, entry to the market – unlike to the state – was essentially voluntary, and this ensured the liberty of the individual. Thus in the mind of the believer the ethical idea of the sovereign individual fighting a battle for liberty translates easily into a more prosaic and materialistic economic individualism.

In this way 'free markets' became one of the security and foreign-policy goals of the West. For instance NATO was no longer to continue as a defence pact but would instead become a military alliance dedicated to change, to remaking the world on Western lines. It would, according to Colin Powell, testifying before the Senate Foreign Relations Committee in July 2002, 'promote democracy, the rule of law, and *promote free markets*, and peace throughout Eurasia'. For the first time NATO possessed a specifically economic agenda. In a big win for the market revolutionaries, 'free markets' were to be backed up by bayonets, another example of Wall Street's objectives signed on to by the Pentagon.

Thus the market developed a moral and political content, for it was not only by far the best way of allocating resources, it was also virtuous – both efficient and good. And the roots of its goodness lay in its protection of the individual – the sovereign individual. Thus the market and individualism became one.

And, for the true believers, if the market was an essential engine for individual freedom then, by contrast, 'the state' – in all its guises, federal, state and local – was a serious threat. Thus was 'the state' demonised. A flavour of the near-religious fervour behind much of this contemporary anti-state impulse is provided by this intriguing passage from a 1980s new-right propagandist:

> The New Right must propagandise mercilessly against the state. It must stress unremittingly the enduring moral bankruptcy of government. It must constantly compare the burden borne by the taxpayer, to fill the government trough from which the interest groups are feeding with the benefits received by the swine at the trough…we must underscore relentlessly to our un-organised fellow taxpayers their direct interest in the unremitting attenuation of the state.[16]

SOCIALISTS FOR THE GLOBAL MARKET

One intriguing aspect of this renaissance of the 'free market' was the number of former socialists and social democrats who began to break cover and support market solutions and a reduced role for the state. The initial issue for many of them was non-economic – they supported the defence build-up during the Cold War and rejected what they considered to be their fellow socialists' growing anti-Western attitudes. But this was a time when the social-democratic consensus – built by Roosevelt in the USA and the Attlee government in Britain – was seemingly failing on the economic front. Big government welfare had not solved the problems of the American inner cities, problems which were literally going up in flames; and in Britain many of the country's economic problems were put down to the 'over-mighty' public sector – with its powerful, 'over-mighty' public-sector unions. It was an environment tailor-made for a systematic critique of the mainstream left's assumptions, not just about defence and NATO, but also about the role of the state and the market. And the list of 'left' public intellectuals who moved across to associate themselves with many key aspects of the broad Thatcherite and Reaganite 'revolution' was considerable. It included Robert Nozick, Peter Berger, Norman Podhoretz, Paul Johnson, Evan Luard, Irving Kristol and – less so – Sidney Hook, Daniel Bell, Robert Skidelsky, New York senator Daniel Patrick Moynihan and former British chancellor of the exchequer and European Commission president Roy Jenkins.

A new, somewhat misleading, political term took hold to describe these former left-of-centre thinkers. They were called 'neo-conservatives'.

And although they varied in their approach to social and economic policy, they succeeded in playing a major role in the 1980s in moving the centre of political gravity towards a more market-based world.

Two magazines became the home for this transatlantic generation of 'neo-cons' – as they came to be dubbed by the American media. In the USA the American Jewish Committee's *Commentary* magazine – edited by the redoubtable Norman Podhoretz – not only focused on winning the Cold War but also, month after month, systematically attacked the social and economic agenda of the American 'liberals', including what they considered to be the overblown US welfare state. In Britain, *Encounter* magazine, led by the equally redoubtable Melvyn Lasky, did not set itself against social democracy quite so strongly (in the early 1980s it supported the social democrats' political exit from the increasingly leftist Labour Party), but it did provide a platform for serious arguments from Thatcherite economists and social scientists.

As well as these social-democratic allies, the anti-statist market revolution secured support from another, somewhat surprising, quarter. Traditionalist conservatives – numerous in Britain and Europe, less numerous in the USA – were always suspicious of individualism and consumerism, tended to be neutral about the power and reach of the state, and saw the market as destructive of traditional values and ways of life. Yet a number of these British 'paleo-conservative' thinkers – such people as Michael Novak, Roger Scruton, John Casey and Peregrine Worsthorne – were swept up in the market revolution and rode shotgun with the free-market conservatives. If they saw real contradictions between the new, raw, global capitalism and Tory tradition they rarely spoke up about it. (Worsthorne, a former editor of the *Sunday Telegraph*, was an exception: he was later to resolve the 'conservative contradiction' in favour of the state, and the EU state at that!) During the 1980s the *Spectator* magazine began to straddle both this traditional conservatism (often with a very 'county' twist) and the new, more 'neo-con', American meritocratic capitalist agenda. In the 1990s, under the Canadian mogul Conrad Black's proprietorship (and Frank and Boris Johnson's editorships), it essentially threw its lot in with both Wall Street minimal-state capitalism and the 'neo-con' idea of an American empire.

LOWER AND LOWER TAXES: RACE TO THE BOTTOM

Market and business-friendly politicians noticed something that the socialists and social democrats of the 1970s and 1980s had ignored. One of the most pronounced social changes since the 1950s was the hugely increased number of people paying taxes. Low, and even average, wage-earners were not really in the income-tax brackets in any numbers until well into the 1960s. But as they, and the growing army of women in the workforce, flooded onto the labour market in the 1970s the anti-tax appeal of conservative politicians achieved a previously unknown resonance.

So successful, so total, was this victory of business over government on the issue of taxes that by the turn of the century not a single politician in Britain or the West was even trying to associate him- or herself with a regime of higher taxes. Gone too was the mid-1990s rhetoric – tried out for a bit by left-of-centre politicians like Tony Blair, Bill Clinton and Gordon Brown – about how public services should come first even if it meant slightly higher tax rates. New Labour's public-sector spending did involve tax increases – the so-called 'stealth' taxes – but business pressure for lower taxes continued into the new century, and was only contained so long as growing amounts of tax money were being spent on the private sector through the growth of outsourcing.

In 2006, towards the end of his premiership, at the CBI (Confederation of British Industry) conference in London, Blair was still acting as a cheerleader for the low-tax regime desired by business; and he was selling it by appealing to the well-worn formula: We must, he argued, 'keep our tax system here competitive... with the new economies as well as the more traditional economies against which we compete'.[17] In other words 'globalisation', which we must 'accept', demanded it. It was still difficult for any aspiring politician to say otherwise.

'LIGHT TOUCH' REGULATION (OF THE BANKS TOO!)

This minimal state would also be a minimal, or 'light touch', regulator. The minimalist revolutionaries based their deregulation agenda on the need to 'free up' business from the 'dead hand' of state regulation – a freedom that would lead, in financial services as much as elsewhere, to higher levels of innovation and productivity – and profits. One of the leading voices behind the campaign for deregulation was the American

Nobel laureate and minimal-statist George Stigler, who argued that regulation too often ended up favouring the regulated through cosy deals between the private and public sectors and led business into the inadequacies and corruptions of the political process.[18]

In the Anglo–American world in the 1990s the deregulators won the battle, particularly in the banking and financial sector. Britain's chancellor Gordon Brown set out his 'light touch' vision in a speech to the CBI on 28 November 2005: he wanted, he argued, 'no inspection without justification, no information requirements without justification, not just a light touch but a limited touch'.

And it was this 'light touch' that, in essence, opened the door to the massive overleveraging that, over a decade after its introduction, was to lead to financial catastrophe. So powerful was this push for deregulation that, even after 2007 – even after the banking failures, and even after the fallout from Enron and WorldCom – the voices of the minimalists could still be heard from Wall Street to the European Commission urging a new round of deregulation – this time in the labour market. And even as late as October 2007, when it was clear that something had gone seriously wrong with the financial sector, Hector Sants of Britain's financial regulator, the FSA, was still committing the agency to a 'principles-based' regulatory regime, seen by many as meaning a 'light touch' one.

A key demand of the minimalists had been a deregulation of the labour market – in order to create a 'flexible' workforce. And the key point of the 'flexibility' advocates was the need to establish a legal ability of corporations to hire and fire at will, to enable them to respond quickly to changing profit margins caused by changes in demand. Some extreme supporters of these 'reforms' saw an endgame in which corporations not governments would determine the labour market, and would be free not just to hire and fire but to employ a whole range of labour – full-time, part-time, hourly, full benefits, no benefits, and so on. Again, 'reforming' the labour market – making it more 'flexible' – was a policy propounded beyond Downing Street, in Wall Street, and most insistently by the European Commission.

THE MARKETISATION OF THE STATE

Of course even for Blair's New Labour there were going to be limits to dismantling the state. When Blair came to power there were few enterprises left that could reasonably be privatised. Nonetheless, the continuing pressures from the big-business community could still be satisfied, this time through a new idea of 'quasi-privatisation' – or, as it became known, 'the marketisation of the state'.

John Major had taken the lead in this in the early 1990s. He had argued that 'some areas would not readily, or perhaps ever, be privatised…to rest our fortunes entirely on privatisation seemed to me to be too ideological, too lacking in vision or ambition.' At the first meeting with his policy unit in January 1991 Major told his staff that

> we ought to have pressed on more boldly in the past with work on the privatisation of British Rail and British Coal, but that I had reservations in the case of the Royal Mail. I said that central and local government contracting-out…must be part of our armoury. I was also concerned that those parts of Whitehall which had been moved 'offshore' into agencies should continue to involve and embrace the private sector and its skills. I wanted to bring the discipline and effectiveness of the private sector into the public services.

And he went on,

> in areas where the introduction of true competition and choice was impractical, I was certain that publishing the performances of different schools, hospitals, local authorities or transport services would act as a kind of surrogate competition to raise standards. Those bodies which were seen to be underperforming would come under pressure to explain why, and to improve. If we could at the same time, as I intended, also devolve more management responsibility to the local service level, then local governors, teachers, managers, train operators and others would have the opportunity to improve standards as well as the incentive to do so.[19]

Within the Labour Party, while policies such as a quasi-market for the NHS were controversial and widely opposed within the broader labour movement, there were some on the left who saw merit in the marketisation of the state idea. Michael Barber, the first head of Blair's delivery unit from 2001–5, was a central figure in pushing this agenda. During the 1980s he worked in the Education Department of the National Union of Teachers. From this vantage point he witnessed, and approved of, Thatcherite Conservative education policy, which he described in these terms:

> through the national curriculum and national testing, the government had decided to set standards and then to check whether they were being achieved; through devolving power and money to schools they were giving headteachers the responsibility for meeting those standards.

Meanwhile, the influence of local education authorities – those bêtes noires of Thatcherites – was steadily reduced. Increasingly, schools were encouraged to 'opt out' of them altogether and receive funding direct from Whitehall. The school, in effect, had become the point of accountability. Later in 1992, the theme of transparency was added – school results would be published and a new agency, Ofsted, incorporating the old Inspectorate, was established to inspect all schools once every four years instead of on an occasional basis.

Barber felt that 'the principles behind the reform were bold and sensible,' though they were not implemented properly. He regretted that the NUT did not embrace these reforms.[20]

Barber helped put a particular left slant on Blair's programme of marketising the state. As he told the House of Commons Public Administration Select Committee in 2003,

> The Government wants to achieve high quality public services which means rising average standards of performance across those public services and particularly it means faster progress in the most disadvantaged communities so as to ensure equity. In the pursuit of that vision there are significant sustained levels of investment going into the public services for which the tax payer expects to see a return. Targets and league tables... are essential parts of an overall approach to achieving that vision.[21]

Another influential thinker who, like Barber, saw some merit in the marketisation of the state as practised from the 1980s onwards and viewed it as a means of pursuing socially progressive goals was Julian Le Grand. Also like Barber, he became an adviser to Blair at Number 10 between 2003 and 2005, on secondment from the LSE, where he was Richard Titmuss Professor of Social Policy. Le Grand's approach was to become extremely influential in New Labour thinking; and he made a statement of his philosophy and its possible practical application in a book, *Motivation, Agency and Public Policy: Of knights and knaves, pawns and queens,* published in 2006. He noted how

> During the 1980s and the early 1990s, there was something of a revolution in...social policy. In several countries where a combination of state provision and state finance had been the norm, the state, while retaining control of finance, began to pull back from provision. Instead of providing the service through monolithic state bureaucracies, provision became competitive with independent providers competing for custom in market or 'quasi-market' settings.[22]

Le Grand described how, in these 'quasi-markets' 'the state retains control of financing the service...However, instead of also providing the service concerned, the state allows provision to be undertaken by independent providers competing with one another for custom.' On reviewing 'two market-orientated policies that have been tried in British health care and education: the holding of budgets for hospital care by organisations of primary-care physicians...and parental choice and competition in primary school education' he concluded 'these schemes have been broadly effective'. Le Grand justified quasi-market mechanisms on the grounds that they empowered users and enabled the harnessing of both the altruistic and self-interested tendencies of individuals across society.[23]

Under the influence of these radical ideas drawn from the Thatcher era the marketisation of the state continued apace under Blair and after him Gordon Brown. In 1998 a system of public service agreements (PSAs) was introduced in 1998 for every Whitehall department, containing within them performance targets and reform commitments. While targets are not unique to the private sector, being used in statist regimes such as the Soviet Union under Stalin, the context in which they were used under Major, Blair and then Brown seemed to be as part of an attempt to import practices from the private sector.

Jack Cunningham, an old Labour politico who converted to New Labour, became minister for the Cabinet Office, and in 1999 set out 'a clear statement by the Government of what government is for – not government for those who work in government; but government for people as consumers, people as citizens'. Cunningham argued that 'we need to make sure that government services are brought forward using the best and most modern techniques, to match the best of the private sector including one-stop shops, single contacts which link in to a range of government Departments and especially electronic information-age services.'[24]

It all amounted to a clear preference by New Labour for the private sector (competitive, efficient) over the state (slothful, inefficient). And Blair's government set out to use the marketisation mechanism to, as it saw it, 'devolve more local power to the frontline to deliver those high standards, establish more flexible working to keep pace with constant change and better rewards and incentives, and bring about more choice for customers and the ability, if provision is poor, to have an alternative provider.'

At the heart of the new 'public-service reforms' pushed forward under the Blair governments were the controversial 'public–private partnerships' (PPPs). These contrivances were much beloved by banks. They were defined by the Treasury as

> arrangements typified by joint working between the public and private sector. In the broadest sense, PPPs covered all types of collaboration across the interface between public and private sectors to deliver policies, services and infrastructure. Where delivery of public services involve private sector investment in infrastructure, the most common form of PPP was the private finance initiative [PFI].

PFIs were an inheritance from the Major period but were retained and pushed by Labour. They were a means of securing private-sector investment in projects such as prisons, hospitals and school buildings, which the private sector would build and the public sector use and repay. A problem with this PFI – at least for the British taxpayer – emerged in acute form later, once the boom times were over: for taxpayers remained on the hook to investors way into the future – for instance in October 2007 the total capital value of PFI contracts signed in the UK was £68 billion, and the cost to the taxpayer in future spending amounted to £215 billion.

Blair's New Labour admired the private sector so much that government hired private consultants like they were going out of style. In 2006 the National Audit Office noted that between 2003 and 2006 the public-sector consulting market grew by 33 per cent from a value of £2.1 billion in 2003–4 to £2.8 billion in 2005–6.[25] The most favoured firms were IBM (£275 million), LogicaCMG (£175 million), Accenture (£130 million), PA Consulting (£102 million) and Capgemini (£85 million). The National Audit Office expressed some concern, noting that

> Consultants, when used correctly and in the appropriate circumstances, can provide great benefit to clients – achieving things that clients do not have the capacity or capability to do themselves. On the other hand, when used incorrectly, consultants can drain budgets very quickly, with little or no productive results.[26]

The New Labour administration also saw that the somewhat incestuous interchange of personnel between consultancy firms and Whitehall continued apace. For instance Michael Barber, after stepping down as head of the delivery unit in 2005, joined McKinsey; Barber's successor, Ian Watmore, had previously been managing director of Accenture UK.

WHAT OF THE WELFARE STATE?

Of all the projects of the minimum state, reducing welfare, unlike privatisation and lower taxes, was the most difficult to sell. Britain, like most European countries, had a welfare state that, though reformable at the margins, was so entrenched that any dismantling – particularly in health provision – could well lead to political revolt. The Thatcherite governments from 1979 to 1997 were constantly straining to make 'neo-liberal' reforms to the welfare state, but in the end made no real structural changes, and Margaret Thatcher herself argued that the NHS was safe in her hands. New Labour under Blair and Brown added an interesting twist to the welfare argument: the idea was that the universal welfare state (which it supported) and an increasingly free – and global – market went together. Thus a market economy and a marketised society would increase economic growth out of which welfare could be sustained. In a specific example of such thinking Blair and Brown gave the City of London free reign (a regulatory 'light touch') and in return the burgeoning finance sector would contribute to tax revenues. It was, though, a strategy that was completely dependent upon boom times continuing. What would happen – both to government spending and to tax revenues – in a 'bust' was hardly contemplated.

And as Blair's time in government came to an end 'the bust' was just around the corner.

PART 6

The reckoning

18 THE CRASH

GORDON BROWN

Tony Blair left Downing Street on 27 June 2007. And he left with his head held high – for in public-relations terms, notwithstanding the fallout from the invasion of Iraq, he could consider himself a success story. And this 'success' was mainly down to the perceived 'success' of the economy under his watch. And to the success of his timing – for he left office only a couple of months before the great banks of the Western world started to freeze up and stop lending.

But there was also about Tony Blair a sense of great missed opportunities. Given the initial political strength of New Labour, and his undoubted leadership qualities, he might well have possessed the potential to be not just a reforming prime minister but the prime minister who changed everything.

He was in a position to end the country's lack of a role in the world, its strategic 'road to nowhere', by adjusting the country, through a victorious referendum, to a new role in Europe. He also possessed the political leverage to make the long-sought-after goal of a written constitution a reality, thus ending the *ancien régime* of a constitution. And in the process he could have modernised the monarchy, cutting down to size the lavish, imperial 'hauteur' of this premier national institution and thus helping forward a new and more modest self-image for the country and its elites. In sum he had had it within his grasp to end the long post-war grand delusion.

But as it turned out Blair was no revolutionary. In reality he stood in the long line of Elizabeth's prime ministers who, rather like Elizabeth herself, could not escape from the afterglow of empire. He thus, like them, and her, continued to pursue an utterly unrealistic 'global role'. Blair's years led to the hugely over-extended global position of the City of London and to the also hugely over-extended military position created by playing with 'the big boys' in Iraq. Just another British leader in thrall to the grand delusion of British power.

When Blair handed over to Gordon Brown as prime minister these illusions were still very much intact. They were, though, about to be shattered by the great financial crash. Indeed the whole edifice – constructed since Britain's post-war leaders threw their lot in with the USA, and then with upper storeys added since Margaret Thatcher opened the way for the financialisation of Britain – was to come crashing down.

In August 2007 inter-bank lending froze, and a year later, in September 2008, Wall Street crashed, and with it Gordon Brown's short premiership, for he was to be engulfed by one crisis after another until he left office.

The month of August 2007 was a real turning point for the American, and therefore the global, and therefore the British, economy. During that fateful month the strains on the American economy – principally the global imbalances and the mountainous private debt linked to the housing bubble – could no longer be contained. What bankers were calling the sub-prime-mortgage crisis finally spilt out into the wider banking industry as American and then other Western banks stopped lending to each other (except, that is, at prohibitive rates of interest). Banks looked vulnerable for the first time since the 1930s.

This debt-bubble covered the world – or at any rate that part of the globalised world run by banks and financial institutions. Its global dimension was soon revealed when news came through of banks in trouble outside the USA. In Britain the bank Northern Rock had to be nationalised (by a market-friendly British government); banks from Spain to France to Germany to Asia, including the People's Bank of China, were all in trouble. It had the feel of major global crisis about it.

This sudden crisis may well have been triggered by the French bank BNP Paribas, whose board took a fateful decision in early August to junk its toxic assets in the USA – for reasons that are still unclear, but may have ultimately been cultural (a Gallic antipathy to Wall Street's 'wild west' lending practices, or a reluctance to take further risks with sub-prime mortgages). In any event the board of the French bank found itself unable to value properly the assets of three sub-prime mortgage funds – and refused to play the game any longer. But by not playing by the rules that were keeping the Wall Street bubble intact, BNP Paribas set off alarm bells all over the global banking system, leading directly to the shutdown in global inter-bank lending. The European Central Bank, seeing the potential for a run throughout the system, immediately stepped in by making available $130 billion in low-interest credit.

The Wall Street bubble burst over Switzerland too. At the height of the housing/debt mania UBS, the giant Swiss bank with $31 trillion in assets, had taken a large slice of American mortgage debt (reckoned to be worth around $80 billion) and when the bubble burst was forced to write-down $37 billion of that debt. This was a bigger write-down than American banks Citigroup and Merrill Lynch. 'What happened here is a scandal,' declared local lawyer and shareholder Thomas Minder at the shareholders' meeting in Basel in early April 2008. 'You're responsible for the biggest loss in the history of the Swiss economy,' he thundered, and, adding a political postscript, demanded that the board 'put an end to the Americanisation of the Swiss economy'.[1]

An important part of the new capitalist global-debt bubble was the so-called 'carry trade' in which speculators and investors borrowed from low-interest countries, like Japan, and placed their money in higher-interest countries, like Iceland, Turkey or the Baltic states. Massive amounts of money were involved. Iceland became what one commentator called a massive 'nordic hedge fund masquerading as a country', a fund that then invested throughout the world in such enterprises as Woolworths, Hamleys toy shops and West Ham football club. The asset base of the Icelandic banking system was a world-record eight times the country's GDP. But it was always fragile. And Max Keiser likened the small, debt-laden country to a money geyser awaiting an eruption. In a television documentary aired just two days before the Western debt bubble burst he told the story of Iceland and the carry trade – and the global financial imbalances that it represented. On the programme Dr Paul Walker of GMFS (Global Monitoring for Food Security) argued that 'the buying up of US debt has been a key component of the global imbalances' and that 'central banks kept putting off the day of reckoning... but the longer they put it off the more serious it will be... and it will come.'[2]

Previously, high inflation and a trade deficit would have brought it all to an early and abrupt end. In the 20 years before the crash, however, the low-cost Chinese economy would keep the system going and the American consumer buying. Americans took on huge debt and the Chinese built up massive reserves. These 'global imbalances' represented a dangerous and fragile balancing act, but even as American debt levels reached Himalayan proportions 'neo-liberal' policy-makers in Washington, Wall Street and London remained confident and upbeat. A soothing thesis was delivered: the Chinese were recycling their reserves into the Western system (including the US government) and would never allow their great new market to contract. In reality, though, the whole Wall Street global edifice was shaking.

It all represented a major defeat for Wall Street – and the 'neo-liberal market' capitalist economy it represented and had been vigorously promoting. And the crisis led to much public soul-searching about the causes and the responsibilities. One thing was clear. The crisis had been triggered by 'sub-prime' lending – that is lending to lower-income people who could not afford to pay back the debt, either because the teaser interest rates suddenly rose or because of job losses or income weakness. And the banks – the lenders – were in the dock both for 'predatory' lending and for parcelling up the 'bad loans' in collective debt packages, a process known as 'securitisation'.

Surprisingly, the bankers' bank, the Bank for International Settlements (BIS), became a harsh critic of the Wall Street-led banking establishment. Indeed it 'startled the financial world' by pinning the blame firmly on the US central bank for what it considered to be its lax monetary policy, arguing that 'cleaning up' a property bubble once it had burst was not easy. A year later the BIS stated, through its seventy-eighth annual report, written primarily by its chief economist Bill White, 'the magnitude of the problems we now face could be much greater than many now perceive. It is not impossible that the unwinding of the credit bubble could, after a temporary period of higher inflation, culminate in a deflation that might be hard to manage, all the more so given the high debt levels.'[3]

NORTHERN ROCK, BEAR STEARNS

On 13 August a Bank of England loan to the British bank Northern Rock was made public, and this led to the first run on the deposits of a British bank in living memory – with 24-hour news channels broadcasting pictures of the lengthy queues around the world. Four days later the Treasury guaranteed the deposits of Northern Rock, and four-and-a-half months later the bank was nationalised.

Bear Stearns was a Wall Street institution. Founded in 1923 it grew to become one of the largest investment banks on Wall Street – with a sizeable equities business. It employed over fifteen thousand people. At the beginning of 2007 its total capital was well over $65 billion and it had total assets of $350 billion. The public got to know of trouble when on 22 June 2007 it sought to bail out one of its funds, which was trading in collateralised debt obligations. It was at real risk of bankruptcy when on 14 March 2008 JP Morgan Chase, in a highly unusual deal involving the Federal Reserve Bank (of New York), provided Bear Stearns with a mammoth emergency loan.

On 16 March JP Morgan Chase effectively bought Bear Stearns. The Federal Reserve had 'tossed out the rulebook when it assumed the role of white knight', temporarily bailing out Bear Stearns with a short-term loan 'to help avoid a collapse that might send other dominoes falling'.[4] Just days before, the Federal Reserve had announced a $200 billion lending programme for investment banks and a $100 billion credit line for banks and building societies. And in what the *New York Times* called a move 'unthinkable until recently' the Federal Reserve agreed to accept risky mortgage-backed securities as collateral.

RBS, HBOS

Hard on the heels of the Bear Stearns crisis in the USA, the giant British Royal Bank of Scotland (RBS) appeared to be in trouble, and in late April 2008 announced a massive £12 billion rights issue. The day before, in response to the obvious dramatic weakening in inter-bank lending and to help banks with the growing overhang of liquid assets (assets they could not sell or secure borrowing on), the Bank of England announced a special liquidity scheme under which £185 billion of Treasury bills were to be lent to the banks to improve liquidity and confidence.

A week later another bank, HBOS, announced a $4 billion rights issue, and two weeks after that the much smaller Bradford and Bingley announced a £300 million issue. And then in late June Barclays joined the party and announced a £4.5 billion share issue. With two of the country's great 'universal' banks, RBS and Barclays, in trouble the Bank of England's special liquidity scheme window saw a lot of traffic over the summer of 2008; but the growing British arm of the worldwide crisis was contained – at least for a few weeks.

FANNIE, FREDDIE, AIG AND THE
DISAPPEARING INVESTMENT BANKS

In July the action moved back to the USA and to the mammoth lenders Freddie Mac and Fannie Mae. On 13 July the US government made the extraordinary announcement that they would bail out the tottering companies. Freddie and Fannie were hybrid organisations – they were stockholder-owned but government-sponsored companies. More importantly, they controlled just about half of the US home-loan market – one worth $12 trillion. The Bush administration agreed to an unspecified and unlimited credit line, borrowing privileges at the discount window and, incredibly, a capital injection into the companies, if needed, in return for which the US government would receive shares.

So severe was the financial crisis, and the panic, that these measures were introduced swiftly in congress and signed with a sigh of relief by the conservative Bush administration. The US government had ditched decades of history – not to mention half its belief system – and guaranteed the debt of a private company. With the 'full faith and credit' of the US taxpayer behind them they were just one step away from socialist nationalisation – indeed to all intents and purposes they were in fact nationalised but with shareholders continuing to take the profits – should there be any.

In September the US government went further. It effectively nationalised both Freddie and Fannie by taking them into 'conservatorship', sacking the top executives and placing them under the management of the Federal Housing Finance Agency.

Later in September two other investment banks, Lehman Brothers and Merrill Lynch, effectively collapsed. Following a historic meeting in which the US Treasury brought all the top US bankers together, Lehman was forced to file for bankruptcy and Merrill was engineered (by the US government) into being purchased by Bank of America. And on the very next day the 'free market' Bush administration was forced into rescuing (effectively nationalising) the huge insurer AIG. This outright state takeover was a measure of how dire the problems of the US financial system had become: for without it the USA, and the world, might well have faced an immediate financial meltdown as the now all-important foreign holders of US dollars rushed to unload. The Chinese government was particularly interested in how the USA was going to deal with the Fannie and Freddie bankruptcy – as, according to an National Public Radio report on 7 September by Adam Davidson, almost one-tenth of China's GDP was invested in the outcome.

BRITAIN'S BANKS ARE RESCUED

The collapse of Lehman Brothers amounted to a US government-backed default, and its repercussions were to be felt worldwide among an array of other parties, not least in the UK financial sector. On 18 September the British government forced Lloyds TSB and HBOS to merge (a deal finalised in January 2009) and the British regulator, the FSA, announced a ban on 'short selling'. Ten days later, on the twenty-ninth, Bradford and Bingley joined Northern Rock in becoming a nationalised bank (with Abbey buying its retail deposit trade). And then on 13 October the British government took on a great and unprecedented new burden as further details were released about a £37 billion programme of government support for the recapitalisation of RBS, Lloyds and HBOS – all of this just after the UK had announced that, in the wake of the Icelandic banking collapse, it would protect British retail depositors.

November saw the UK government formalise its extraordinary socialising (or nationalising) of Britain's major banks when it set up the UK Finance Institute (UKFI) to manage the government's investments in the banks. And, after a short lull, January saw yet another quantum leap in socialising the City with the announcement of the government's asset protection scheme, asset-backed securities guarantee scheme and the extension of government help via the credit direct swap draw-down window.

By March of the following year the banking system of the City had been stabilised – at least for the moment – and the Brown government then turned its attention to the broader economy – with a singular and dramatic new policy. On 5 March the Bank of England introduced a new term into the vocabulary of socialised finance by announcing that it was organising a 'quantitative easing' (QE) of £75 billion. This was later to increase to over £175 billion by August, and then again to over £200 billion by November 2009.

BRITAIN ON THE BRINK

This socialising of the debt by the Brown government may well have temporarily stabilised the banking system, but it led directly to a growing financial crisis for the British government itself – a phenomenon that was to become more widely described as a 'sovereign debt crisis'. In short, British taxpayers had bailed out British banks; but this had put such pressure on the public finances that Britain itself could go bust.

The country, no longer a global imperial power, was simply too small to carry these huge, over-extended global banks. The over-extension of RBS told the awesome story: by the end of June 2008 this one bank had a balance sheet of almost £2 trillion – whereas its backer and seeming guarantor, the UK, had a GDP that amounted to just £1.5 trillion.

It was becoming clear that the continuing set of Britain's political/financial elites – with its hubristic over-importance and its consequent financial over-extension – was coming home to roost.

The economist Willem Buiter could argue that Britain's political/financial establishment had acted as recklessly as that of another island with an egregiously over-extended global banking system – Iceland.

> Returning from Reykjavik last night was like coming home from home. Allowing for the differences of scale…there are disturbing economic parallels…Relaxation of regulatory norms was consciously used by the British government as an instrument for attracting financial business to London, mainly from New York City. Fiscal policy in both countries became strongly pro-cyclical during the boom years…Households were permitted, indeed encouraged, to accumulate excessive debt – around 170% of household disposable income in the UK, over 210% in Iceland.

And on top of this irresponsibility, there was another, related, irresponsibility: the British had allowed, and encouraged, the 'Dutch disease' to take hold – that is the crowding out of other sectors of the British economy by the financial sector in the City of London and the housing and construction sector. It was a highly shortsighted national strategy leading to a deadly imbalance in the economy; and all this on top of the imbalances created by Britain as a petro-dollar economy, built up since the discovery of North Sea oil. As Buiter could argue, referring again to Britain and Iceland, 'in neither country have the responsible parties (the prime minister, the minister of finance, the governor of the central bank and the head of banking regulation and supervision) admitted any personal responsibility for the disaster'.[5] The 'responsible parties' named here would include: Tony Blair and Gordon Brown (both as chancellor of the exchequer and prime minister), Alistair Darling (chancellor of the exchequer after Brown), Eddie George and Mervyn King (both governors of the Bank of England), and Callum McCarthy and Howard Davies (both chairmen of the FSA) – although their 'responsibility' needs to be placed in the context of a general supportive political/financial elite (hence the honours, including baronetcies, knighthoods and other awards, bestowed on them).

'ANGLO–AMERICA' FAILS

Of course the British crisis as it unfolded in 2008–9 was but part of a more general crisis of the 'Anglo–American' economic and geoeconomic model. During Tony Blair's premiership Britain remained out of the euro-zone and instead increasingly hitched itself to the American Wall Street-led way of doing economics. And it also joined the USA in both constructing and operating the new global financial capitalist system as it was evolving during the years after the collapse of communism. The old maxim used to be that 'when America sneezes Europe catches a cold.' Now it had become 'when America catches a cold Britain catches pneumonia.' Indeed the story of Britain's financial crisis cannot be told without placing the country's plight in the broader context of her earlier choice, a choice not made by France or Germany, to take part in the American-led global debt scam – that is the pursuit of an economic model with stagnant wages, no savings and huge personal credit based upon a housing bubble, with people living beyond their means and funded by rising, low-cost Asia. In other words by 2007 Britain had got caught up in a broader unfolding disaster – that of American weakness and decline, the rise of China, and the stalling and eroding of 'globalisation'.

THE END OF AMERICAN ASCENDANCY

The world at the end of the George W. Bush presidency was very different from the world envisaged at its beginning. At its start, on 20 January 2000, Americans – and much of the world – still saw an ascendant America at the heart of a global economic system. The driver of this economy was something called 'globalisation' – an essentially Americanising dynamic that was fashioning the world's economy on American economic lines with American capitalist values and rules. It was also seemingly a global economy in which the US consumer was the engine driving global growth.

America was also ascendant politically. In January 2001 American influence was still spreading east through the NATO expansion into Eurasia inaugurated by Bush's father and continued by Bill Clinton. Poland, Hungary and the Czech Republic had joined in 1999, and even the Baltic countries, former states of the Soviet Union, were slated to join. They were all very pro-American, seeing Washington as their liberator. And with successes in the first Gulf War and in the Kosovo campaign against

Milosevic, the USA stood tall. So tall that George Bush during his election campaign could promise a 'humbler foreign policy', and in his inaugural speech could suggest a global engagement 'without arrogance'.

But eight years later, as the Bush presidency drew to its momentous close, the promise of American ascendancy had shrivelled. The reckless 2003 attempt to remake the Middle East had failed, and the American political class was divided about how to extricate its troops from Iraq. And neither big nor small nations were listening to the USA as carefully as they had done. Iran was successfully rebuffing the USA over the question of its nuclear programme with its potential to produce nuclear weapons; EU leaders had turned down an American request to bring Georgia and Ukraine into NATO; Russia was reasserting its Soviet-era influence in the Caucasus as it pressured Georgia, a US satellite, to disgorge two of its regions with majority Russian-speaking populations – all while the USA was unable to offer any serious counter-pressure; and China was determining its own economic path – and had refused to revalue the renmimbi after very insistent American pressure.

And on top of all this the American economy was in deep structural recession. For the first time since 1945 American power in the world was becoming a live issue – and the question could well be asked: what kind of superpower is it that is no longer economically independent, relying for its very financial stability and living standards on another power? Of course few were openly asking this question. London university professor Iwan Morgan was an exception. He was suggesting that America was an 'indebted empire' and prophesied that 'when Asia stops buying dollars, the American economy will experience problems that will have implications for America's global power.'[6]

After any turning point the times that went before it can, with hindsight, look very different. And looking back – from a vantage-point in 2008 at the end of the Bush/Greenspan regime – the great era of 'globalisation' did indeed look rather different. It looked far less comprehensive than it appeared during the heady days of expansion. In fact it began to look as though it may never really have existed at all – at least not in the sense that the world was becoming a single global system.

What had decidedly existed, though, was a 'partial globalisation', if such a phenomenon was possible. This 'partial globalisation' amounted to an increasing trilateral integration and economic lift-off across North America, Asia and Europe (and parts of Latin America, Brazil certainly), but it left huge swaths of the world outside the system, still without an industrial or commercial base or internal market.

What was also increasingly clear was that, whatever the precise dimensions of the power and influence of the various players in the coming multipolar world, the twenty-first century was not going to be the second American century.

BAD NEWS FOR BRITAIN

This was very bad news for Britain's political and financial elites, who had progressively from Margaret Thatcher's third term onwards hitched themselves both to Wall Street financial capitalism and to American power.

It was a decision that was assuming the proportions of a fatal and fateful blunder.

PART 7

Jubilee year:
celebrating an
illusion

19 A JUBILEE FOR THE BRITISH: HOLLOWED OUT AND IN DEBT

The great crash of 2007–8 led, for a short while, to great soul-searching among Britain's financial elites, and indeed to bitter criticism of the un-reformed, over-bloated City. No less a figure than the governor of the Bank of England Mervyn King could say on 20 October 2009, 'to paraphrase a great war-time leader, never in the field of financial endeavour has so much been owed by so few to so many. And, one might add with little real reform.' And FSA chairman Lord Turner described much of the City's activities as 'socially useless' and questioned whether the City had become too large.

On top of these 'official' critiques, reassessments and *mea culpas* were coming fast and furious from London's financial commentariat – not least from those erstwhile doyens of the neo-liberal globalisation consensus like Martin Wolf of the *Financial Times* and Anatole Kaletsky of the *Times,* who became as eloquent in their denunciations of capitalist finance as they had been earlier in their support.

And there was also a search for causes. And it soon became clear that chief among the culprits was the heady mix of financialisation and 'light touch' regulation (of the economy) and the over-extension of Britain's financial sector (primarily the banks in the City). But deeper causes still were also starting to be exhumed. And attention began turning to how global finance had driven the 'hollowing out' of the country.

'Hollowing out' was the new, apt, catchphrase to describe the process that had forced the destruction of jobs in Britain. Indeed, ever since the 1980s huge swaths of British industry and manufacturing had been declared 'uncompetitive' compared with low-cost Asia, and Britain's leaders – Thatcher, Major, Blair and Brown – had seen no point in trying to keep them. They all accepted an unrefined version of 'free trade' theory in which the service sector, including the City, would make up for this loss as China allowed us to penetrate their burgeoning domestic market. It did not happen – and the 'hollowing out' of Britain continued.

This 'hollowing out' – its growing unemployment, low wages, part-time work, all leading to stagnant incomes – was filled for a while by the unsustainable debt boom. But this debt mountain began to collapse in 2007. By jubilee year, 2012, as London hosted both the jubilee celebrations and the Olympic Games – which its organisers were dubbing 'the greatest show on earth' – the country had ended up in a more vulnerable debt position than any of its competitors. And many of its households were in varying levels of financial distress.

DROWNING IN DEBT

By the time of the crash the British people had amassed the highest amount of debt of any European country, accounting for about one-third of all EU private indebtedness. In 2001 personal debt in the UK was estimated to be an astronomical £1000 billion, much of this mortgage debt; between 2001 and 2005 average earnings grew by only 22 per cent, while mortgage debt increased by 94 per cent. Five years later the indebtedness was even worse. In 2010 average household debt was £57,888; excluding mortgages it was £18,784, so the average owed by every UK adult was £30,226. Total UK personal debt stood at £1459 billion.[1]

However, during the 1990s for any commentator to raise this issue as a potential threat – certainly to raise it as a problem that the market could not rectify – was considered somewhat crankish. The Bank of England, the Treasury, the political class in Westminster, and most financial journalists all missed its significance. Yet debt was building up huge problems for the British. As economists Larry Elliot and Dan Atkinson, among the first to warn about it, could argue, somewhat understatedly, 'astronomical levels of personal indebtedness will, we believe, prove a millstone around the economy's neck in the decade to come.'[2]

Britain saw two private-sector borrowing booms, one following the other. In the late 1990s corporate liability grew rapidly during the dot-com bubble and the so-called 'new economy'. Then, following the dot-com crash, the authorities, with help from low inflation derived from low costs in Asia, kept interest rates low – and the great 2002–7 housing boom was born.

But Britain's debt disaster was two-pronged – for while British families were borrowing at home, British-based financial institutions were over-extended abroad – big time! And by the time of the banking crash Britain's external debt was causing serious credibility problems and was by far the largest of all the Western economies. This debt – largely private debt owed to non-residents repayable in foreign currency, goods or services – amounted to a staggering $9,191,104 million or $150,673 per (British) person. This was almost four times the debt of the USA (only $42,343 per person), three times that of Germany ($54,604 per person) and well over twice that of France ($68,183 per person). Britain's debt to foreigners as a percentage of GDP was 365 per cent, a very high percentage compared to that of the USA (95 per cent), Germany (160 per cent) and France (211 per cent).[3]

Britain's banks were the most vulnerable of all the banking systems in the advanced economies and were increasingly being compared to Iceland and Ireland, two countries whose banks were too big for their respective nations to support. So when the crash threatened the UK's entire banking system, the government bailout had to be substantial. The Treasury footed part of the bill – with consequent high levels of government liabilities, and the Bank of England began a money-printing operation, euphemistically called 'quantitative easing'. In the process Britain's central bank itself became over-extended. Central bank balance sheets told the story: between September 2008 and July 2009 all the major central banks expanded their balance sheets – the ECB by 39 per cent, the Swiss National Bank by 80 per cent, the US Federal Reserve by 119 per cent but the Bank of England by more than any of these, 127 per cent increase.[4]

BANKING: NEW MARKETS IN ASIA?

This mountainous level of liability had not been built up accidentally, or by chance. It had been a key part of public policy promoted by governments and central banks and financial-industry lobbyists. For a generation of British politicians the 'financialisation' of the economy had become the easy way out of an increasingly difficult economic dilemma caused by Britain's lack of competitiveness in the heavy industrial and manufacturing sector, the changing global order and the shift of wealth to low-cost Asia.

Britain saw its future in services. A key component of the Thatcherite revolution was the necessary break-up of old Labourist Britain with its full employment policies and its large 'uncompetitive' manufacturing and industrial base. In the era of globalisation the country should concentrate on 'what it does best', and financial services was one such area. This strategy dominated British government thinking from 1979 right through to 2007. Blair's New Labour was a particularly enthusiastic supporter of adapting to the global market, rejecting 'industrial policy' and emphasising a future based upon financial services, 'the creative industries' and 'the knowledge economy'. During the 1990s other Western economies, though not France and Germany, were developing along the same lines, but Britain was an extreme case.

This great and reckless strategic switch to a 'service-based', 'knowledge-based', economy had a deadly effect. Over time the economy became seriously unbalanced. The domestic economy had become overly financialised: and although British people 'selling insurance to each other' made good business during a boom, it added little to long-term economic wellbeing. More importantly the country became far too dependent upon the burgeoning global financial-services industry in the City of London, which, though benefiting the country in good times, was to become a catastrophic burden in a downturn. Although it was clear from the early days of 'globalisation' that China would not seriously open her vast market to Britain's finance and service sector, the British financial elite remained fixated by a 'free trade' belief that the East, and particularly China, would become a big and lasting market for British services. There was an assumption that 'Chinese people can't do banking.' So by 2007 both the downturn and the emergence of Asian protected markets was creating real trouble for the City and its global debt industry.

THE GREAT HOLLOWING-OUT JOBS CRISIS

As a direct result of this three-decades-long gamble on a rosy global future for the British service sector the country witnessed the 'hollowing out' of its manufacturing jobs, and its more general wage base. As jobs were lost and wage levels remained stagnant, Britain's growth rate and living standards were slated to fall. It was here that debt came in – for, with official blessing, the British would fill this vacuum with a vast expansion of credit: of loans, credit-card debt and easy and lavish mortgages.

The great British debt crisis was therefore part of a deeper underlying three-decade-long structural change in the British economy as it adapted to globalisation. This 'jobs crisis' or 'hollowing out' had started with

Thatcher's market reforms, but gathered pace under Major and then, powerfully, under Blair. And because it was slow-burning, and living standards were kept up by rising debt and oil revenues – and real employment figures were difficult to assess properly – for many commentators the jobs 'hollowing out' was, *at any one time*, hardly discernible. And it was under-reported – after all the leaders of media corporations and many of their journalists were high-net-worth individuals and continued to do well, shielded from the growing strains on normal family budgets.

This jobs crisis was also masked by the systematic rise of part-time working and the creation of a huge 'contingent' workforce. In Britain all types of households saw part-time work increasing: 5.9 million worked part-time in December 1992, rising to 6.3 million in September 1996 (5 million of these being women). In Britain between 1979 and 1993 full-time work fell dramatically – by a huge 10 per cent. Will Hutton has calculated that between 1975 and 1993 the proportion of the adult population in full-time tenured jobs fell from 55 to 35 per cent. Many of these new part-time workers, whose incomes ranged widely from high to low, were increasingly defined by their insecurity.[5]

Of course this new system of contingent labour and, more generally, the flexible labour market demanded by the global economy does in some sense serve the needs of people, of labour as well as of capital. Flexibility and part-time working appeals to many women and some men because it fits in with their family responsibilities. And in principle labour flexibility is a highly appropriate mechanism for an advanced, complex society. However the 'hire and fire' economy of the Anglo–American globalised system was not essentially a response to these changing social needs; rather it was a cost-cutting operation. Contingent labour often relieves the employer of expensive 'on costs' such as pensions.

HIDDEN UNEMPLOYMENT

Karl Marx famously coined the idea of a 'reserve army of the unemployed' acting as a weapon that could be used by employers to discipline workers. As the number of core workers has shrunk and that of contingent workers risen, modern global capitalism now has its own 'reserve army' available – and, in a sense unknown to Marx, on a global scale! Of course many part-time workers, unlike the unemployed of old, are not seeking full-time work and therefore cannot be counted as 'reserve' in the Marxist sense; however, many are; and with welfare being pared down, with more income needed in traditional households, and with the growth of single-parent families and people living alone (who need a proper wage, not a supplementary one), the demand for full-time work will always be high.

Contingent, part-time work serves another function too. In this public-relations-dominated media age Western governments are constantly fighting a battle of presentation. The growth in part-time work hides the extent of unemployment. During the 1970s the unemployment rate began to rise across the Western world – up from 3 per cent at the beginning of the decade to an average of about 6 per cent at the end. The 1980s saw unemployment rise further, denting the view that unemployment was a passing phase, linked to economic cycles.

In the early 1990s, with the corporate mania for downsizing in full swing, it became obvious that structural factors such as changing technology and footloose global capital in search of low costs were causing high unemployment. Harry Shutt has pointed to technology as being partly responsible for this higher unemployment, and as a reason for the new phenomenon known as 'jobless growth', particularly in Europe. He argues that 'taking the 1974 to 1994 period as a whole, there has been negligible growth in the numbers of employed people in the countries of the European Union at a time when the level of economic activity (GDP) has expanded significantly,' and he points to the example of Spain, where employment fell by over 8 per cent during the period while the economy virtually doubled in size![6]

NAGGING INSECURITY AT WORK

But perhaps the most important consequence of the new 'flexible labour market' was the widespread and profound insecurity it engendered. Insecurity is indefinable, and its extent is not statistically provable. Yet over the last two decades it has been interwoven into the very fabric of the working populations of the 'free market' economies. The signs of anxiety are there for everyone to see: employees work longer and longer hours, workers stay late at the office, not in order to finish necessary work but to secure their positions, and there is an increase in useless paperwork to justify jobs and salaries.

Of course job insecurity certainly keeps people on their toes, as well as on other people's toes, but there is no evidence that it produces higher growth rates than was the case in the more regulated and structured labour markets of the 1950s, 1960s and early 1970s. The jury is still out, and may always be out, on whether labour-market competition and insecurity, or alternatively stability and cooperation, produce a more efficient workforce.

JOB INSECURITY AND THE MIDDLE CLASS

For most people in Britain under pensionable age, income from employment remains the very foundation of their lifestyle, if not their life. Other sources of income – dividends from shares, interest from bonds, small inheritances, rent – may help out, but tend to be marginal. Jobs remain the name of the game, and the character of employment – particularly its security – becomes important. For the employed majority, if not for those who employ them, the new capitalism's destruction of traditional job security was a real blow. And by destroying the good secure job (with pensions and benefits) it was also destroying one of the building blocks of the middle class.

Flexible 'hire and fire' labour policies may also have caused some wider problems in society. The world of disposable jobs may well have induced a short-termism into the work culture that would feed through into broader social values. Richard Sennett, in his fascinating book *The Corrosion of Character: The personal consequences of work in the new capitalism*, argues that this connection is very real. It appears that 'when people talk in earnest about family values [short-termism] is no way to raise children. We want them, for instance to learn how to be loyal; a management consultant told me he felt stupid talking to his children about commitment, since at work he does not practice it.' Sennett also argues, intriguingly, that hire-and-fire labour flexibility may undermine the work ethic: 'the classic work ethic was one of delayed gratification: coping with immediate frustration usually requires a sense of sustaining purpose, of long-term goals. The flexible work ethic undermines such self-discipline; you must seize the moment, delay may prove fatal.'[7]

THE DEVALUATION OF WORK

The British (and Western) middle class was forged on the work ethic. The capitalist system of the twentieth century, which created this middle class, differed from the old aristocratic system it replaced by elevating productivity and creativity – that is, work – over lineage. And by mid-century almost everyone – the medium and small businesses, the professional classes, even the big corporate bosses – was defining themselves by their work, and by securing their money 'the old-fashioned way' – by earning it.

Yet the new globalised economy, and the new capitalism it created, was turning this value system on its head. Work itself was becoming devalued. Earning, as opposed to 'making' or having, money was becoming more and more difficult. It was a stark fact that in the 1990s earned income (wages and salaries) actually fell as a percentage of total income. Global capitalism was at least becoming clear about its priorities: lower rewards from work, higher rewards from investments and inheritance. And there were big rewards too for going into debt. The average Briton no longer worked to pay for a house – you could buy it, and sell it, for a huge profit, all in the same week by the clever use of debt.

Looking at the same issue from a different vantage point, in Britain income from employment (wages) was diminishing as a ratio of all household disposable income – from 90.4 per cent in 1977 to 73.3 per cent in 1994, while income from rents, dividends and interest grew from 10.7 per cent to 13.6 per cent, and even benefits rose as a proportion of income. An IFS (Institute for Fiscal Studies) study in 2005 reported that since 2001/2 household earnings had barely risen in real terms, while at the same time self-employment incomes had fallen considerably, by a startling 30 per cent over the same period.[8]

WAGES, INVESTMENTS, INHERITANCE

One look at the riches and rewards created by investments – as opposed to wages and salaries – shows the advantages in the new economy of investing for a living over working for a living. Charles Handy calculated – in boom times – that

A £10 million investment, for example, which is made on the expectation that it will recover its costs in ten years' time and provide a 20% compound return, will, in the next ten years, if the expectation is met and if things continue the same, earn an extra £26.4 million, and even more in the years following.'[9]

Of all the income coming into all the households in the British and US economies during the height of the global capitalist boom the share of pay went down and the share from interest, dividends and straight gifts (inheritance) went up. Of course much of this was concentrated at the top. Take shares: in Britain in boom times there remained a marked difference between the wealth holdings of the top 1 per cent and the rest – the top 1 per cent holding almost half of their portfolios in shares whereas less wealthy groups held progressively less in shares.[10]

THE WORKING POOR: THE WONDERFUL
WORLD OF McJOBS

Perhaps, though, the biggest single attack on the value of work is the rise of the working poor. Millions of people in Britain put in 'a fair day's work' but end up without 'a fair day's pay'. In the early years of the new century the American 'new economy' retailer Walmart became the symbol of such low pay and conditions. There were even reports that in parts of the Walmart empire workers were depending on federal food stamps and the use of hospital emergency rooms for basic medical care.[11] From being the darling brand of the new 'flexible economy' in the 1990s Walmart's labour practices became highly controversial – so much so that by 2007 Democratic politicians in the presidential campaign found the company an easy target.

In Britain, where there is no official count of the number living in poverty, low pay – in reality 'poverty pay' – is also a feature of the employment landscape. In 1991 a staggering 28 per cent of those with incomes of less than half the national average were in households in some kind of work, and a third of these were self-employed.[12] Over a decade-and-a-half later – with 'low pay' now defined as 60–70 per cent of median pay – around 20–30 per cent of all incomes were designated 'low pay'.[13] And since the crash and the economic downturn, with pay freezes in an inflationary period, low pay is growing as a real concern.

Of course for some, poverty pay is simply an addition to family income. As Paul Gregg and Jonathan Wadsworth have reported about Britain before the crash, 'new jobs – often McJobs – are taken disproportionately by those with another household member already at work.'[14] For others low pay is acceptable as a step on the ladder to higher pay. And for some, work, any work at virtually any pay, will suffice because of the need to be in a working environment.

However, none of these arguments outweighs the damage that low pay does to the work ethic. If work is underpaid it will ultimately be undervalued. Nor do these arguments justify the extreme differences between the top of the income scale and the bottom. It is difficult to argue that the gap between the ability, creativity and dedication of the millions of working poor and that of the top earners (let alone the top 'unearners') is large enough to justify the gap in income and wealth.

20 A JUBILEE FOR THE SUPER-RICH

Following the popular success of the royal wedding in April of 2011, when the country was given a bank holiday in order to celebrate the occasion, Downing Street announced that for the Queen's jubilee celebrations in 2012 two days' holiday would be granted. The Labour government had begun the planning for the jubilee in 2010, and Peter Mandelson, who had in his younger days left the country to escape the royal wedding of Charles and Diana, was effusive in his hopes for the event. He went on television to speak for the government: 'the country as a whole and the Commonwealth will want to mark a remarkable 60 years on the throne.' He announced that a diamond-jubilee medal would be struck and plans were later unveiled that the Queen would lead a jubilee pageant flotilla of a hundred boats down the Thames. And all of this would set the scene for what was to follow – 'the greatest show on earth', the London Olympic Games.

This assumption by Britain's official class of a celebratory national mood that would sweep the country in 2012 was to be seriously reviewed when in the summer of 2011 violent rioting broke out in many British cities, and with it extensive looting. Police recorded that three thousand offences had taken place in London alone. In the debate that followed the prime minister David Cameron argued that 'there are deep problems in our society that have been growing for a long time' and that there was a moral issue involved: 'a decline in responsibility, a rise in selfishness'. The former prime minister Tony Blair also pitched in. He argued that there was at work a gang culture and that 'the truth is that many of these people [looters] are from families that are profoundly dysfunctional, operating on completely different terms from the rest of society...'[1]

WHITHER THE 'MIDDLE CLASS'?

As the country entered jubilee year the celebratory mood was somewhat muted – as it was becoming clear that the effects of the economic downturn were spreading beyond the underclass and the poor. A broad swath of Britain's middle-class households were beginning to feel real economic anxiety.

The country's late-twentieth-century experiment with financialised capitalism was supposed to create a stable and prosperous middle-class society. It was certainly sold as such by its proponents. They predicted that by sweeping away post-war social democracy and the industrial society it represented we would also sweep away the old 'us and them' frozen class divisions of Britain – the entrenched class warfare between the paternalist business-cum-aristocratic class at the top and the large traditional highly unionised working class. Instead, and over time, the market would ensure social mobility and we would all become 'middle class'. It would also, necessarily, be a society with big disparities of income and wealth, but this would not matter for it would also be a society in which, broadly speaking, 'all ships were rising' with the tide of growth. As long as 'all ships were rising' we would be at ease with ourselves – and we would not particularly care, we would be 'supremely relaxed', about the super- and mega-rich. And so, particularly during the early years of Blair and New Labour, when for a few years average wages were rising, we were. Issues of inequality began to seem like yesterday's debate.

It was a beguiling prospect. But by the turn of the millennium, and after two decades of full-on marketised capitalism, British society was not evolving as envisaged. For a start, there may have been many 'rising ships', but there were also many ships in the fleet that were sinking, and many more that were taking in water. The fact is that Britain has seen a marked increase in economic inequality over the three decades of the neo-liberal period, and by 2010 these inequalities had become striking. In January of 2010 a report, commissioned by the minister for women and equality, Harriet Harman, and chaired by Professor John Hills, stated that 'inequalities in earnings and income are high in Britain, both compared with other industrialised countries, and compared with thirty years ago.' The report also showed that disparities in wealth were even more striking. It argued that 'for some readers the sheer scale of the inequalities which we present will be shocking,' and then concluded, dramatically, and rather ruefully, that 'whether or not people's positions reflect some form of merit or desert, the sheer scale of the differences in wealth, for instance, may imply that it is impossible to create a cohesive society.' And an IFS study published in 2009 at the very end of the neo-liberal period reported that 'income inequality has risen for a second successive year, and is now equal to its highest-ever level (in 1961)'.[2]

THE SUPER-RICH PROBLEM

But it was only after the crash, and the bankers' pay and bonuses revelations in 2008, that Britain's unequal society was firmly back in the spotlight, and with it the issue of the super- and mega-rich. The economist Paul Krugman has argued that the much-vaunted 'Anglo-Saxon' new capitalism model is not only not producing a middle class of so-called 'knowledge workers', but rather the model is generating 'the rise of a narrow oligarchy' with 'income and wealth becoming increasingly concentrated in the hands of a small privileged elite'.[3]

The problem now, though, is not just growing 'concentration' of wealth and income, or growing inequality – it is much deeper, and much more worrying. For what the three decades of neo-liberal capitalism has wrought in the 'Anglo–American' market economies, in Britain and the USA, is the entrenching of classes and the virtual end of mobility. During those years virtually every political tendency in Anglo–America, from right-wing conservative Republican to left-wing socialist Labour, could at least agree with the aim of 'equality of opportunity'. Yet even achieving this meritocratic objective, long promised by market enthusiasts, was not so easy. Indeed from the 1990s onwards things may have gone into reverse. In 2009 the New Labour Blairite meritocrat *par excellence*, Alan Milburn, issued a report called 'Unleashing Aspiration' which was greeted with praise from many quarters (including from London mayor Boris Johnson and neo-con Tory *Telegraph* commentator Janet Daley).[4] Milburn argued that 'the huge growth in professional employment that took place after the Second World War was the engine that made Britain such a mobile society. By opening their doors to people from a rich variety of backgrounds, the professions created unheard of opportunities for millions of men and women.' Yet, in a devastating admission of failure, he also argues that 'in the decades since then, of course, social mobility has slowed down in our society. Birth, not worth, has become more and more a determinant of people's life chances.' As the Harman Report in 2010 argued, achieving this mobility 'is very hard when there are such wide differences between the resources which people and their families have to help them fulfil their diverse potentials'.[5]

So, in a startling reversal, it is continental Europe's so-called 'sclerotic' societies that are arguably more socially mobile that those of the 'dynamic' 'Anglo-Saxons'. Even after the crash Britain's neo-liberal elites, however, were finding this proposition very difficult to accept.

THE NEW PLUTOCRACY

Of course income inequality is only one measure of the social division in Western nations. Wealth also counts. And the story of wealth distribution in the highly globalised 'new capitalist' states of Britain and the USA since the late 1970s is a striking one.

The situation in the 1990s is illustrated by the fact that in 1995 in America the mega-wealthy (the top 0.5 per cent, or 500,000 families) controlled 24.2 per cent of assets and 27.5 per cent of net worth, the top 1 per cent of American households (about one million) possessed 31 per cent of assets and 35.1 per cent of net worth, the next 9 per cent (the affluent) possessed 31 per cent of assets and 33.2 per cent of net worth, and all the rest (over 89 million households) only possessed 37.9 per cent of assets and 31.5 per cent of net worth.'[6]

By 2004 wealth inequality had grown even further, and there was evidence that the mega- and super-rich were leaving greater and greater gaps between themselves and everyone else, including the merely affluent. Figures show that the top quartile (25 per cent of people) owned 87 per cent of the country's wealth, the upper-middle owned 10 per cent, the lower-middle 3 per cent and the bottom zero. They also show that between 1995 and 2004 the gap between the top quartile and the 'lower-middle' had risen by almost a third. A 2007 report from Harvard University argued that 'by the early 1990s, the United States had surpassed all industrial societies in the extent of inequality of household wealth'; and it also argued that the economic growth of the most recent decade or so, from 1995 onwards, had seen 'growing inequality [of wealth] accompanying [this] wealth growth.'[7]

Not surprisingly Britain increasingly resembled the USA in this 'wealth gap'. In Britain an unhealthy concentration of wealth is not new. In the 1930s the top 1 per cent owned as much 58 per cent of all the country's wealth while the mass of Britons were capital-less and property-less. As R.H. Tawney poignantly argued, Britons who fought during the First World War on the Somme and at Passchendale 'probably do not own wealth to the value of the kit they took into battle'. In the first seven decades of the twentieth century there were significant – indeed dramatic – changes to the wealth of the top 1 per cent, which declined from 68 per cent in 1911 (for England and Wales) to 20 per cent in 1976 (for the UK as a whole). This half-century-long spreading of wealth, primarily the product of progressive tax policies, amounted to what Charles Feinstein has called 'a major economic and social revolution'.

However, in a clear measure of the reactionary effects of the new global market capitalism, this wealth 'revolution' stalled as the British economy became more globalised during the 1980s and 1990s, while wealth distribution remained static. By the end of the 1980s – after a decade of Thatcherite market radicalism – the top 10 per cent of adults owned 45 per cent of the wealth, and 30 per cent of adults still had less than £5000 in assets. In the early 1990s the British super-rich – the top 1 per cent of the population, with an average wealth of $1.3 million each – owned a huge 18 per cent of the country's marketable wealth and the top 5 per cent owned a staggering 37 per cent of all wealth.[8]

BRITAIN'S LANDED CASTE

Even after Thatcher's 'popular capitalist' revolution – with its rhetoric of 'spreading the wealth' beyond the traditional landowning class – wealth and land still tended to go hand in hand. In the most sophisticated analysis available, John Scott has described the 'top twenty' of the British league of wealth as 'a mixture of urban and rural rentier landowners and entrepreneurial capitalists'. Scott argues that because research into this very murky area can only concentrate on relatively visible sources of wealth, and is often unable to penetrate into the anonymity of most shareholdings and bank accounts, rentiers, whose assets are concentrated in such anonymous investment portfolios, are normally underrepresented in any hierarchy of wealth holders. Even so, he argues that land and entrepreneurial capital remained the major sources of really large fortunes in the 1980s, and that 'the wealthiest landowners are the long established landowning families of Cadogan, Grosvenor, and Portman, most of whom own substantial urban estates as well as their country acres'.[9]

A particular feature of the British super-rich scene is the concentration in very few hands of land ownership. Britain – or rather the land area known as the United Kingdom – is, quite literally, owned by a very small caste; as is the capital city, London. It remains a poignant commentary on wealth concentration that large tracts of London are owned by just a few individuals. The Duke of Westminster, through the Grosvenor estate, owns around 200 acres of Belgravia and 100 acres of Mayfair – a dynastic inheritance created by the seventeenth-century marriage of Cheshire baronet Thomas Grosvenor to Mary Davies, the '12 year old heiress to a London manor that at the time included 200 acres of Pimlico'. Viscount Portman owns 110 acres north of Oxford Street. Lord Howard de Walden's four daughters, through a holding company, own 90 acres of Marylebone. Elizabeth Windsor, the Queen, remains the 'official' owner of 150 acres of 'crown estates' in central London, as the eight crown estates commissioners address their annual report to her.

A SELF-PERPETUATING PLUTOCRACY:
THE INHERITING CLASSES

'Old money' is still very prominent in free-market Britain; and the traditional aristocracy remains a highly privileged group. Tom Nicholas has suggested that 'becoming a business leader in Britain is still largely determined by the interconnected characteristics of a wealthy family and a privileged education...there has been no democratisation of British business over the last century and a half.'[10] For all the rhetoric of 'the need to reward enterprise and skill', 'old money' has done extremely well out of the Thatcher–Reagan revolution and the global market economics that it spawned. Like all capital, 'old capital' was bound to survive and prosper in a low-tax, deregulated economy. And 'new inheritance' – that is the wealth of the sons and daughters of the self-made of the post-war years – has now joined 'old inheritance' in an economy (and culture) dominated by inherited wealth.

The amounts are staggering – and were being reported long before the great crash of 2007–8 raised issues of wealth distribution within mainstream thinking. The economist Robert Avery of Cornell University argued as early as the beginning of the 1990s that 'we...will soon be seeing the largest transfer of income in the history of the world' as the older generation leaves wealth to the 'baby-boomers'. And apart from straight gifts during the lifetime of the giver, there is also the mammoth transfer of unearned wealth – including whole businesses – upon the death (or retirement) of the super-rich giver. And this inheritance culture will continue to grow. Two dynamics will see to that. First, the global economy has made the present generation of super-rich wealthier than any before. Second, this burst of super-wealth coincides (or, is the cause of) the increasing financial pressures on the young. Hence, as leading political scientist Kevin Phillips saw clearly as early as 1993,

> for those under thirty or thirty-five, two decades of polarisation had brought a special, though widely unappreciated, irony: not only were they (and those younger) in danger of being the first generation...to suffer a lower standard of living than their parents, but they would be the first generation to receive – or not receive – much of their economic opportunity from family inheritance, not personal achievement.[11]

A troublesome feature of this new economy and culture of inheritance is the growth in the number of recipients of unearned cash income – using inherited money to consume and live on. There are a considerable number of people within super-rich families whose unearned annual income is not derived from their own net worth, but rather from their parents' or grandparents' net worth. But partly because it is often shrouded in mystery some of the egregious sums involved are, unlike huge salaries, rarely exposed to public view.

The sting is often taken out of the censure of super-rich inheritance because in the modern economy many middle-class families and individuals now inherit money themselves (albeit fairly small amounts). And this inheritance – normally the family house – is a very welcome addition to the stretched household economies of millions. The great housing and debt boom of the early twenty-first century priced many younger middle-class people out of housing altogether, and as a result passing housing down the generations was the least the older generation could do for their offspring. The middle-class housing crisis creates a considerable constituency of approval for inheritance, from which the super-rich inheriting classes benefit. So politicians in the West (particularly in the housing-boom-and-bust lands of Britain and America) either accept inheritance as untouchable – except at the margins – or even support it ideologically as creating 'islands of independence' from the state.

Neo-liberals and 'free-marketeers' – who philosophically may remain meritocrats – nevertheless often support the idea of wealth 'cascading down the generations' as a bulwark against socialism. Yet, ironically, what has now begun to emerge is a capitalist version of the much-derided state welfare 'dependency culture'. For too many, dependency upon the family inheritance has been substituted for dependency on the state.

TAX-DODGING: 'ONLY THE LITTLE PEOPLE PAY TAXES'

As well inheriting large portions of their fortunes, many British super-rich people are also dodging taxes. The late Leona Helmsley, the billionaire New Yorker, famously made her name when she bragged that 'we [the super-rich] don't pay taxes. Only the little people pay taxes.'

And in Britain too tax-dodging by rich people has become a way of wealth. Queen Elizabeth has set a bad example. Until 1994 the Queen was allowed by successive governments to pay no taxes at all, and since then has only had to pay some of them. Particularly egregious is the continuing exemption from inheritance tax that monarchs enjoy. For instance she has paid no tax at all on the money left to her by her mother, 'the Queen Mother' and her own successor will not be taxed at all on this inheritance, which will remain the basis of royal personal wealth. Thus as the laws that pertain to all of her subjects do not pertain to her, the Queen is literally above the law as far as tax is concerned, and remains a role model for tax-dodging, as does her son, the heir to the British throne. Charles Windsor has also been placed above the law by British governments, as he is specifically exempt from paying corporation tax, capital-gains tax and death duties. The Duchy of Cornwall, providing income for Charles and run as a company, has not been liable for tax since 1921.[12]

Other British super-rich people, who unlike the royals are not 'above the laws' of taxation, nonetheless manage to avoid their share of taxes. Lloyd's 'names' are a striking example.

> According to Robson Rhodes, the accountants, the most striking advantage
> is that Names are treated like businesses ... so losses incurred in the market

can be offset against other earnings…they enjoy business property relief for inheritance tax purposes on their deposits and funds which support their underwriting.[13]

Dodging taxes – even in global capital's highly friendly tax environment – is final proof, should it be needed, of the lack of even a residual loyalty to nation and home society on the part of many super-rich families.

During the Blair government in the late 1990s London became a haven for a species of super- and mega-rich called 'non-doms' – shorthand for rich people domiciled elsewhere. These 'non-doms' paid no tax at all to the British government – who refused to tax them, unlike other countries including the USA, on their worldwide income. And while the 'little people' were compelled to pay their taxes, in Britain, under the Labour government elected in 1997, private-equity partners paid tax on income at 10 per cent and 'entrepreneurs', who turn their income into capital gains, also got taxed at 10 per cent of their income. As the economist and commentator Martin Wolf argued, this super-rich tax haven had become so egregious that it was 'subversive of any enduring political compact amongst citizens', leading to a situation in which the 'political community will collapse'.[14]

Companies – huge, large and medium-sized – are also well into the tax-dodging game. One scam, made possible by global economics, is 'transfer pricing', which allows companies to pay tax where they want to, which naturally is the country or haven with the lowest tax regime. They can engineer this by doing much of their spending in the high-tax countries, thus cutting their tax obligations, and making most of their profits – using subsidiaries with little more than a front office with a few staff – in low-tax countries.

For super-rich tax-dodgers a helpful dynamic often sets in. Home governments make strenuous attempts to keep money at home by lowering even further the tax burden on rich people. The idea, not always fanciful, grew that more tax money could be attracted by taxing less. In Britain the top rate of tax was reduced from 98 per cent to 40 per cent during the country's move to market capitalism, and in the USA, even after a decade-and-a-half of falling taxes for the upper-income groups, by the late 1990s the authorities were still struggling manfully to lower the 'burden' further by even lower capital-gains taxes.

Nonetheless the amount of 'offshore' money is growing rapidly. The IMF reported that a staggering $2000 billion is located beyond the reach of the countries in which the money was made – in the growing number of safe-haven tax shelters, ranging from the Cayman Islands, through the Channel Islands and Liechtenstein to Singapore. In the late 1990s German commentators estimated that a hundred thousand tax-evading rich people had transferred many of their assets to a new favourite safe haven: the rock of Gibraltar.[15] 'Trickle down' – the 1980s public-relations term for the idea that wealth trickles down to the masses from those who make and own large chunks of it – has now been replaced by 'gush up and out'.

In earlier times many very rich people saw their destinies as linked to their countries of birth, and they spent considerable amounts of money (and acquiesced to relatively high tax regimes) in order to stabilise and ameliorate social changes that might otherwise threaten their interests. Now, though, should a local environment turn hostile to them, they can simply up sticks and leave, both financially and in person. And often the mere threat, or assumption of a threat, to withdraw their assets and patronage is enough to persuade the domestic politicians to secure a friendly environment. Such threats are now regularly made, either implicitly by corporations (who take jobs with them) or explicitly by high-profile, super-rich individuals, as was the case before the 1997 British general election with the musical entrepreneur Andrew Lloyd Webber, the actor Michael Caine and the boxer Frank Bruno.

THE COMING MISERY OF THE MAJORITY

The future can rarely be depicted with any precision. But should today's trends continue, and the global financial market still rule, then one thing is certain: Britain will see emerging a new social structure in which the lives now lived by its poorest people will be the future of more and more citizens, and maybe even a majority.

Should global capital still set the rules, this misery of the British majority will, though, likely exist side by side with a wealthy and self-perpetuating globally oriented 'aristocracy' who will define itself by its ownership of capital.

It is a combustible prospect, for it will exist in an era, unlike any before, in which this poor majority will also be assertive. The social and political deference to 'authority' that existed at the beginning of the twentieth century is, at the beginning of this century, long gone. So it would seem likely that such a future majority will demand major, even revolutionary, changes in the economic and political system.

It amounts to a classic pre-revolutionary situation – as critical and as dangerous as the last time – in the 1930s – the West faced economic collapse and total political change. Britain had a relatively benign depression in the 1930s, certainly when compared to Germany or the USA. Then it was protected by an imperial economic system, and the blows were somewhat softened. Today, though, the country faces the global economy alone.

21 CAN BRITANNIA ADJUST?

When in May 2010 David Cameron entered Downing Street at the head of a coalition with the Liberal Democrats this change of government was heralded as a new dawn. But a new vision of Britain's future and its role in the world did not dawn with it. In fact in the midst of one of the deepest crises facing the country in modern times the political and financial class carried on as usual. The broad strategic position inherited from Margaret Thatcher would remain. We would stay outside the European mainstream, and continue with our search for a separate 'global role' – as a military and financial power.

Over one hundred and fifty years ago, at the height of the country's world empire, British troops were stationed and fighting in Afghanistan to keep the Russians at bay and weaken the Himalayan tribes. In Jubilee year, 2012, with the country now representing only 1 per cent of the world's population and 4 per cent (and falling) of the world's GDP, British troops were there again. Prime minister Harold Wilson could say in the late 1960s that 'our frontiers are on the Himalayas', but few then believed it could last much longer. But it did, and David Cameron, reaffirmed Britain's commitment to Afghanistan.

He also reaffirmed, indeed more than reaffirmed, Labour's semi-detached European policy. Cameron came from the Eurosceptic wing of the Conservative Party, and reasserted the country's standoffish attitude to Europe by legislating that no more powers would be transferred to the EU without triggering a referendum. And then on 7 December 2011 he took the unprecedented and momentous step of vetoing a new EU treaty on further integration. The rest of the EU then proceeded, without Britain, with this integration. Britain had become more isolated than at any time since she joined the EEC in the early 1970s. This decision by the Cameron coalition government was the culmination of thirty years of growing Euroscepticism in London.

NEW GOVERNMENT, SAME FINANCE-LED ECONOMY

The new Cameron government blamed Labour for the debt crisis it inherited but found no fault with the fundamentals of the neo-liberal financial and economic system that had caused it. And it proclaimed, sticking fast to orthodoxy, that it was the government deficit – not the 'hollowing out' or the unemployment or the economic imbalance – that was the overriding problem facing the country. The new Liberal Democrat deputy prime minister, Nick Clegg, had talked during the election campaign of the need for 'savage' cuts.

From this neo-liberal perspective Britain's deficit was indeed a huge and dangerous problem. And by the time of the general election of 2010 it was clear that Britain was one of the worst cases. The budget deficit was higher than in any of its major European neighbours – in late 2009 it was standing, and rising, at 12.6 per cent of GDP (in normal times 3 per cent was the preferred limit in the EU); and in late March 2009 the total British 'national' debt stood at 55 per cent of GDP and was rising quite sharply.[1] The Labour government had not only financed the rescue of the hugely over-extended banking system but, as the recession bit and unemployment grew, was sustaining a growing welfare budget. These debt and deficit figures were placing great strains on sterling, and there was a widespread fear of a serious run on the pound. Prime minister Gordon Brown and chancellor of the exchequer Alistair Darling had been caught between Scylla and Charybdis, increasing public expenditure (private investment and consumption were anaemic) in order to engender growth and employment, while at the same time retaining some measure of fiscal responsibility in order to defend sterling in the speculative markets. It was a high-wire act, only sustained by the promise to cut the deficit in half from 2011. The Conservative policy was to cut the deficit sooner and more deeply.[2]

The only debate was over timing – how quickly to set about cutting (or raising taxes). There was, however, a growing body of opinion arguing that the sheer size of these projected and demanded cuts, if introduced too soon, would likely lead to a further downturn (and perhaps too to a currency crisis – caused by the prospect of a downward spiral of low growth and low tax receipts leading back to high deficits, and doubtless further demands for further cuts). George Magnus, a senior economics advisor at the UBS bank, proclaimed that any premature cut could provoke a 'savage' reaction in currency markets and would 'endanger the recovery of the banking sector and the UK labour market' – a view publicly supported by Britain's leading Keynesian economist Robert Skidelsky and other leading economic thinkers.[3] Britain's economy was so low in the water that a currency crisis was being confidently predicted on all sides of the debate.

Yet the new Conservative–Liberal Democrat government took the view that the maintenance of Britain's triple-A bond rating from the rating agencies in New York – which rated government's ability to repay debt – over-rode all other consideration; and within two weeks of taking office the new chancellor of the exchequer, George Osborne, embarked upon over £6 billion in savings, and later, in an emergency budget in June, started down the road to cutting the deficit mainly by public-expenditure cuts. He raised VAT to 20 per cent.

With these self-styled 'savage' cuts on the agenda the desperate prospect for Britain's future was of high levels of unemployment likely to last for many years – as was a hardening of wealth and income divisions, a further growth of the dependency (welfare) culture, and greater national, ethnic and religious divisions, particularly growing tension between the indigenous and Islamic populations. There was a further problem – that these existing sharp social divisions in Britain had only been held together by a growing and booming economy. So, lose the dynamism and hope of boom times, and the tearing, indeed rupture, of Britain's social fabric was becoming a distinct possibility. It was so serious that some commentators were suggesting that should unemployment rise significantly, say to 1930s proportions, then the question would arise: could Britain survive as a liberal-democratic, civilised advanced society?

As the new coalition government bedded in during 2010 and into 2011 it soon began to seem as if the great Wall Street and global banking crash had been a figment of the imagination. For the same old British financial and political elites, in all parties and none, who had supported the old deregulated City-dominated financial system were still running the show. And they still had no answers. There had been no revolution in thinking at the top – whether in government, in the opposition, in the Bank of England or among the opinion-forming London-based journalist class. The dominant narrative presented to the people was a simple and comforting one: the financial system had been 'saved' and the country was on the road to 'recovery'. The recovery would be difficult, and some tough budget-cutting times lay ahead, but there was no need to change the fundamental structures of the capitalist system or of the global system within which it operated. The patient would return to full strength soon, as soon as the private sector revived and the life-support machine of the state could be removed.

It was an environment in which bold new thinking was largely absent. In 2011 few leaders of opinion in Britain were even faintly echoing the radical views of the American economist Paul Krugman that a big new 'Keynesian plus' stimulus was needed. And absolutely no mainstream voice was suggesting a radical overhaul of the entire capitalist financial system.

It was obvious that this phase of the crisis was not going to be used as the reason for major structural changes in the economic system. President Obama's chief of staff, Rahm Emmanuel, may well have declaimed that we should 'never let a good crisis go to waste'. But in Britain it was 'as you were'. There was much anger at bankers and the size of banks (with proposals to split them up), there was also increasing talk about inequality and bonuses, but there was no serious or systematic critique of the fundamentals. In other words: Anglo-Saxon capitalism has failed, long live Anglo-Saxon capitalism!

BRITAIN ALONE IN A PROTECTIONIST WORLD

In the summer of 2011 the political mood suddenly worsened. For as data poured forth from the USA, Europe and Asia it was becoming clear that growth had stalled, and with it the famed 'recovery'. Without a recovery then deficits and debt would likely remain dangerously high.

Britain faced a double crisis: an era of austerity because of its unbalanced, overly credit-based economy, and massive public-expenditure cuts (whichever party won the next general election). But unlike previous economic crises it was also facing the need to adjust to a rapidly changing world order – nothing less than the collapse of economic globalism, or 'globalisation'. This collapse had been long in the making. By the late 1990s the growing imbalances of trade between Asia and the West were becoming unsustainable as they systematically destroyed both the employment base and its balanced economies; early in the new century the resultant global financial imbalances (primarily between China and the USA) were reaching critical proportions. The evil day was put off by a few years by a seriously irresponsible explosion of credit in the West, including Britain. The banking and credit crash was in essence the crash of globalisation. And as the various states around the world moved in to shore up the banks these essentially protectionist moves further collapsed the globalist model.

The 'rules' of global markets, both formal and informal, were increasingly broken, for as recession, depression and massive unemployment threatened, states acted unilaterally, and asked questions afterwards. The bank bailouts and quasi-nationalisations broke the rules; so too did the stimulus packages; so too did the often-unilateral moves to regulate financial markets. As Daniel Price, an assistant to President George W. Bush on international economic affairs, referred in September 2009 to 'regulatory reform measures that, if unchecked, will foster a disintegration of the global economy and re-raise the very barriers to cross-border trade and investment that the world has spent the past 60 years dismantling.'[4]

At its most intense in France, the growth of protectionist sentiment could be seen during the 2005 referendum on the European constitutional treaty when French popular opposition to the neo-liberal globalist agenda of the European Commission led to the victory of the 'no' campaign. Even in the USA protectionist sentiment was on a rising curve. The refusal of the politburo in China to raise its currency against the dollar (and therefore to ease its exports to the USA) was a constant source of tension, and a bi-partisan alliance in the US Senate, led by senators Chuck Schumer and Lindsay Graham, was constantly threatening China with sizeable tariffs should it continue its currency policy. Also, the issue of 'outsourcing jobs' was a key feature of the successive Democratic presidential campaigns of John Kerry and later Barack Obama; and the US public was increasingly supportive of protectionist intervention in the 'global' market.

BRITAIN AND THE NEW PROTECTIONISM

The signs were there for all to see, but Britain's elites remained in denial that anything was fundamentally wrong with the global economy and global finance. Indeed the New Labour administration of Tony Blair not only pursued a globalist policy but also became a cheerleader and proselytiser for globalisation. His argument was that there was no alternative to accepting its rules, and that British economic strategy should be based not on attempting (with its neighbours) to shape the global system, but rather on equipping the people with skills so that they could compete (with Asians) in the world economy.

So Britain remained, under both Conservatives and New Labour, the most open of all the G8 countries to the global economy. More than any other major Western nation Britain threw its lot in with, and thus placed its fate in the hands of, the globalisers. Indeed it extended its reach, both financially – through the City of London's worldwide operation – and through its interventionist foreign and military policy (as it became the chief ally of the American empire in Iraq and Afghanistan). And, largely because of the global impulses of its elites, Britain remained outside an integrating Europe and the euro-zone (though still, awkwardly, within the EU).

During the boom years of the 1990s onwards 'globalisation' seemingly served Britain well – for although global market forces eroded the country's 'uncompetitive' industrial sector they also engineered a quite dramatic switchover to the booming service sector – primarily financial services. Yet many realised that should globalisation fail, Britain would be disproportionately hurt. Even so, throughout the 1990s and on into the new century Britain's elites remained in thrall to global markets (and their alluring limitless possibilities for profits). They remained in denial about the inherent weaknesses of the global economy right up until the global crisis hit the City of London in 2007–8 and beyond. And they could not see that the great banking crash was also a national train wreck in which everything that Britain's financial, and financialised, elites stood for was up-ended – virtually overnight.

JOBS, JOBS, JOBS

Of course following the crash Britain's *zeitgeist* slowly began to change: some, small, voices began to critique systematically the global capitalist system and even proffer an alternative – a 'protectionist' strategy for the country which would put jobs first, centre its economic policy on employment and growth, and resist the siren demands of the global economy to become ever more 'competitive' . In March 2010 *Guardian* economics editor Larry Elliot argued that such a strategy, with its echoes of the Labour left's 'alternative economic strategy' of the 1970s, had some merit, though it would not be likely to be tried, at least not for some time. He quoted from a London University (SOAS) research paper which argued that such a strategy would involve

> devaluation followed by cessation of payments and restructuring of debt. Banks would have to be nationalised and public control extended over utilities, transport, energy and telecommunications. There would be industrial policy, including strategies to improve productivity, infrastructure and environmentally sensitive investment, and support equitable growth. This option requires a decisive shift in the balance of political power in favour of labour.[5]

It would also require a decisive shift away from the three-decades-long strategy of accommodating to 'economic globalisation', and instituting increased forms of protectionism.

As the recession began to bite, 'protectionist' sentiments, if not policies, were breaking cover from France to the USA, and in Britain mainly on the British left – not just among left-leaning academics and journalists but also among trade-unionists and lower-income 'working people'. 'Protecting jobs' was becoming a number one issue. Indeed before the crash, on the eve of becoming prime minister in 2007, Gordon Brown had said, 'It is time to train British workers for the British jobs that will be available over the coming few years and to make sure that people who are inactive and unemployed are able to take the new jobs on offer in our country.' This 'British jobs for British workers' approach subsequently – following a strike at the Lindsey oil refinery in North Lincolnshire about UK construction jobs being awarded to European workers – got caught up in charges about racism and xenophobia, and was attacked by columnists from all sides of the spectrum. But Brown stood by his remarks: he said, 'I don't see any reason to regret [my statement]' and 'I understand people's worries about their jobs'.[6] 'Job protection' for the City had been embedded in the great bailout of the banks and financial services, although it was not openly acknowledged.

By the time of the 2010 general election 'protectionism' was no longer likely to frighten. The 2007–8 bank and credit crash had raised fears about unemployment to the top of the domestic agenda, with real concerns about whether global market capitalism could any longer deliver on the promises made for it by all governments from Thatcher onwards. Global markets, by encouraging 'competitiveness' and a constant 'race to the bottom' on costs, were seen as driving down Western wage levels and employment prospects. 'Competing' with rising Asia was becoming an impossibility. Previously this employment and wage crisis facing millions had been smoothed over by abundant, cheap credit. But that prop was now being removed. So, with living standards under serious threat, the idea of 'protecting' people – rather than making them ever more 'competitive' in the global economy – seemed increasingly attractive. 'Protectionism' – whether industrial policy for long-term jobs, or trade protection against unfair competition, or 'social protection' when unemployed – was suddenly much more acceptable in the British political discourse.

BUT IS BRITAIN BIG ENOUGH?

Yet there remained one overwhelming problem with any 'protectionist' strategy for Britain – the country's size and economic imbalance. Only large, continent-states or blocs can embark upon a workable neo-protectionist economic strategy as they were potentially self-sufficient. The USA, the EU and the euro-zone are such economies. They may indeed have benefited from the global trade upturn during the boom times, but they were also big enough to withstand a serious trade downturn (with only about a 10–12 per cent of GDP exposure to foreign trade). And these continent-states also possessed a relatively healthy balance between manufacturing and services, between industrial and agricultural, and between the real economy and the financial.

By contrast, Britain, a medium-sized European state with a skewed and imbalanced economy and far higher global trade exposure, was not nearly self-sufficient. On its own it was simply too small and too vulnerable in an increasingly protectionist world. It had placed itself in grave danger, as it could hardly afford to bail out its over-extended banking system during the crisis of late 2008.

How big then is the British economy? Britain's good growth rates have helped her grow from her relative position in the early 1980s when she was lying with Italy for third place in the EU. By 2006 the UK economy amounted to $2,201,473 million or 4.9 per cent of the global GDP. Britain ranked fifth in the world (behind the USA, Japan, Germany and Mainland China), and was roughly the same size as France and just ahead of Italy. And it was only one-sixth the size of the total EU economy, and also of the total US economy.

These figures tell the story of a Britain that during the 1980s and 1990s had stabilised its shaky situation. But in truth it did little more than that. For by the end of the 1990s British national income was almost exactly equal to that of France and only about 20 per cent higher than that of Italy. (Figures show: UK 1403, France 1453, Germany 2103, Italy 1162.) These are exchange-rate sensitive, and could easily change by 10–20 per cent. They also show growth rates for the UK [1965–99] lower than France, Belgium, Italy and most of the then EEC nations; figures for Germany are unavailable because of the addition of the eastern states. By 2009 Britain's position had worsened. The country's GDP, $2,183,607 million, was behind France (at $2,675,251 million) and Germany (at $3,352,742 million) – with the EU total standing at $16,447,259 million, the USA at $14,256,059 million and China at $4,908,982 million.[7]

Taking the longer view – that of the whole post-war period – Bernard Alford, at the end of his exhaustive work on Britain's recent economic history, came to a clear conclusion: 'the thrust of our analysis,' he wrote in 1996, 'is that there are few signs that Britain has reversed the condition of relative economic decline that has been endemic to its development since the late nineteenth-century.' He adds, though, that the status of nations is often a matter of perception, 'but that perception is so easily clouded by delusion'. In the decade since Alford's report very little has changed that would alter his assessment.[8]

Yet, no matter its status and size, is the British economy strong enough to withstand pressures from the global economy, from downturns and shocks? And here there remains a problem – for Britain, even with good growth rates, remains a very vulnerable economy, much more so than many other advanced economies. One vulnerability is that the country remains highly dependent on the continuing robust health of the global economy. Britain's economic growth rates have largely been sustained by global growth, which in turn has been sustained by the low-inflation era caused by China's low costs. This virtuous low-inflation cycle has allowed Britain to pursue low interest rates and a massive increase in private debt levels (based on a housing boom). This whole economic structure is heavily trade-dependent, more so than is the case in many of its competitors, and in any downturn would be hurt disproportionately.

And by the second decade of the new century it was becoming clear that in this coming age of protectionism Britain needed, for its own survival, to be part of a bigger integrated economy; and that could only mean the EU.

This of course raised the thorny subject of Britain's proper role in the world and the vital linkage between this role and the domestic economy. After seven-plus decades of maintaining at all costs a 'global role', of 'punching above our weight', and three decades of grandiose financial over-extension within the booming global economy, the country was vastly overstretched. It had huge 'universal' banks which reached into every corner of the world. Its limited military had taken part – the major European part – in actions from Iraq to Afghanistan (where in early 2010 British troops were dying almost daily) and its defence budget was the largest (in percentage of GDP terms) of all the USA's NATO allies. As of 2010 the country's political parties were still committed to the hugely expensive Trident nuclear system, and to continuing with its next generation. The elites who ran the Foreign Office and the Ministry of Defence still retained the culture of empire and 'greatness', as did Britain's top politicians. And few, now that the boom was over, were arguing that Britain needed to face a future in which the country 'punched *within* its weight'. They were still resisting an adjustment to a more realistic and modest approach.

But can the country so adjust? Such an adjustment would demand much more than economic changes, including great institutional, political and psychological ones. The country still possessed a pompous *ancien régime* that fitted an imperial era – a lavish, imperial-style monarchy, a still unelected House of Lords, and strange secretive institutions like the Privy Council. Politically, this imperial legacy exhibited itself in a continuing fear of losing 'sovereignty' and of becoming a normal European power. In sum, even as late as 2010 and the collapse of Anglo–American financial capitalism, our elites, our institutions and our very collective DNA were all far too grand to allow us to abandon our 'global role' in favour of becoming a mere regional power, like Germany or even France. Nowhere is this national hubris more perfectly illustrated than in the over-extended City of London.

Britain's financial-services industry had done extremely well in the post-Cold War global economy. In 2003 Britain's trade surplus in financial services was reported to be 'more than double that of any other country'.[9]

004 researchers at the University of Sheffield analysed the
economy as an atlas, demonstrating that Britain was becoming
iated by London (or rather the City of London), and that to the
.h and west there was 'an archipelago of the provinces – city islands
that appear to be slowly sinking demographically, socially and
economically.'[10] It was an analysis which led a *Guardian* economist to
argue that the 'City wields more power than ever' and that 'Britain has
become a huge hedge fund making big bets on the markets.' And he
asserted, presciently, that 'one day the luck will run out.'[11] In his powerful
2006 study of Britain's elites, Hywel Williams reckoned that 'The City,
in combination with New York, now controls 90 per cent of the world's
wholesale financial activity.' And he recorded that at the end of 2003
310,000 people were employed in the City (and nearly 150,000 in
financial services).[12] But what goes up also comes down – and by 2008
and the beginning of the financial meltdown London's financial district
was already laying off large numbers of workers.

Yet two questions stand out: can 'the City' and its allied commerce
continue to carry on its shoulders a country of 60 million people? Or,
looking at it inversely, can 60 million people succeed in bailing out such
a mammoth operation as the City when it fails? And what happens
when China and India start seriously competing in financial services as
well as in manufacturing? Merely posing these questions serves to show
the vulnerability of a national economy which includes such a formerly
successful sector.

Whether the City can or cannot continue to carry the country, its
leading players will certainly remain highly influential, if not dominant,
in determining Britain's overseas economic policy and alignment – more
so even than the media moguls. And within the City elite there was
considerable support for a 'go it alone' policy, for standing offshore (of
the continent) and seeing the global economy as our market. This was
the 'tiger option' – after the smallish Asian 'tiger' economies that were
doing so well in the global market before the Asian financial crash. And
as financial services prospered in the Blair era many in the square mile
turned their thinking towards 'the world' and increasingly away from
Europe and the EU.

This dominant view not only saw London's financial services as a
global player working in a global market – very much a 'tiger' – but
went further, seeing London as the world's most successful 'tiger' in
the global financial jungle. And by 2007, on the eve of the global
financial meltdown, all the talk was of London overtaking New York

as the world's leading financial centre. By comparison, in this hubristic atmosphere, 'tying the City down in Europe' – even should the City become the EU's primary financial centre (similar to New York in North America) – was dismissed as too restrictive a vision. In a December 2006 after-dinner speech to London financiers, the EU's financial-services action plan ('MiFID') was introduced by Charlie McCreevy, the internal market commissioner, and was given a less than enthusiastic reception – much less so than that accorded to the American comedienne Ruby Wax who, bizarrely, but perhaps aptly, followed him with top billing. A *Financial Times* report by Gideon Rachman at the time suggested that 'as the biggest financial centre in Europe [the City] would do well in a huge liberalised [EU] market'.[13] However, the EU remains too regulated for City tastes; as does even Wall Street following the Sarbanes-Oxley Act passed in the aftermath of the Enron scandal (a tough US regulatory regime providing a huge – though temporary – boost for the City).

The successful and profitable world of British finance created, though, another vulnerability in the British economy – that of the debt culture. For it was the dynamic and innovative credit systems and culture of 'the City' that helped, together with a willing Westminster political class, to create the country's mountainous private debt. A report commissioned by the Conservative Party in 2005 reported that 'personal debt levels of more than £1 trillion mean that about 15 million people are exposed to external shocks such as a sharp rise in the price of oil,' and went on to call the debt issue a 'time bomb'. These debt levels had been fuelled by the 'wealth effect' of rising house prices.[14]

These vulnerabilities in the British economy – the reverse side of its successes – make Britain's 'tiger option' a huge gamble. Britain is more exposed to global forces than any other major Western country (including the USA). And should the country leave the EU, then everything will depend upon a continuingly robust global economy – and one in which competition in the service sector from China and India remains weak.

Britain's 'successful' economy – no matter its vulnerable and exposed global position – will likely continue to convince a powerful faction of opinion-formers that the country can, with confidence, 'go it alone'. After all, the 'tiger option' will continue to appeal to more than just the profit-makers; it will have an abiding resonance with the popular instincts of English exceptionalism – of a uniquely entrepreneurial people surviving and prospering alone on the global 'open seas'. This appeal combines short-term profits and nationalist romance – the two impulses that built the empire and will be difficult to combat.

Yet the romance of the 'island story' will come face to face with the realities of the great de-leveraging, and with the lower living standards inevitably involved. Also, Britain comes out of its neo-liberal era a more unequal society than it was at the beginning. It has succeeded in building up something of an American-style 'middle class' – increasingly travelled, self-confident and with considerable expectations – based upon a mountain of debt. As they are marched down the mountain this middle class will inevitably fracture, creating a growing pool of 'losers'. For a time, Britain's welfare mechanisms will help to cushion the blows; but sooner or later the increased pressure on welfare services will need to be funded by higher taxes (which will be resisted by the remaining middle class and the super-rich) or, alternatively, by government deficits and inflation. Both of these courses of action will decrease the global competitiveness of a very globally oriented economy.

One way of limiting the damage of a global recession or depression would be to take a decision to integrate more fully the British economy into the wider European one. With a declining global demand for financial services the EU would at the very least provide a hinterland for the City of London (in much the same way as the American market provides a hinterland for New York). Once the broad strategic move – away from Wall Street-dominated economics and towards Europe – has been made, then whether Britain should go for a quick entry into the euro-zone would become a technical matter.

However, this radical change in the geopolitical course will be very difficult to engineer; it will run right up against the British attachment to 'sovereignty', to its history as an imperial and independent power, and to its rigid constitution based upon ancient 'sovereignties', including the monarchy and the culture of 'Queen and country'. In this sense the traditional political culture of Britain's elites directly damages the future economic health of its people.

ENGLAND'S IDENTITY CRISIS

Yet even if we can downsize our thinking, and see ourselves as we really are, then the great question remains: in the emerging multipolar world of trade blocs, where do we British fit in? Is it within the 'American empire' or in the 'European home'? Or can we continue to avoid this choice and become a smallish 'little England' offshore island scratching a living in what remains of the globalised economy (and maybe acting as a European base for rising China?)

For a time during the decade-long premiership of Tony Blair the country was as enmeshed in the American empire as it had ever been. Indeed when Blair left office British troops were still in American-occupied Iraq and Britain had intensified her status as Washington's chief European outpost. The country was geopolitically tied to Washington, economically under the sway of the neo-liberal American model, and culturally, through television and the tabloidisation of the mass media, increasingly Americanised.

This 'American option' for Britain – of tying the country more and more to America's political and economic coat-tails – was, though, to be dealt a real blow following the failure of the American occupation of Iraq, and then again in 2008 when the great crash on Wall Street severely dented the allure of the American economic model. More important than Britain's view of the USA was the changing US view of Britain. Whereas George W. Bush had found Britain useful as political cover for his forward strategy in the Middle East, the election of Barack Obama in 2009 ushered in a new approach, for the new president had little attachment to Britain (his father had been born in colonial Kenya), and anyway was slowly reorienting American foreign policy away from its historic concentration on Europe and towards a more Asia-centred perspective.

On the face of it the comparative decline of the USA should have improved the chances of Britain adopting the European option. Yet, at the time of the 2010 election the Conservative Party was still divided between those who were hostile to further integration and those who wanted to pull out of the EU altogether, while Gordon's Brown's New Labour, under the influence of the City, was still tied to an off-shore, 'competitiveness' agenda. In reality Britain's political leadership was not yet willing to make a choice between America and Europe – Blair even argued publicly the case that 'to choose between America and Europe is a false choice.' He simply did not see the need to choose. 'It would be insane – yes, I would put it as strongly as that – for us to give up either relationship.'[15] After the crash Gordon Brown started edging ever more closely towards the European option, but as the global financial crisis hit the euro-zone and the deficits and debt of Greece and other 'Club Med' countries caused strains with Germany, questions were raised about the long-term viability of the euro-zone and 'the European option'.

All in all, the fallout from the great crash could not have come at a worse time for Britain. With the US special relationship in decline and the country still outside the euro-zone, and increasingly isolated in Europe, Britain had to engineer the bailout of its banks alone. This bailout – which stretched Britain's public debt to almost impossible limits – allowed the illusory 'go it alone' mentality to flourish. A former US State Department official, Kendall Myers, an Anglophile with a good understanding of contemporary Britain, summed up Britain's 'stand-alone mentality' rather well. He said, 'I think and fear that Britain will draw back from the US without moving closer to Europe. In that sense London bridge is falling down.'[16]

A body of opinion in the City, and in the coalition government formed in 2010, saw Britain's future in these isolationist terms. Some even believed that the future lay in standing offshore from Europe as a global financial centre and host to hedge funds and low-tax operations. This finance-led, strategy-led approach would, though, only be sensible if Britain could also remain in the EU single market. And Tony Blair himself had hinted at this as a viable option. 'Of course Britain could survive outside the EU,' he had argued in 2000, and 'we could possibly get access to the single market as Norway and Switzerland do.'[17]

Even Eurosceptics were anxious to seek arrangements with the EU which would allow Britain continued access to the single market. Some hoped that Britain could come up with an ingenious scheme to stay in the single market through rejoining EFTA (the European Free Trade Association) and through EFTA join Norway in the AEA (Associated Economic Area). Yet the idea that after the controversy, rupture and pain of withdrawing from the EU the union would then grant Britain special continuing access to its single market remains highly fanciful. And even should Britain get the same deal as Norway it will then become a so-called 'Euro fax' country – subject to the rules of the single market, sent out by fax, but having no say in drawing them up. A British withdrawal would thus likely be exactly what it says – a full withdrawal. It would amount to a 'go it alone' strategy – and face the country with the urgent need to make a living outside of the trade bloc. It would be a dramatic, bold and risky move. Yet during the 1990s some British opinion-formers were becoming more and more confident in the viability of this 'go it alone' strategy.

It is a high-risk strategy in which 'little England', facing the global economy alone, would prosper by remaining highly competitive and entrepreneurial. It would amount to a future role for the country that its supporters – such as the novelist Frederick Forsyth – describe as creating 'an independent, global Britain'. Taking this road, 'little England' would, in effect, become a 'tiger economy'.

But the big question remains: can this go-it-alone strategy actually work? Supporters of the option assume that once outside the EU and its single market, relations with the EU will, maybe after an initial hiccup, remain amicable. In reality there is no such guarantee. After all, Britain would have left in order to seek a competitive advantage (lower costs and taxes) and in such a competitive environment the EU could easily erect trade barriers against British goods and services. In a trade war, trying to live outside a trading bloc could become a very uncomfortable position.

These isolationist instincts – renewed by xenophobic Englishness and the continuing woes of the culture of 'Queen and Country' – run directly counter to the realities of the world in which the British people actually live. For instance, in this real world seriously urgent problems are lapping at the shores – problems like carbon emissions, mass immigration, terrorism and the social and economic effects of globalisation, let alone support against speculation and manic market forces. Not one of these problems can be solved by national solutions alone. But national solutions, based upon 'national sovereignty' and an old ideology of national separateness, were, in 2010, all that was on offer from Britain's established elites.

WHAT KIND OF PEOPLE? ANY 'BETTER ANGELS'?

This geopolitical identity-crisis was – is – a symptom of something deeper. For, certainly at the turn of the century, there was no certainty about how to answer a crucial question: what kind of people are the British? Are we an 'Anglo-sphere' nation ruled by an elite whose political language will forever tie us to Washington? And what are the geopolitical implications of the growth of English nationalism? Will Scotland and Wales gravitate to a European future should England stay out? What are the implications of a multicultural society, and sizeable Islamic populations, for foreign policy? And what of vast, cosmopolitan London? Will London and its environs lead the way into Europe while much of the rest of England resists? And will the British elite's love affair with the US neo-liberal economic model propel the country away from Europe's 'social model' and towards increasing inequality – with a protected class of super-rich side by side with a sinking and impoverished middle class and a deeply alienated underclass?

A lot will turn on how the English define themselves over the coming years. It could go either way. England, and 'Englishness', may well be defined by its worst angels, by that narrow xenophobia that still lurks and can be so easily aroused by media moguls and ultra-conservative politicians. In a declining economy and conflicted society this kind of visceral 'little England' impulse could turn the English in on themselves – leading not just to the break-up of the union but also to the politics of authoritarianism – to what could become a 'very English' form of mild 'gentleman fascism'. And it might not be so mild.

Alternatively, England and Englishness could yet be defined by the country's better angels – that is by those informed by the country's historical tradition of liberty, democratic reform and relative openness. But mass prosperity is needed if these better angels are to negotiate the shoals without losing their balance.

A lot more, though, will turn on what happens in the wider West. In facing the global economic crisis and the coming multipolar world (particularly the rise of Asia) will there be one West or two? And if two, then will Britain's elites, their minds and culture strangely still likely imbued with the imperial hangover, ever be capable of joining with others in helping to secure the European future?

If we are going to a enter protracted period of lower living standards – with an all-but-certain associated increase in class and ethnic tensions – then it is absolutely vital that we are serious about 'all being in this together'. A more equal society becomes an urgent necessity. It is no exaggeration to assert that without it we could lose our liberal democracy and could lapse into something akin to a 1950s Latin American-style military slum state governed by a Latin American-style super-rich elite.

QUEEN AND COUNTRY

Yet, a question remains: can we adjust? Can our elites finally stop living in the past and warming themselves on the embers of empire? Can we indeed deal with growing inequality and make a reality of 'all being in this together'?

The omens are not good. In 2012, in the midst of the gravest economic crisis since the 1930s, with the households of Britain facing widespread financial insecurity, official Britain nonetheless deemed that the people should celebrate – not their country or their citizenship, but a Queen who, for all her service, most perfectly represents both the imperial past and super-rich present. That in itself stands testimony to the continuing power of the 'grand delusion'.

NOTES

CHAPTER 1

1. Randolph Churchill, *The Story of the Coronation*, London, 1953, p. 19. John Maynard Keynes quotation from Correlli Barnett, *The Lost Victory*, London, 1995.
2. See Barnett, *The Lost Victory*, p. 55. For Barnett's thesis that Britain was vastly over-extended during these years see Chapters 1, 2 and 3.
3. Cited in Barnett, *The Lost Victory*, p. 52.
4. Volume 6 of Winston Churchill's *History of the Second World War* was entitled *Triumph and Tragedy*.
5. Cited in Barnett, *The Lost Victory*, p. 54.
6. J.R. Seeley, *The Expansion of England*, 1884, p. 350.
7. For the most perceptive and scholarly account and analysis of Chamberlain's appeasement policy see Robert Self, *Neville Chamberlain: A biography*, London, 2006.
8. The views of C.A. Vlieland of the Malayan Civil Service as communicated to Correlli Barnett: see Correlli Barnett, *The Collapse of British Power*, London, 1972, p. 28.
9. From George Laming's *In the Castle of My Skin*, cited in Jack Lively and Adam Lively (eds), *Democracy in Britain: A Reader*, Oxford, 1994, p. 238.
10. R.C.K. Ensor, *England 1870–1914?*, Oxford, 1966, p. 137.
11. W.K. Hancock and M.M. Gowing, *British War Economy*, London, 1953, p. 116.
12. The chancellor of the exchequer in the cabinet minutes, CAB 66/11 324, 21 August 1940.
13. Barnett, *The Collapse of British Power*, London, 1972, pp. 14–15.
14. Ibid., p. 592. Some of the figures about British military and technical dependence on America during the Second World War come from Barnett, *The Collapse of British Power*, Chapter 6.
15. Speech in London, 10 November 1942.
16. *The War Speeches of Winston Churchill*, compiled by Charles Eade, London, n.d., vol. 3, p. 512.
17. John Charmley, *Churchill: The end of glory*, London, 1993, p. 649.

18. D.R. Thorpe, *Eden: The life and times of Anthony Eden, First Earl of Avon, 1897–1977*, London, 2003, p.270.
19. Data and quotation from John Dickie, *Special No More: Anglo–American relations, rhetoric and reality*, London, 1974, p.35–36.
20. Barnett, *The Lost Victory*, p.41.
21. Dickie, p.38.
22. Cabinet minutes, 6 November 1945.
23. Hugo Young, *This Blessed Plot: Britain and Europe from Churchill to Blair*, London, 1998, p. 27.

CHAPTER 2

1. Speech in London, 10 November 1942.
2. Quote about Wilson from Pankaj Mishra, 'The Unquiet American', *New York Review of Books*, 12 January 2006.
3. Alan Bullock, *Ernest Bevin: Foreign Secretary, 1945–1951*, London, 1983, p.111.
4. Quoted in Kathryn Tidrick, *The Empire and English Character*, London, 1992, p.227.
5. Correlli Barnett, *The Lost Victory*, London, 1995, pp.120, 176.
6. Tidrick, p.232.
7. Quoted in Bullock, p.352.
8. The quotation was from Sir Michael Perrin and was unearthed by Professor Peter Hennessey in an article in the *Times*, 30 September 1982. Reported in Bullock, p.352.
9. Bullock, p.353.
10. See John Scott, *Who Rules Britain?*, London, 1991, Tables in Chapter 6.
11. Barnett, p.24.
12. Tidrick, p.43.
13. Quotation cited in Hugh Cunningham, 'The Conservative Party and patriotism', in Robert Colls and Philip Dodd (eds), *Englishness*, Beckenham, 1986, p.298.
14. Quoted in Ian Gilmour, *Inside Right: A study in conservatism*, London, 1977, p.77.
15. Frank Reeves, *British Radical Discourse: A study of British political discourse about race and race-related matters*, Cambridge, 1983, p.114.
16. Andrew Roberts, *Eminent Churchillians*, London, 1994, pp.213–14.
17. Quoted in Alan S. Milward, *The European Rescue of the Nation-state*, London, 1992, p.432.
18. First quotation from Lady Selina Hastings, in Phyllis Hatfield, *Pencil Me In: A memoir of Stanley Olsen*, London, 1994, p.94. Second quotation, ibid., p.95.
19. Tidrick, p.3.

CHAPTER 3

1. From D.R. Thorpe, *Eden: The life and times of Anthony Eden, First Earl of Avon, 1897–1977*, London, 2003.
2. See Thorpe. For a more critical biography see David Carlton, *Anthony Eden*, London, 1981.
3. Speech to NATO Council in Paris, December 1953.
4. Speech at Columbia University, 11 January 1952.
5. Thorpe, p.453.
6. Thorpe, p.382.
7. See Thorpe, p.383ff.
8. Quoted in Simon Heffer, *Like The Roman: The life of Enoch Powell*, London, 1998, p.122–23.
9. See David Carlton, *Anthony Eden: A biography*, London 1982, p.460.
10. Interview with Michael Charlton, 'Last step sideways', *Encounter*, September, 1981.
11. See Anthony Nutting, *No End of a Lesson: The story of Suez*, London, 1962.

CHAPTER 4

1. Macmillan in conversation with John Colville, in John Colville, *The Fringes of Power, Downing Street Diaries, 1939–55*, London, 1985, 30 May 1952.
2. Andrew Marr, *The Diamond Queen: Elizabeth II and her people*, London, 2011, p.246.
3. For the most detailed account of these negotiations over Skybolt and Polaris see Richard Lamb, *The Macmillan Years 1957–1963: The emerging truth*, London, 1995, Chapter 14.
4. Reported in the *Sunday Telegraph*, 9 February 1964.
5. Peter Riddell, *Hug Them Close: Blair, Clinton, Bush and the 'Special Relationship'*, London, 2003, p.31.
6. Broadcast on *Booktalk* on BBC Parliament channel, 14 January 2006.
7. Martin Holmes, 'The Conservative Party and Europe', the Bruges Group, paper no 17 (http://brugesgroup.com/mediacentre/index.live?article=73).
8. From the Campaign For Democratic Socialism's bulletin, *Campaign*, 18 July 1962.
9. Roy Jenkins, *The Chancellors*, London, 1998, p.70.
10. See Stephen Haseler, *The Gaitskellites*, London, 1969 for a survey of the views of these social democrats.
11. See John Goldthorpe, David Lockwood, Frank Beechofer and Jennifer Platt, *The Affluent Worker in the Class Structure*, Cambridge, 1969.

CHAPTER 5

1. *Sunday Telegraph*, 26 January 1964. Macleod's article appeared in the *Spectator*, 17 January 1964.
2. Michael Young, *The Rise of the Meritocracy*, London, 1958, p.22.
3. John Vaizey, 'The Public Schools' in Hugh Thomas (ed.), *The Establishment*, London, 1959, p.26.
4. Hugh Thomas, 'The establishment and society', in Thomas (ed.), p.20.
5. Thomas, p.15.
6. See Thomas Balogh, 'The Apotheosis of the Dilettante', in Thomas (ed.), p.85.
7. Henry Fairlie, 'The BBC', in Thomas (ed.), p.205.
8. Vaizey, p.2.
9. Geoffrey Owen, *From Empire To Europe: The decline and revival of British industry since the Second World War*, London, 1999, p.30.
10. Owen, p.31, Table 3.1.
11. Michael Shanks, *The Stagnant Society*, London, 1961, p.47.
12. Martin Weiner, *English Culture and the Decline of the Industrial Spirit 1850–1980*, New York, 1981, Preface.

CHAPTER 6

1. Hugh Thomas, 'The establishment and society', in Hugh Thomas (ed.), *The Establishment*, London, 1959, p.20.
2. Henry Fairlie, 'The BBC', in Thomas (ed.), p.205.
3. Philip Ziegler, 'Leadership and change: prime ministers in the post-war world – Harold Wilson', lecture at Gresham College, 21 February 2006 (http://www.gresham.ac.uk/lectures-and-events/leadership-and-change-prime-ministers-in-the-post-war-world-harold-wilson).
4. Andrew Marr, *The Diamond Queen: Elizabeth II and her people*, London, 2011, p.204.
5. Martin Weiner, *English Culture and the Decline of the Industrial Spirit 1850–1980*, New York, 1981, p.92.
6. Anthony Crosland, *Socialism Now and Other Essays*, London, 1974, p.49.

CHAPTER 7

1. Quoted in *Sunday Telegraph*, 30 September 1973.
2. Quoted in Martin Weiner, *English Culture and the Decline of the Industrial Spirit 1850–1980*, New York, 1981, p.163.
3. See *The Cecil King Diary 1965–70*, London, 1972.

4. Quoted in Andrew Gamble, *The Conservative Nation*, London, 1974, p.219. Barber made these comments on 17 December 1973.
5. *Times*, 2 January 1976.
6. Correlli Barnett, *The Collapse of British Power*, London, 1972, p.9.
7. Barnett in Richard English and Michael Kenny (eds), *Rethinking British Decline*, London, 2000, p.42.
8. English and Kenny (eds), p.41.
9. Andrew Gamble, *Theories and Explanations of British Decline*, in English and Kenny (eds), Chapter 1. The second quote is from Andrew Gamble, *The Conservative Nation*, London, 1974, Introduction.
10. The academics Richard English and Michael Kenny produced a superb summary of these varying approaches in the final chapter of *Rethinking British Decline*. Books and works cited include Martin Weiner, *English Culture and the Decline of the Industrial Spirit 1850–1980*, Stuart Holland, *Strategy For Socialism: The challenge of Labour's programme*, London, 1975, James Bellini, *Rule Britannia: A progress report for Doomesday 1986*, London, 1981. See also David Marquand, 'Reflections on British Decline', in English and Kenny (eds), pp.117–20.
11. Both quotes from Peter Riddell, *The Thatcher Era and its Legacy*, Oxford, 1989, p.7.
12. Ian Gilmour's memoirs of this period, *Dancing With Dogma: Britain under Thatcherism*, London, 1993, recounted, as in its title, his deep frustrations with Thatcherism.
13. Marie-Therese Fay and Elizabeth Meehan, 'British Decline and European Integration', in English and Kenny (eds), p.210.
14. Henry Kissinger, *The White House Years*, London, 1979, p.964.
15. Reported in the *Times*, 4 December 1973.
16. Reported in John Campbell, *Edward Heath: A biography*, London, 1993, p.558.
17. Kissinger, p.993.
18. Kissinger, p.933.

CHAPTER 8

1. From a report in the *Times*, July 1973, reported in Stephen Haseler, *The Death of British Democracy*, London, 1976, p.119.
2. From the unpublished memoirs of Reg Prentice.
3. Set out in James Callaghan, *Time and Chance*, London, 1987, pp.425–26.
4. William Keegan, *Observer*, 17 December 2006.
5. See Bernard Donoughue, *Prime Minister*, London, 1987, p.168.
6. Quoted in Antony Jay, *Oxford Dictionary of Political Quotations*, London, 2001.

CHAPTER 9

1. ITN/Harris exit poll, 11 June 1987.
2. *New York Times*, 13 June 1987.
3. From the unpublished memoirs of Reg Prentice.
4. Ibid.
5. *Sunday Times*, 23 August 1987 (review of *Family Quartet* by John Catlin).

CHAPTER 10

1. Jonathan Raban, *Soft City*, London, 1974, p.59.
2. Quote from Margaret Thatcher, *Statecraft: Strategies for a changing world,* London, 2002, pp.19–20.
3. Ibid.
4. *Times*, 6 October 1999.
5. Reported in David Reynolds, *Britannia Overruled: British policy and the world*, London, 1991, p.276.
6. Quoted in Michael Smith, 'Britain and the United States: beyond the special relationship', in Peter Byrd (ed.), *British Foreign Policy Under Thatcher*, London, 1988, p.9.
7. Thatcher, pp.19–20.
8. Quoted in *Woman's Own*, 31 October 1987.
9. Arthur Seldon, *Capitalism*, Oxford, 1990.
10. John Redwood, *Stars and Strife: The coming conflicts between the USA and the European Union*, London, 2001, p.28.
11. Martin Weiner, *English Culture and the Decline of the Industrial Spirit 1850–1980*, New York, 1981, Preface.
12. For statistics on the British economy during the Thatcher years see B.W.E. Alford, *Britain in the World Economy Since 1880*, London, 1996, tables and figures in Chapter 10, and Geoffrey Owen, *From Empire To Europe*, London, 1999, various tables.
13. Reported in the *Guardian* ('Business'), 28 February 2008.

CHAPTER 11

1. Samuel Beer, *Britain Against Itself*, London, 1965, p.179.
2. *Sunday Telegraph*, 27 December 1987.
3. Speech to Cambridge University Conservative Association, 25 January 1987.
4. Speech to Conservative Central Council, Buxton, 19 March 1988.
5. Norman Tebbit, Inaugural Lecture to the Radical Society, London, 25 April 1988.
6. Quoted in the *Sunday Times*, 31 May 1987.
7. Reported in the *Times*, 27 April 1988.

8. From George Orwell, 'The lion and the unicorn: socialism and the English genius', *Collected Essays*, London, 1941, vol. II.
9. See Anthony Crosland, *Socialism Now and Other Essays*, London, 1974, p. 152.
10. Joel Krieger, *Reagan, Thatcher and the Politics of Decline*, Oxford, 1986, p. 74.
11. Quoted from Stephen Haseler, 'The spectacle of Tory radicals hoist by their own petard', *Independent*, 16 June 1988.
12. *Times*, 3 February 1988.
13. Jeremy Paxman, *On Royalty*, London 2006, p. 208.

CHAPTER 12

1. Quoted in, among other sources, John Cherion, 'Balkan scapegoat', in *Frontline*, India's national magazine, vol. 23, issue 6 (March–April 2006).
2. Ibid.
3. Speech on 23 September 1992, quoted in Bernard Connolly, *The Rotten Heart of Europe: The dirty war for Europe's money*, London, 1995, p. 165. See this book for a stimulating and powerful Eurosceptic account of the politics of the currency crises of the 1990s.
4. See *Financial Times*, 28 December. It reported that the value of euro notes in circulation overtook those of the dollar during 2006.
5. Bob Worcester's remarks during an account of the politics of the euro given at a European Research Forum seminar on 'The British and the Euro' at London Metropolitan University, February 2001. For full transcript see http://www.europeanresearchforum.com. See also Stephen Haseler and Jacques Reland (eds) *Britain and Euroland*, The Federal Trust, 2000.

CHAPTER 13

1. Figures from the Audit Bureau of Circulation for 1997.
2. Mencken quote from *Chicago Tribune*, 19 September 1926. Greenslade quote from Roy Greenslade, *Press Gang: How newspapers make profits from propaganda*, London, 2003, p. 59.
3. Delors was in provocative mode again in the aftermath of Thatcher's ouster from Downing Street. With Thatcher's anti-EU posture widely thought to be the reason for her dismissal, the Commission president grandly opined that should Britain continue to be unhelpful in Europe he 'would not hesitate to provoke a crisis'. Reported in Bernard Connolly, *The Rotten Heart of Europe: The dirty war for Europe's money*, London, 1995, p. 106.
4. Hugo Young, *One Of Us: A biography of Margaret Thatcher*, London, 1989, p. 419.

5. See http://web.unic-pau.fr/~parsons/antigerm.html.
6. Frank Johnson, former editor of the *Spectator*, to the author, January 2005.
7. Speech to the FCO leadership conference, Queen Elizabeth II Conference Centre, 7 January 2003.
8. See Norman Tebbit, *Upwardly Mobile: An autobiography*, London, 1991.
9. Anatol Lieven, *America Right or Wrong: An anatomy of American nationalism*, London, 2005. See particularly Chapter 3, 'The embittered heartland'.

CHAPTER 14

1. See for these Blair quotes Labour Party Conference Report, 1997 and 1999.
2. See Ben Pimlott, *The Queen: A biography of Elizabeth II*, London, 2001, p.626.
3. See Anthony Seldon (with Peter Snowdon and Daniel Collings), *Blair Unbound*, London, 2007, pp.288–89.
4. Seldon, p.289.
5. Report from *The Alistair Campbell Diaries*, vol.II, serialised in the *Guardian*, 16 January 2011.
6. Tony Blair, *A Journey*, London, 2011, p.132.
7. Ibid., p.144.
8. See ibid., Chapter 5.
9. Both quotes from *The Alistair Campbell Diaries*, extracted in the *Guardian*, 1 July 2011.
10. Reported in *The Alistair Campbell Diaries*.
11. Ibid.
12. Ibid.
13. House of Commons Public Accounts Committee, oral evidence session, 7 February 2005.
14. Ministry of Justice, July 2007, CM 7170.
15. Ibid.
16. *The Alistair Campbell Diaries*, vol.II.
17. Hugo Young, *This Blessed Plot: Britain and Europe from Churchill to Blair*, London, 1998.
18. For full text of conference see http://www.cnn.com/ALLPOLITICS/1997/05/29/clinton.blair.
19. *Guardian*, 19 April 2004.

CHAPTER 15

1. See Stephen Haseler, *The English Tribe: Identity, nation and Europe*, London, 1996, pp.56–64, for an analysis of 'theme-park' Englishness or Englishness for export. Since the mid-1990s globalisation, travel and tourism have tended to reinforce this industry.

2. Reported in *Time* magazine, 30 July 1984. Blair quote from Tony Blair, *A Journey*, London, 2011, p.42.
3. Reported in the *Times*, 6 April 1994.
4. Quoted in Joe Rogaly 'A dangerous battleground', *Financial Times*, 6 December 1994. The comment is from Rogaly in the same article.
5. Quoted in BBC News, *Open Politics* (Open University programming), 12 February 2007.
6. For aspects of this perceived relationship between the Almighty and the English see Christopher Hill, *God's Englishman: Oliver Cromwell and the English revolution*, London, 1970.
7. Quoted in Jack Lively and Adam Lively (eds) *Democracy in Britain*, Oxford, 1994, p.15.
8. Geoffrey Elton, *The English*, Oxford, 1992, p.235.
9. Elton, p.70.
10. See Paul Johnson, *The Offshore Islanders: England's people from Roman occupation to the present*, London, 1972.
11. See note 9 in Chapter 2.
12. Cited in Hywel Williams, *Britain's Power Elites: The rebirth of a ruling class*, London, 2006, p.735.
13. Quoted in D. Gowland and A. Turner, *Reluctant Europeans: Britain and European integration, 1945–98*, London, 1998, Introduction.
14. Alan Bullock, Peter Hennesey and Brian Bravati, *Ernest Bevin: A Biography*, London, 2002, p.111.

CHAPTER 16

1. Francis Fukuyama, *The End of History and the Last Man*, London, 1992.
2. Full Blair speech to Chicago Economic Club, 22 April 1999 on http://www.pbs.org/newshour/jan-june/99/blair.
3. Labour Party Conference Report, 2001.
4. *Guardian*, 19 September 2005.
5. Downing Street press briefing on 12 March 2003 for Tony Blair's response to Rumsfeld's remarks, posted on Downing Street website.
6. Reported in the *Guardian*, 17 August 2006.
7. This was written in 1951. Quoted in Alex Danchev and Oliver Franks, *Founding Father*, Oxford, 1993. I have used the American spelling of 'counselor', as in this quotation it is appropriate.
8. Peter Riddell, *Hug Them Close: Blair, Clinton, Bush and the special relationship*, London, 2003. The words 'hug them close' were reportedly those used by a senior Blair advisor.
9. Report in the *Independent*, 18 September 2005.
10. Article by Tony Blair in *Newsweek*, available in *Newsweek* 2006 series on msnbc.msn.com.

11. Hywell Williams, 'Britain's ruling elites now exercise power with a shameless rapacity', *Guardian*, 11 April 2006. See Hywell Williams, *Britain's Power Elites: The rebirth of a ruling class*, London, 2006.
12. Paul Krugman's most recent book is *The Return of Depression Economics and the Crisis of 2008*, New York, 2008.
13. 'Global Capitalism is in Full Retreat', *International Herald Tribune*, 10 September 1998. See Chapter 6 for an analysis of Thatcherite economics and inequality.
14. See Neil Chenoweth, *Virtual Murdoch: Reality wars on the information highway*, London, 2001, p.247.
15. British newspapers broke the story of Ruth Kelly's association with Opus Dei on 22 December 2004. See the *Times* for that day.
16. A conversation recorded in Andrew Neil's memoir, and referred to in 'Rupert Murdoch, bending with the wind', Tina Brown, *Washington Post*, 15 September 2005.
17. Chenoweth, p.203.
18. Chenoweth, p.202.
19. Chenoweth, p.274.
20. Chenoweth, p.277.
21. *Mail on Sunday*, 18 September 2005. Price's exact words were later disputed.
22. Reported in the *Guardian*, 1 July 2007.
23. Williams, 'Britain's Ruling Elites Now Exercise Power With a Shameless Rapacity'.
24. Jackie Ashley 'Quiet rise of the King of Downing Street', *Guardian*, 14 July 2004.
25. The MI6 chief Richard Dearlove, for instance, was reported to have believed that the USA 'fixed' the intelligence to create the need to go to war. Reported in the *Sunday Times*, 20 March 2005.

CHAPTER 17

1. Quoted in the *Independent*, 24 February 2000.
2. Speech at University of California, Berkeley, 29 January 2002.
3. Westminster Cathedral lecture, 3 April 2008.
4. See 'The second globalisation debate', a talk with Anthony Giddens, 30 January 2000, http://www.edge.org/3rd_culture/giddens/giddens_index.html.
5. John Ralston Saul, *The Collapse of Globalism*, London, 2003, p.20.
6. Joseph Stiglitz, *The Roaring Nineties*, London, 2003, p.231.
7. William Easterly, *The White Man's Burden: Why the West's efforts to aid the rest have done so much ill and so little good*, New York, 2006, p.10.
8. See D. Nielson, 'Delegation to international organisations: agency theory and World Bank reform' in *International Organisation*, vol.57 (2003).
9. Quoted in Ralston Saul, p.34.

10. Ralston Saul, p.164.
11. Speech at World Economic Forum, Davos, Switzerland, 1999.
12. George Soros, 'The crisis of global capitalism', extract in the *Times*, 30 November 1998.
13. Robert Samuelson, 'Global capitalism, once triumphant, is in full retreat', *International Herald Tribune*, 10 September 1998.
14. 'America: an empire in denial', *Chronicle of Higher Education*, 28 March 2003.
15. William Greider, *One World, Ready Or Not*, New York, 1997, p.473; Edward Luttwak, *Turbo Capitalism: Winners and losers in the global economy*, London, 1998, p.187.
16. Martin J. Anderson, 'In defence of chaos', in Arthur Seldon (ed.), *The New Right Enlightenment*, London, 1985.
17. Speech to the CBI, London, 27 November 2006.
18. George Stigler, *The Citizen and the State*, Chicago, 1975.
19. John Major, *The Autobiography*, London, 2000, pp.245–51.
20. Michael Barber, *Instruction to Deliver: Tony Blair, public services and the challenge of achieving targets*, London, 2007, p.18.
21. House of Commons Public Administration Select Committee, oral evidence, 27 February 2003, Q.486.
22. Julian Le Grand, *Motivation, Agency and Public Policy: Of knights and knaves, pawns and queens*, London, 2006, p.3.
23. Ibid., pp.10, 18, 163.
24. Introduction by Jack Cunningham to *Modernising Government*, London, 1999.
25. 'Central government's use of consultants', National Audit Office, 15 December 2006, HC 128, p.4.
26 Ibid.

CHAPTER 18

1. See Swissinfo.ch, 1 April 2008.
2. Film broadcast by Al-Jazeera, 20 April 2007.
3. BIS report cited in, and quotes taken from Ambrose Evans Pritchard, 'BIS slams central banks, warns of worse crunch to come', *Daily Telegraph*, 1 July 2008.
4. *New York Times*, 16 March 2008.
5. Quotations from Willem Buiter, ft.com/maverecon, 20 January 2009.
6. Iwan Morgan, 'The indebted American empire: America's current account deficit problem', *International Politics*, 45 (2008), pp.92–112.

CHAPTER 19

1. Debt statistics compiled by Credit Action. See creditaction.org.
2. See Larry Elliott and Dan Atkinson, *The Age of Insecurity*, London, 1999.
3. Figures from CIA *World Factbook*, drawn from IMF figures, 2009.
4. From 'Central bank statistics' in *Money Matters: A monthly report*, at www. purusaxena.com.
5. Will Hutton, *The State We're In*, London, 1995, pp. 107–8.
6. Harry Shutt, *The Trouble With Capitalism: An enquiry into the causes of global economic failure*, London, 1998.
7. Both quotes from Richard Sennett, 'Work can screw you up', *Financial Times*, 17 October 1998.
8. *Poverty and Inequality in Britain: 2005*, Institute for Fiscal Studies, 2006.
9. Charles Handy, 'The citizen corporation', presented at seminar, Birkbeck College, London, 23 April 1997.
10. Figures from James Banks, Andrew Dilnot and Hamish Low, 'Patterns of financial wealth holding in the UK', in John Hills, *New Inequalities*, Cambridge, 1996, p. 342.
11. Monica Castillo, *A Profile of the Working Poor*, Report 896, Bureau of Labour Statistics, Washington, DC, 1995, p. 1.
12. Hills, p. 33.
13. *Households Below Average Income Survey*, Department for Work and Pensions, 2008.
14. Paul Gregg and Jonathan Wadsworth, 'More work in fewer households' in Hills, p. 181. Quote from p. 204.

CHAPTER 20

1. Reported on Sky News. Cameron remarks, Sky News, 9 August 2011; Blair remarks, *The Observer*, 20 August 2011.
2. See *Poverty and Inequality in the UK: 2008*, Institute for Fiscal Studies, 2009. Also, quote from the Harman Report, *An Anatomy of Economic Inequality in the UK*, published jointly by the Government Inequalities Office and the Centre for Analysis of Social Exclusion, London School of Economics, p. 1.
3. Paul Krugman, 'America's oligarchs' *International Herald Tribune*, 29 February 2006.
4. *Daily Telegraph*, 21 July 2009.
5. *An Anatomy of Economic Inequality in the UK*, p. 1.
6. Cited in Stephen Haseler, *The Super-Rich*, London, 2001, p. 46 (see note 16, Chapter 3).
7. Zhu Xiao Di, *Growing Wealth, Inequality, and Housing in the United States*, Joint Center For Housing Studies, Cambridge, MA, 2007.
8. Charles Feinstein, 'The equalising of wealth in Britain since the Second World War', *Oxford Review of Economic Policy*, vol. 12, no 1 (Spring 1996).

9. John Scott, *Who Rules Britain?*, Cambridge, 1991, p.83.
10. Tom Nicholas, *The Myth of Meritocracy: An enquiry into the social origins of Britain's business leaders since 1850*, London, 1999, p.26.
11. Kevin Phillips, *Boiling Point: Republicans, Democrats and the decline of middle class prosperity*, New York, 1993. The quote from Avery is also cited there, p.191. These analyses refer to the USA, but can easily also apply to Britain, where like the USA there is no wealth tax and low inheritance taxes.
12. For a detailed account of royal finances see Jon Temple, *Living Off the State: A critical guide to royal finance*, London, 2008.
13. *Guardian*, 7 June 1997.
14. Martin Wolf, 'Leona Helmsley is alive in Britain', *Financial Times*, 7 March 2008.
15. The IMF and Gibraltar figures cited in Hans-Peter Martin and Harald Schumann, *The Global Trap: Globalisation and the assault on prosperity and democracy*, London and New York, 1997, p.63. This book was a relatively early and highly articulate critique of post-Cold War globalisation.

CHAPTER 21

1. Debt figures from Office of National Statistics at www.statistics.gov.uk.
2. George Osborne's Emergency Budget was introduced 22 June 2010.
3. See Robert Skidelsky, 'The paradox of thrift', *New Statesman*, 17 May 2010 and David Marquand, *Guardian*, 26 May 2010.
4. 'The new face of protectionism' *International Herald Tribune*, 2 September 2009.
5. Larry Elliot, *Guardian*, 15 March 2010.
6. Reported in http://www.guardian.co.uk, 30 January 2009. See also 'British jobs for British workers is the cry of our worst instincts' by Mary Riddell, *Daily Telegraph*, 4 February 2009.
7. IMF figures for nominal GDP. These rankings depend on exchange-rate fluctuations.
8. B.W.E. Alford, *Britain in the World Economy Since 1880*, London, 1996, p.33.
9. See Hywel Williams, *Britain's Power Elites: The rebirth of a ruling class*, London, 2006, p.163.
10. Daniel Dorling and Bethan Thomas, *People and Places: A 2001 Census atlas of the UK*, Bristol, 2004.
11. *Guardian*, 5 July 2004.
12. Williams, p.163. See his Chapter 4 on 'The financial and business elites; Dividing the Spoils'.
13. Reported in, and quoted from, Gideon Rachman, 'How the square mile fell out of love with Brussels', *Financial Times*, 12 December 2006.

14. Reported on the BBC News website, http://news.bbc.co.uk/1/hi/business/4366225.stm.
15. Speech at Lord Mayor's banquet, 13 September 2006.
16. Quoted in Stephen Haseler, *Sidekick*, 2006, p.211.
17. Blair speech 23 February 2000 in Ghent, Belgium, reported on news.bbc.co.uk/2/hi/vlc.

INDEX